I0825468

Stevie Nicks

IN 50 SONGS

Running Press
Hachette Book Group
1290 Avenue of the Americas, New York, NY 10104
www.runningpress.com
@Running_Press

First Edition: May 2026

Published by Running Press, an imprint of Hachette Book Group, Inc.
The Running Press name and logo are trademarks of Hachette Book Group, Inc.

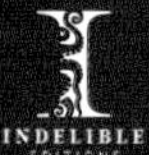

Print book cover and interior design by Jen Quinn of Indelible Editions
Produced by Indelible Editions

Library of Congress Control Number: 2025946244

ISBNs: 979-8-89414-224-1 (hardcover), 979-8-89414-225-8 (ebook)

Printed in China

TLF

10 9 8 7 6 5 4 3 2 1

Stevie Nicks

IN 50 SONGS

Annie Zaleski

NEW YORK TIMES BEST-SELLING AUTHOR

RUNNING PRESS
PHILADELPHIA

Contents

Introduction ix

1 Red Sovine and Goldie Hill, "Are You Mine" (1955) 1

Stevie's Family 3

2 The Mamas & The Papas, "California Dreamin'" (1965) 4

Stevie & Lindsey 6

3 Buffalo Springfield, "For What It's Worth" (1966) 8

4 The Stone Poneys with Linda Ronstadt, "Different Drum" (1967) 10

6 Joni Mitchell, "Blonde in the Bleachers" (1972) 14

5 Buckingham Nicks, "Crying in the Night" (1973) 17

Staying Afloat 18

7 Buckingham Nicks + Fleetwood Mac, "Crystal" (1973/1975/1998) 20

8 Fleetwood Mac, "Landslide" (1975) 25

9 Fleetwood Mac, "Rhiannon" (1975) 28

Witchy Woman 32

10 Fleetwood Mac, "Dreams" (1977) 35

Stevie Gets a Barbie 40

11 Fleetwood Mac, "The Chain" (1977) 42

12 Fleetwood Mac, "Gold Dust Woman" (1977) 45

Shawls & Capes 47

13 Fleetwood Mac, "Silver Springs" (1977) 50

14 Fleetwood Mac, "Don't Stop" (1977) 54

Fashion 56

15 Fleetwood Mac, "Sara" (1979) 59

16 Fleetwood Mac, "Angel" (1979) 62

17 Fleetwood Mac, "Sisters of the Moon" (1979) 64

18 Fleetwood Mac, "Beautiful Child" (1979) 67

Duets & Soundtracks 68

19 Stevie Nicks, "Blue Lamp" (1981) 72

20 Stevie Nicks with Tom Petty & The Heartbreakers, "Stop Draggin' My Heart Around" (1981) 74
The Honorary Heartbreaker 80
21 Stevie Nicks, "Edge of Seventeen" (1981) 82
"Edge of Seventeen" in Pop Music 86
22 Stevie Nicks, "Leather and Lace" (1981) 90
Relationship with Don Henley 93
23 Stevie Nicks, "After the Glitter Fades" (1981) 95
24 Stevie Nicks, "Think About It" (1981) 96
The Enduring Friendship of Stevie and Christine 98
Enchanted Facts About Stevie 100
25 Stevie Nicks, "Sleeping Angel" (1982) 103
Solo Tours 104
26 Fleetwood Mac, "Gypsy" (1982) 106
MTV 109
27 Stevie Nicks, "If Anyone Falls" (1983) 111
28 Stevie Nicks, "Nightbird" (1983) 112
Stevie's Singers 117
29 Stevie Nicks, "Stand Back" (1983) 118
Stevie and Prince 122
30 Stevie Nicks, "Enchanted" (1983) 125
31 Stevie Nicks, "Wild Heart" (1983) 126
32 Stevie Nicks, "Beauty and the Beast" (1983) 128
33 Stevie Nicks, "Talk to Me" (1985) 133
Stevie's Top Hat 134
34 Stevie Nicks, "I Can't Wait" (1985) 136
35 Stevie Nicks, "Has Anyone Ever Written Anything for You" (1985) 139
On Tambourine 140

36 Fleetwood Mac, "Seven Wonders" (1987) . . . 142

American Horror Story . . . 144

Kicking Klonopin . . . 148

37 Stevie Nicks, "Rooms on Fire" (1989) . . . 150

38 Fleetwood Mac, "Affairs of the Heart" (1990) . . . 153

Timeline of the Fleetwood Mac Lineup . . . 154

39 Stevie Nicks, "Every Day" (2001) . . . 156

40 Stevie Nicks, "Fall from Grace" (2001) . . . 158

The Night of 1000 Stevies . . . 160

41 Stevie Nicks, "Planets of the Universe" (2001) . . . 163

42 Stevie Nicks, "Sorcerer" (2001) . . . 164

Sheryl Crow . . . 167

43 Fleetwood Mac, "Say You Will" (2003) . . . 169

44 Stevie Nicks, "Secret Love" (2011) . . . 172

45 Stevie Nicks, "Soldier's Angel" (2011) . . . 174

Supporting Veterans . . . 176

46 Vanessa Carlton, "Carousel" (2011) . . . 179

Stevie as Inspiration . . . 183

47 Harry Styles, "Sunflower, Vol. 6" (2019) . . . 185

48 Daisy Jones & the Six, "Look at Us Now (Honeycomb)" (2023) . . . 190

Stevie in Pop Culture . . . 192

49 Stevie Nicks, "The Lighthouse" (2024) . . . 195

50 Taylor Swift, "Clara Bow" (2024) . . . 196

Select Album Discography . . . 200

Stevie's Tours . . . 204

Photo Credits . . . 206

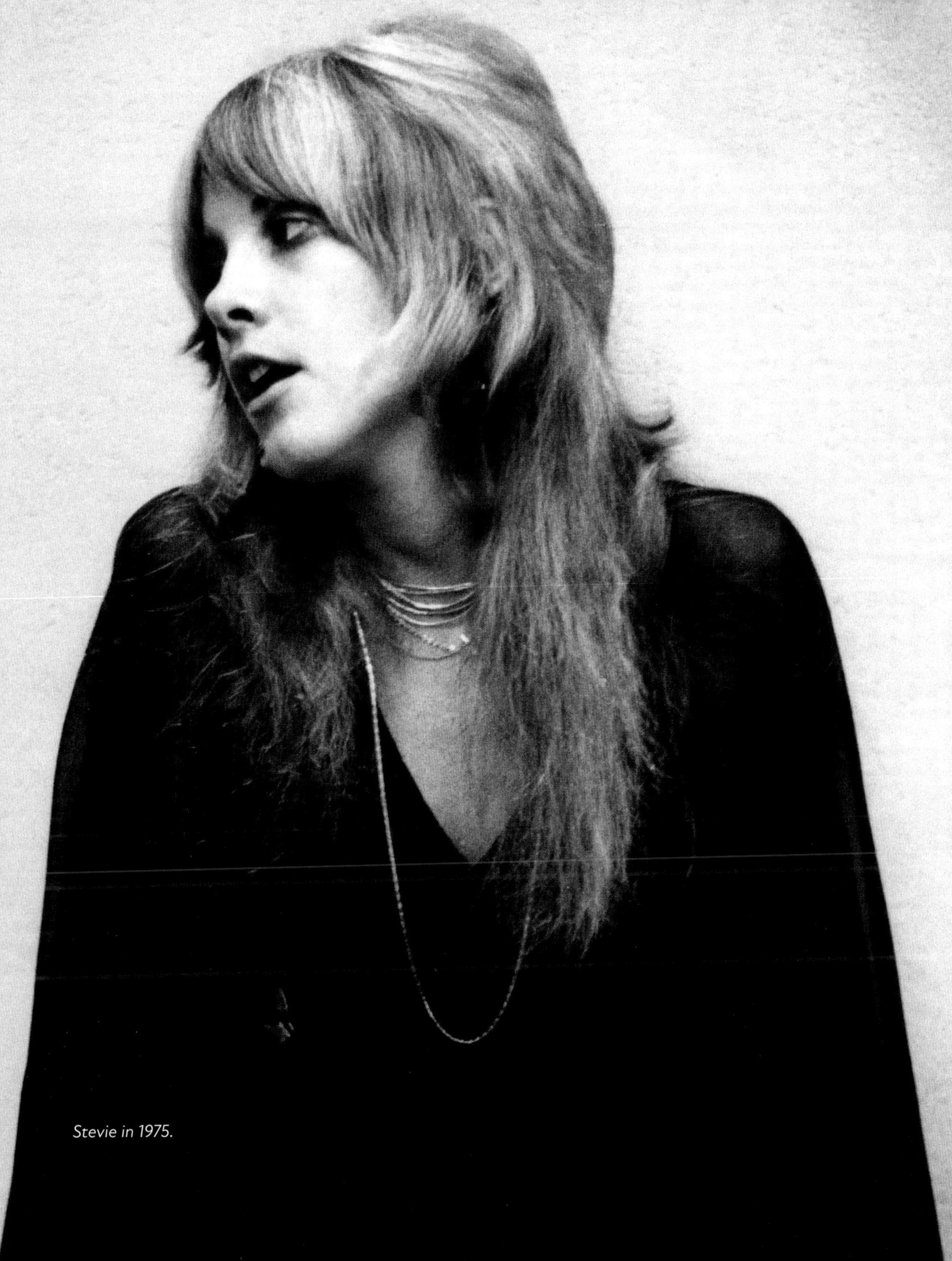

Stevie in 1975.

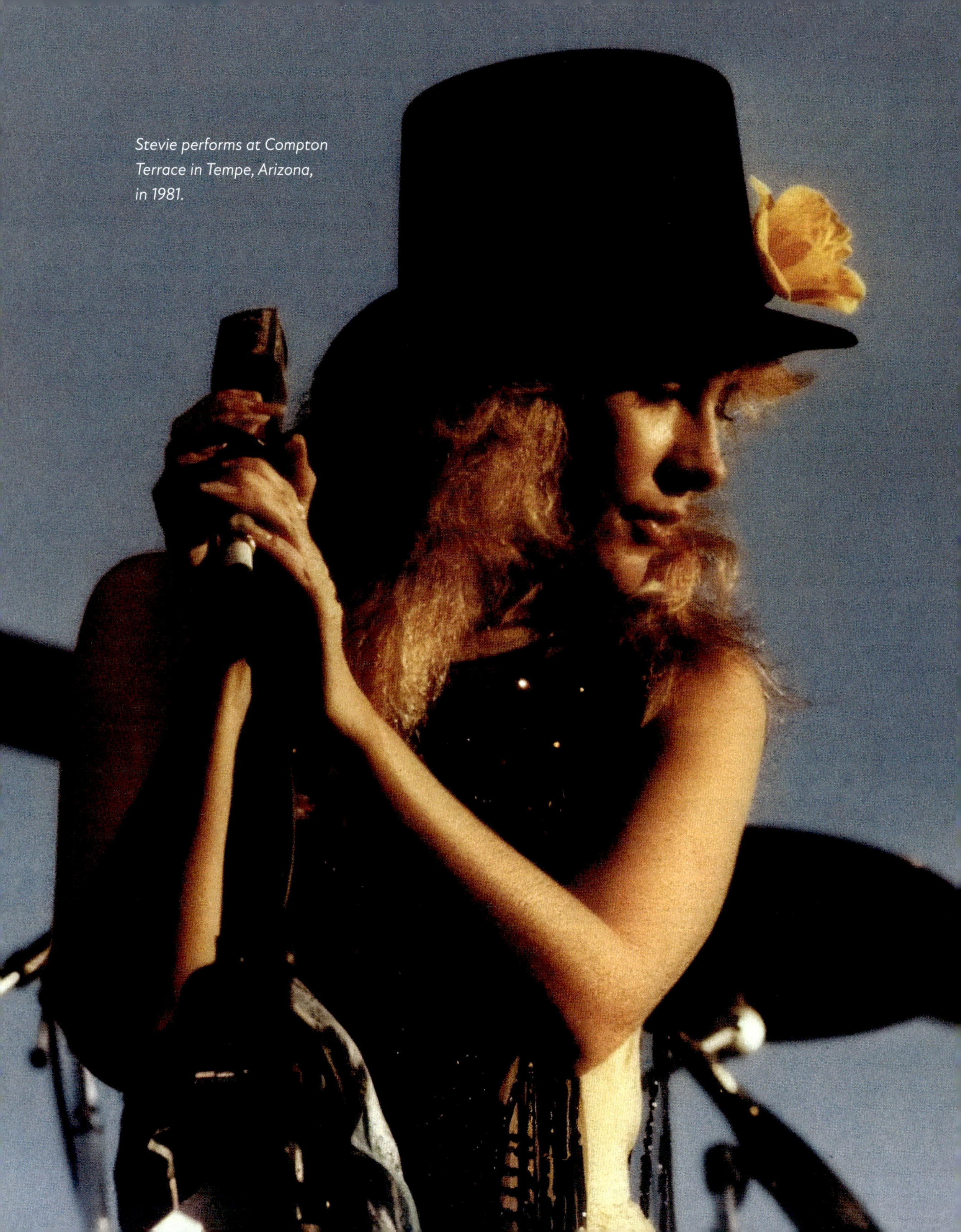

Stevie performs at Compton Terrace in Tempe, Arizona, in 1981.

Introduction

Upon the release of her 1981 solo debut, *Bella Donna*, Stevie Nicks was asked by an interviewer to name her one wish. "I would wish that when this album comes out, people would look at each other and say, 'She really is a very good songwriter,'" Nicks responded. "That's my goal in life, has been to be a writer."

Mission accomplished—and then some. In a career that started well over a half-century ago, Nicks has redefined rock and pop music via songs brimming with elegant imagery and poetic turns of phrase. She's written about the heartache (and anger) of a crumbling romance, but also grieved loved ones, reminisced about youthful innocence, lent comfort to friends, and brought solace to anyone who feels lost.

After joining Fleetwood Mac in the mid-1970s, she helped turn the band members into superstars. With 1977's landmark *Rumours*, Nicks and her bandmates—Lindsey Buckingham, Christine McVie, John McVie, and Mick Fleetwood—crafted a brutally honest chronicle of broken relationships that continues to resonate with younger fans today. Not long after, she launched a solo career and became a superstar on her own, confident her creative direction was the right one.

In the coming pages, you'll read about fifty songs that shaped Stevie Nicks—ones she wrote herself as well as tunes by some of her biggest influences and artists she's mentored. These songs represent her crystal visions and enchanted worldview, but also tell her life story: how a scrappy, poetic dreamer overcame personal loss, romantic turbulence, and musical ups and downs, and emerged stronger than ever. Time hasn't just made her bolder—she's also imparted this wisdom and bravery to everyone else and become a fairy godmother–like presence for countless generations.

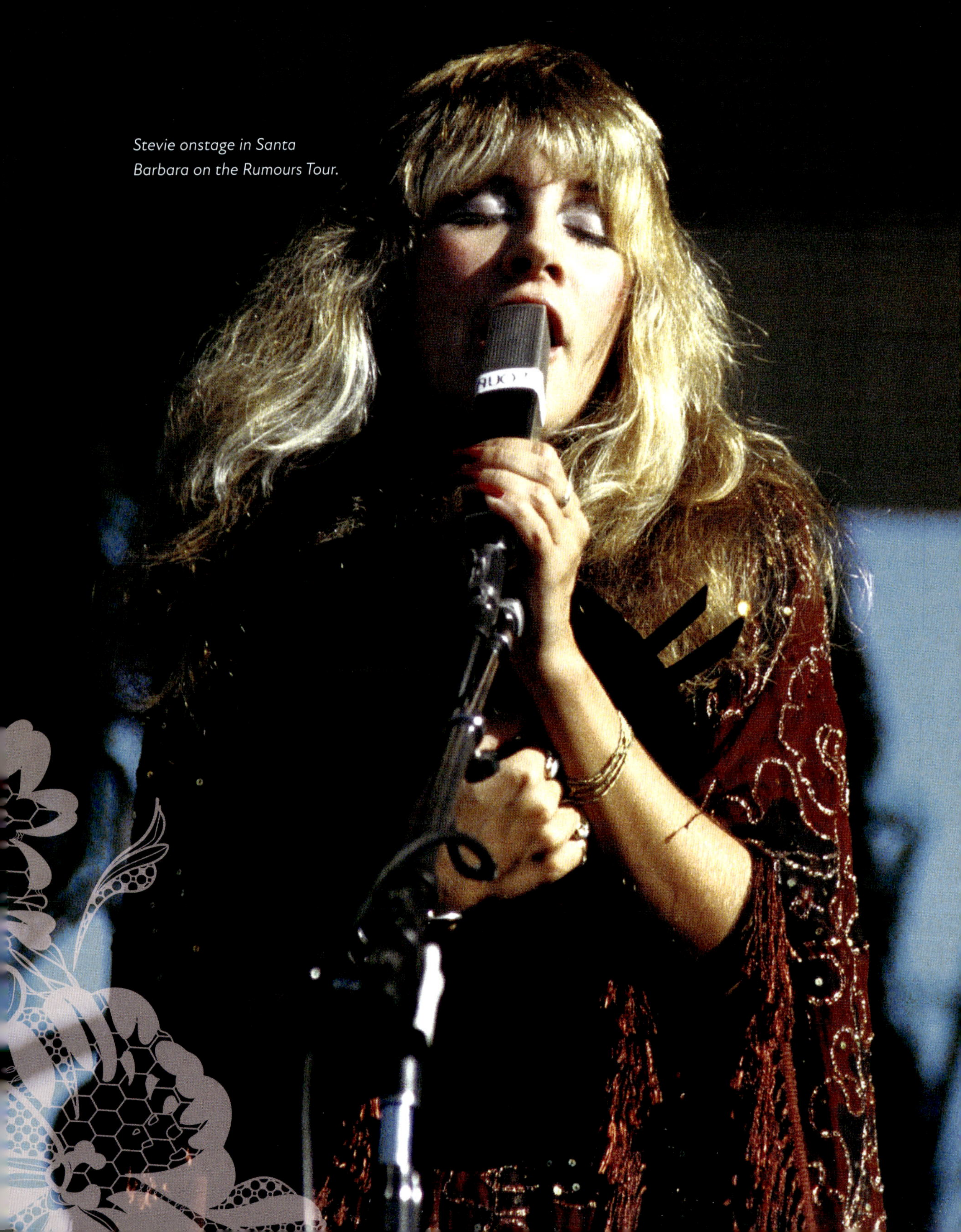

Stevie onstage in Santa Barbara on the Rumours Tour.

1. RED SOVINE AND GOLDIE HILL

"Are You Mine" 1955

Young Stevie learns how to sing from her beloved grandfather.

LIKE MANY ARTISTS, STEVIE NICKS INHERITED HER MUSICAL talents from a family member: her patriarchal grandfather. Aaron Jess "A.J." Nicks was an aspiring country artist who passed down his musical know-how to his young granddaughter. "When she was about four or five years old, her granddad made her a tiny little guitar," Nicks's father, Jess, told *Arizona Living*. "From that point forward, she showed an aptitude and a desire to be involved in music."

Nicks later recalled accompanying her grandfather to gin mills and dancing while he performed. But A.J. also taught her the finer points of singing using country tunes, most memorably the 1955 call-and-response duet "Are You Mine" by Red Sovine and Goldie Hill. That song always stuck with Nicks; in fact, she cut a gorgeous, jazzy demo of it for *The Wild Heart* that featured Roy Bittan on piano.

A.J. later hit the road to try to make it as a musician, bringing back singles by the Everly Brothers and country artists for Stevie. He "wrote beautiful words," Nicks once said. "My dad says it's very strange to go back and see the things that he would write and the things I write, because it's very similar." Unfortunately, A.J. found it difficult to sustain a successful musical career and often made his living instead by playing pool.

Nicks, meanwhile, took her grandfather's lessons to heart. Her musical tastes eventually broadened beyond country to include girl groups like the Supremes and the Shirelles, and she'd belt out their hits while riding in the car with her parents. "It was Motown, full on," she told *The New Yorker*. "And my mom and dad would turn around and look at me and go, 'Who are you?' And that's how I learned to sing."

A.J. died in 1974, just a few months before Nicks joined Fleetwood Mac. Yet he continued to influence her career. She dedicated *Bella Donna* to him and wrote a song in 1973 before he passed called "The Grandfather Song" that detailed their time together and encouraged her passion for country music.

Poignantly, she never played the song for him. "There was a line in it that said, 'I can still hear him playing though he'll soon be gone,'" she told *Rolling Stone*. "I couldn't change that line, and I couldn't sing it to him."

"That was when I decided I would never write another song that I could not play or show to somebody, 'cause he should have heard that song..."

—STEVIE NICKS TO *ROLLING STONE* ON "THE GRANDFATHER SONG"

STEVIE'S FAMILY

Nicks grew up with a younger brother, Christopher, and two loving parents who were married for close to sixty years. Born in Phoenix, Arizona on May 26, 1948, Nicks subsequently lived in many places while growing up, including Salt Lake City, Utah; El Paso, Texas; and Albuquerque, New Mexico. Her family moved around so much because of her dad's jobs: Jess held executive positions in a brewery, the bus company Greyhound, and Armour-Dial. Nicks's mom, Barbara, meanwhile, owned an antique store called the Silver Springs Emporium for decades and was a dedicated philanthropist who supported St. Jude Children's Research Hospital, the Wounded Warrior Project, and the Salvation Army.

Jess retired in 1974 after developing heart issues and launched a second career as a music promoter—he owned and operated the Tempe, Arizona, venue Compton Terrace—and was also on the board of the Arizona Heart Foundation. To honor her dad, Nicks has performed multiple benefits for heart health–related organizations in her career.

Both parents championed Nicks's artistic dreams and even helped her financially if she promised to stay in college while pursuing music. "My mom and dad have been very supportive my whole life," she said in a 1998 online chat. "[Including] before I joined Fleetwood Mac. And they were supportive all through the tumultuous times of Fleetwood Mac, when they didn't see or hear from me. They never got angry with me. So basically they're the only ones who were there before the Mac, they're the only ones who really know me."

The 1960s folk-rock group the Mamas & the Papas.

2. THE MAMAS & THE PAPAS

"California Dreamin'" 1965

A folk-pop hit unwittingly changes the course of Stevie's life.

WHEN STEVIE NICKS WAS A TEENAGER, SHE STARTED TAKING guitar lessons twice a week, learning how to play on a rented classical guitar. Unsurprisingly, she loved the experience—and when her teacher ended up deciding to go abroad and study in Spain, her parents bought his guitar and gifted it to Nicks for her sixteenth birthday.

Inspired, she immediately sat down and wrote a song about a recent heartbreak, "I've Loved and I've Lost." As the title implies, the song was about her "first love affair" with a boy who broke up with her, she told ABC News. The split was a blessing in disguise. "If he hadn't . . . I wouldn't have been spurred on to write that song," she said. "I don't know what would have happened if it hadn't have been for that. And when that song was done, I knew that I was going to be a songwriter."

The next year, while attending Arcadia High School in Southern California, Nicks joined her first band, the Changing Times. Influenced by the Mamas & the Papas—whose haunting hit "California Dreamin'" was a pillar of the psychedelic folk-pop movement—the Changing Times unfortunately didn't make a huge impression. But it did give Nicks a taste of what being in a band was like—and indirectly prepared her to change the course of music history.

Nicks later transferred to Menlo-Atherton High School and graduated in 1966. When she was a senior, Nicks met Lindsey Buckingham at an after-school church event that doubled as a hub for socializing. From their first meeting, the duo's musical chemistry was undeniable. "Lindsey walked into the room and sat down and started playing a song that I just happened to know every word and harmony perfect, 'California Dreamin',"" Nicks recalled in a press interview. "I thought he was absolutely stunning, so I kind of casually maneuvered my way over." His reaction to her singing was nonchalant but positive. "He was somewhat, I guess, ever-so-lightly impressed, not to let me know it," Nicks continued. "But he did sing another song with me, which made me know he did like it."

The two would eventually cross paths again several years later while Nicks was in college, when both ended up playing in the band Fritz. The group, which was also known as the Fritz Rabyne Memorial Band, performed around the Bay Area in the late 1960s and early 1970s, taking cues from psychedelic rock and the blues and opening for big artists such as Chicago and Janis Joplin. Even then Nicks belted out Fritz originals with earnest confidence, bringing sincerity to the music.

DID YOU KNOW?

In recent years, original members of Fritz have released two compilation albums that include rare songs featuring Stevie on vocals.

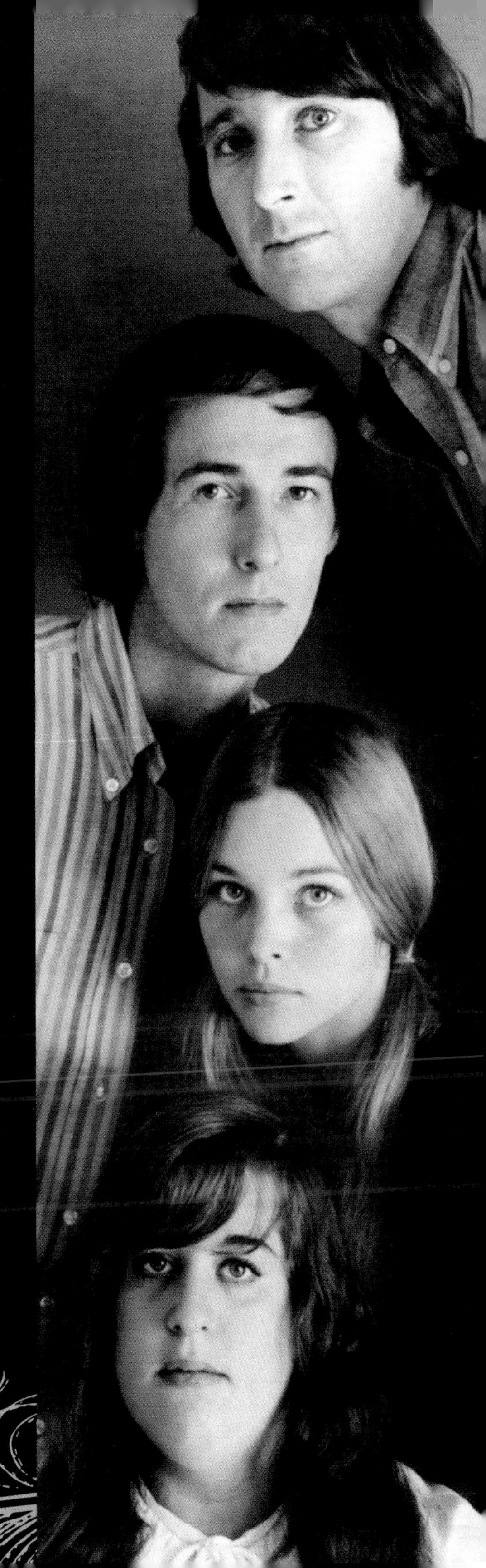

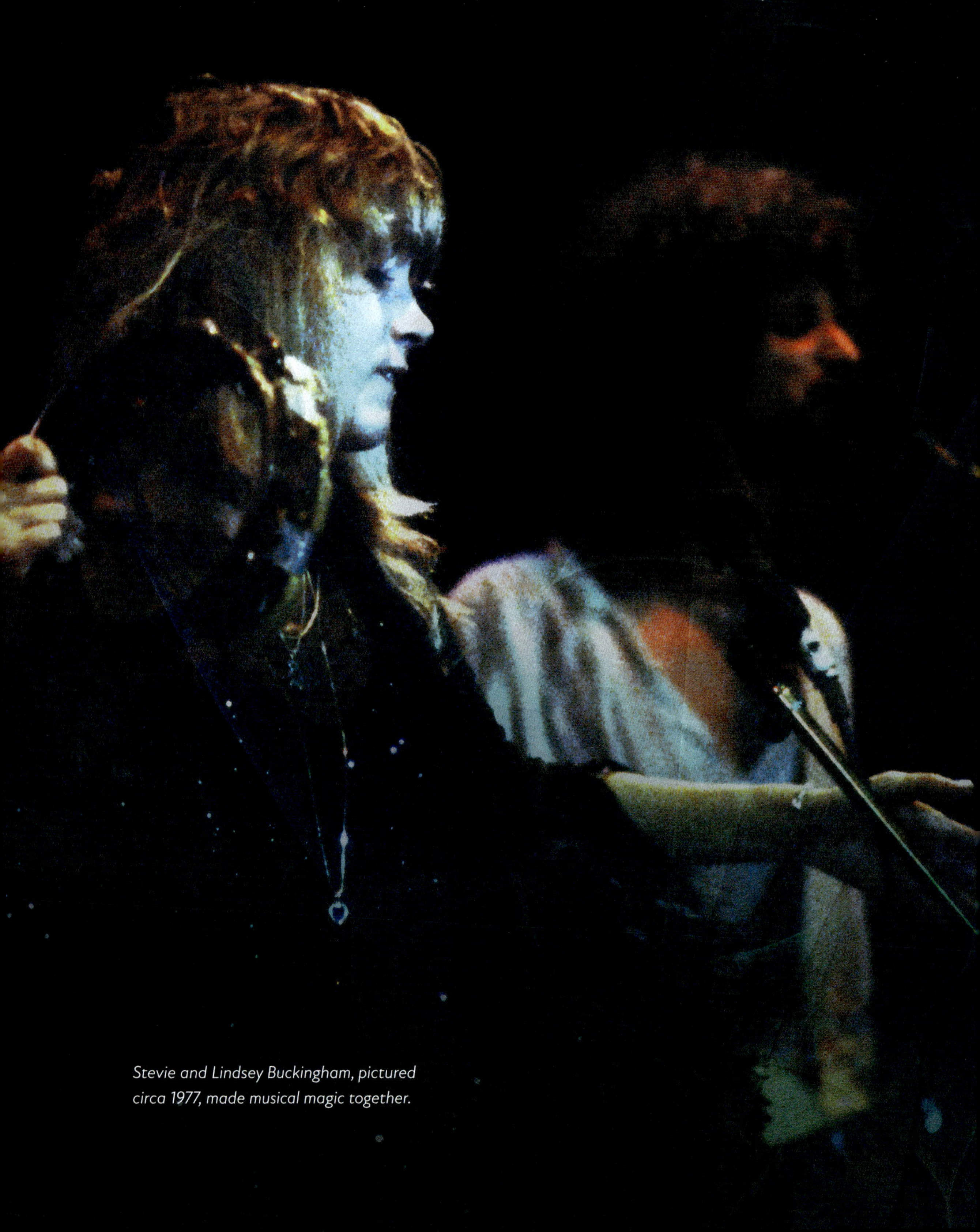

Stevie and Lindsey Buckingham, pictured circa 1977, made musical magic together.

Stevie & Lindsey

In a 1990 interview, Nicks minced no words about her romantic relationship with Buckingham: "He and I were about as compatible as a boa constrictor and a rat." This description shouldn't be a surprise given the duo's well-documented, long-standing disagreements. Still, when the couple's romance was good, it led to plenty of musical magic and was an integral part of the Fleetwood Mac mythology.

Buckingham and Nicks started dating in 1971, after spending three years as bandmates in Fritz. "Our relationship happened because I wanted to move to L.A.," she told Q magazine. "And I don't think either of us would've been brave enough to get in the car and drive to L.A. alone." As Nicks documented in interviews and songs, their relationship had many professional and personal ups and downs, but culminated in the duo joining Fleetwood Mac together at the dawn of 1975.

Nicks and Buckingham split up in spring 1976, with the *Associated Press* delicately noting the couple had "decided to end their long-time living arrangement." In response, Buckingham told the interviewer, "As far as musical likes and dislikes, there is no problem. When we walk up on a stage the band is very close. There are lots of bands who detest each other. We're not one of those." This observation has been true (and not so true) in the last half century or so—but the tension generated by this relationship friction paradoxically helped Fleetwood Mac create some of their best work.

Buffalo Springfield.

3. BUFFALO SPRINGFIELD

"For What It's Worth" 1966

A political song that shaped Stevie's worldview.

IN 1967, BUFFALO SPRINGFIELD REACHED THE TOP 10 OF THE Billboard Hot 100 with "For What It's Worth," a folk-pop song with a pointed message. Guitarist-vocalist Stephen Stills wrote the tune in fall 1966 amidst the backdrop of violent tension on the Sunset Strip in Los Angeles. Police in heavy riot gear clashed with teenagers over curfew and incidents like the closing of the popular club Pandora's Box, leading to weeks of arrests and newspaper headlines.

For Stills, the confrontations came to represent the looming friction between older and younger generations, as cultural shifts changed the fabric of society. "Riot is a ridiculous name," he later told the *Los Angeles Times*. "It was a funeral for Pandora's Box. But it looked like a revolution."

In 2022, Nicks recorded a faithful version of "For What It's Worth," something she had wanted to do literally for decades. (In fact, she had first vowed to cover the song while playing in Fritz.) Her impetus for finally heading into the studio was a sad one: the school shooting in Uvalde, Texas, where twenty-two people died. One week after the tragic incident, Nicks called up producer Greg Kurstin and her longtime guitarist Waddy Wachtel and cut the track, turning in sleek, smoky vocals that were steely with resolve.

Nicks debuted the song live at the Jazz Aspen Snowmass festival in September 2022 and subsequently released her studio version. "It meant something to me then, and it

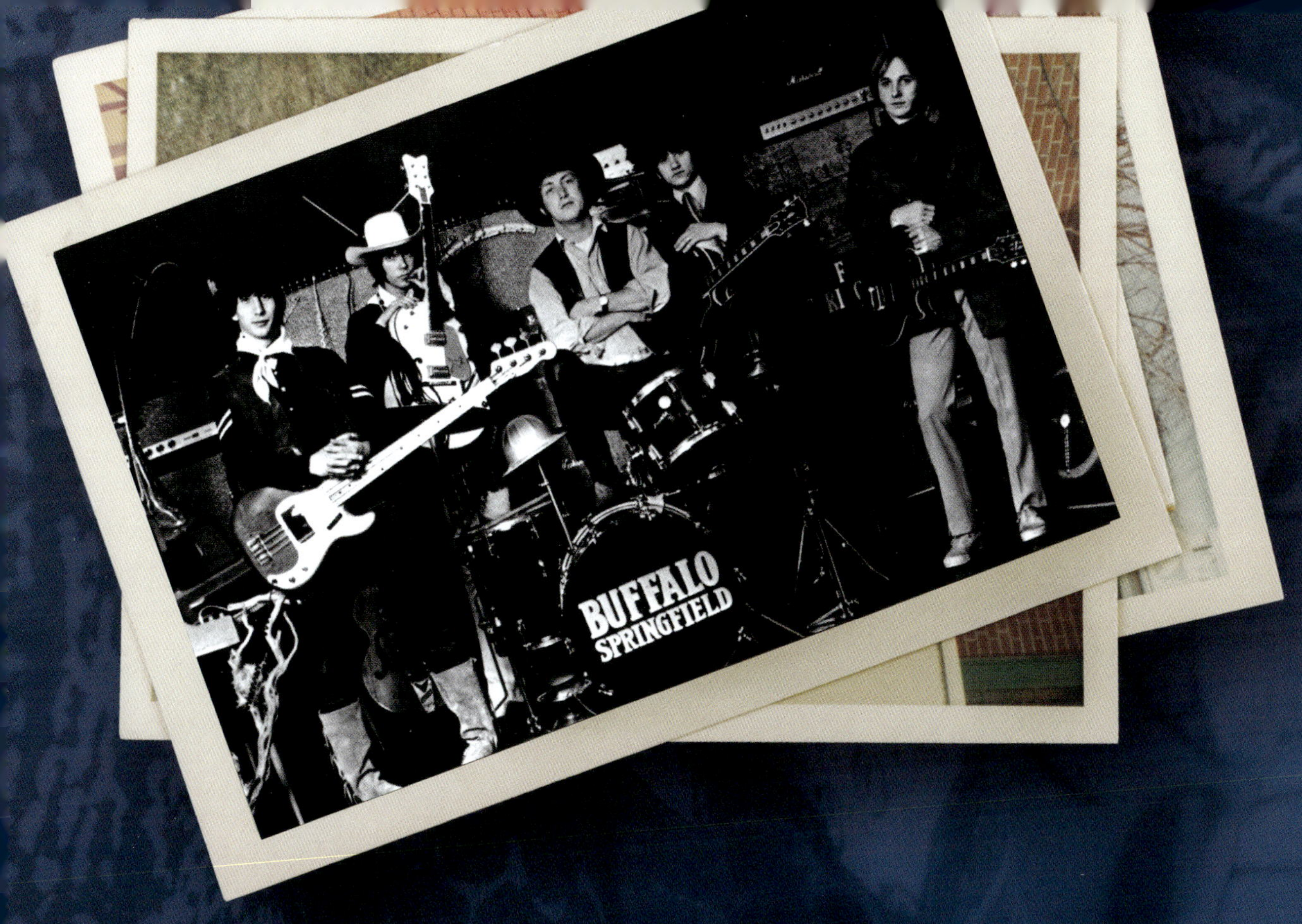

means something to me now," she said on social media about her take on the song. "I always wanted to interpret it through the eyes of a woman—and it seems like today, in the times that we live in—that it has a lot to say."

DID YOU KNOW?

In 2011, Nicks also released an original song called "For What It's Worth" on her solo album *In Your Dreams*.

> "It meant something to me then, and it means something to me now."
>
> —STEVIE NICKS ON "FOR WHAT IT'S WORTH"

Linda Ronstadt, circa 1978.

4. THE STONE PONEYS

"Different Drum" 1967

A country-rock icon helps Stevie find her own voice.

WHEN STEVIE NICKS WAS IN HIGH SCHOOL, SHE DISCOVERED Linda Ronstadt, who was then the lead singer of a group called the Stone Poneys. Nicks learned how to play the band's 1967 hit "Different Drum" on guitar and imitated Ronstadt's sweet-but-confident vocal delivery, admiring the way she was a "rock star" influenced by country music. "She figured out a way to blend those things," Nicks told *Rolling Stone*. "So she was rockin', and she hung out with the rockers, the rock bands. But she still had that little bit of country that went along with her."

Nicks also appreciated Ronstadt's strength, she added. "She was never gonna do a song she didn't love. Because I've gotten in terrible arguments with producers about a song that they'll give me, and they'll go, 'This could be your next hit single.' And I'm like, 'I don't care because I hate it, and I'm not doing it.'"

Fittingly, when Ronstadt was inducted into the Rock & Roll Hall of Fame in 2014, Nicks led an all-star tribute to her icon, belting out "It's So Easy" with a tenacious, twangy warble alongside Carrie Underwood, Bonnie Raitt, Emmylou Harris, Sheryl Crow, and Glenn Frey.

"All of us girl singers that started out after Linda [that] became very famous in a way wanted to be her and wanted to sound like her," Nicks said at the induction ceremony. "And then we had to say, 'But we can't.' So we have to find our own inner Linda and then we can move on with our life and our career."

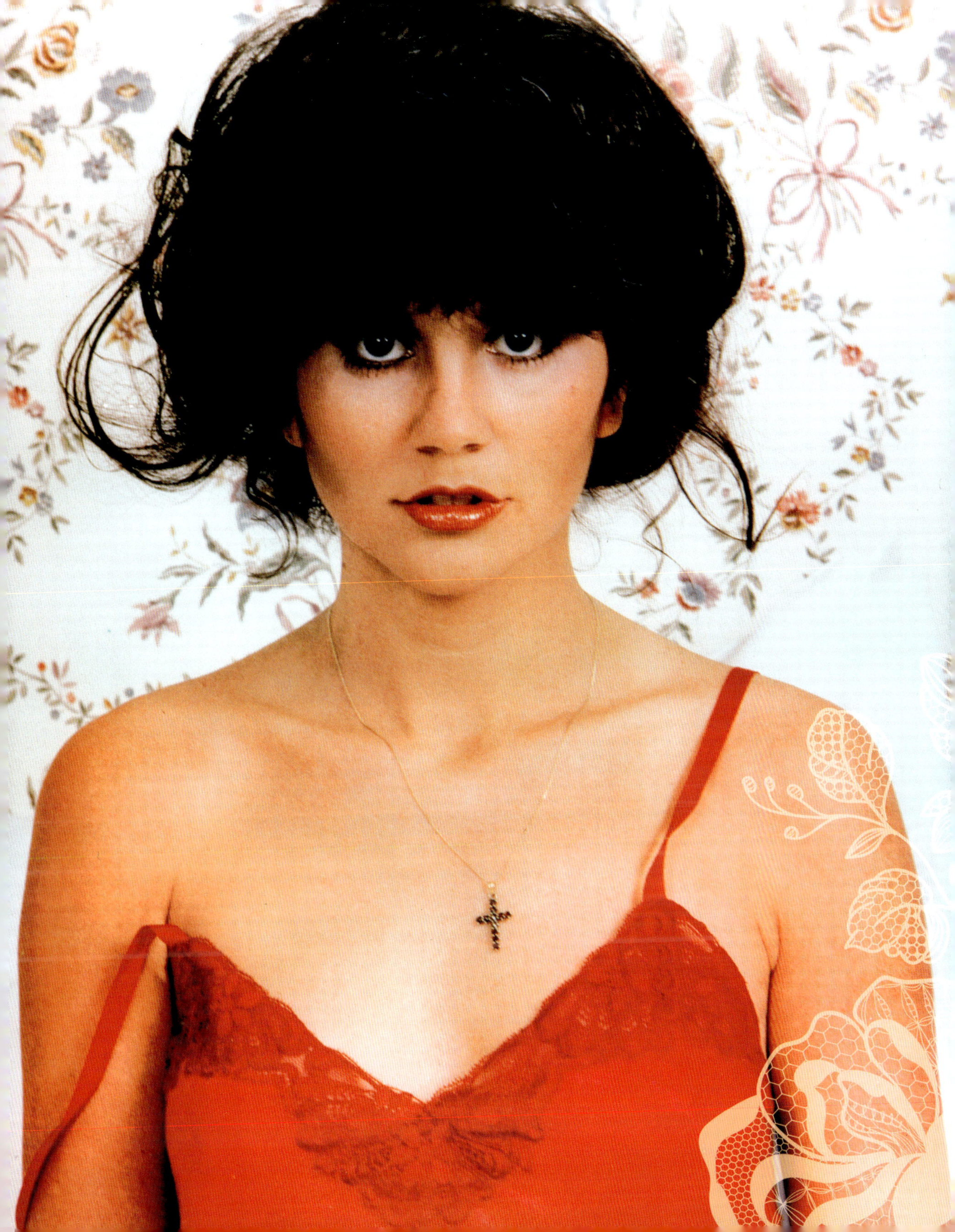

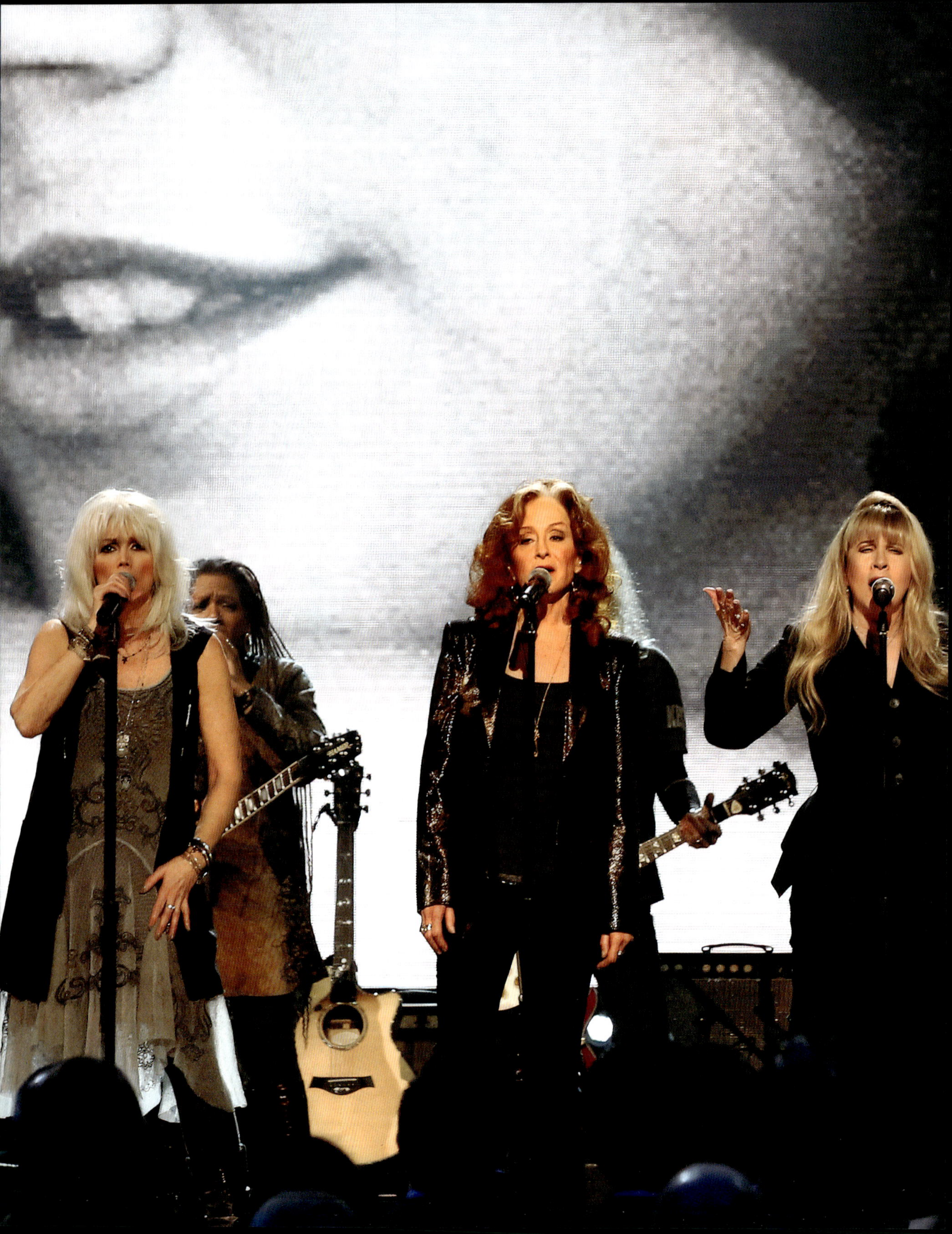

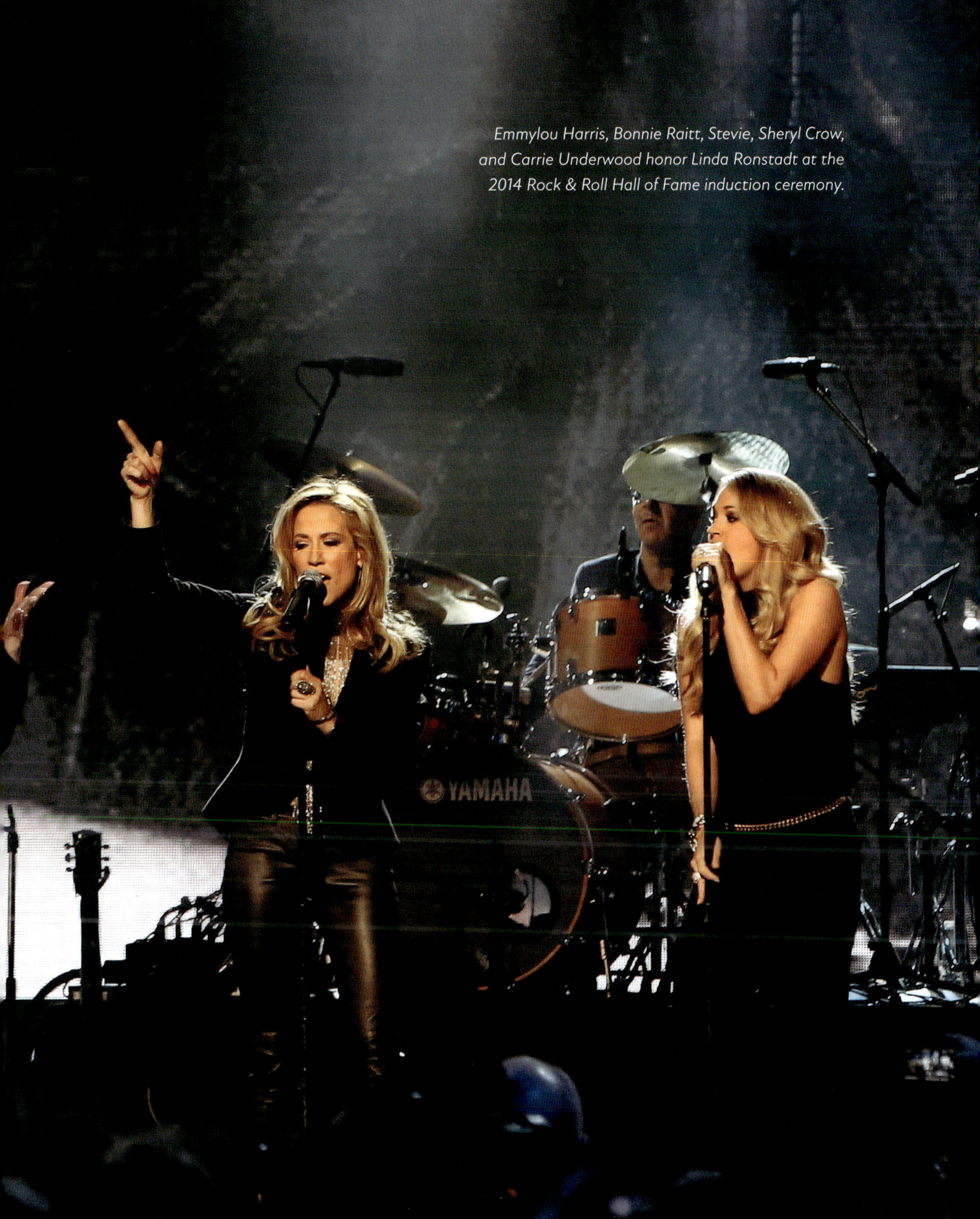

Emmylou Harris, Bonnie Raitt, Stevie, Sheryl Crow, and Carrie Underwood honor Linda Ronstadt at the 2014 Rock & Roll Hall of Fame induction ceremony.

Joni Mitchell was (and is) a musical inspiration for Stevie.

5. JONI MITCHELL

"Blonde in the Bleachers" 1972

The iconic songwriter provides solace and inspiration for Stevie.

STEVIE NICKS WOULD NOT BE WHO SHE IS TODAY WITHOUT JONI Mitchell. "It was her music that showed me I could say everything I wanted to and push it into one sentence and sing it well," Nicks told *BAM* magazine, citing 1970's Ladies of the Canyon as an example. "When she came out with a new album I'd go crazy: 'Don't bother me this week. I'm listening to Joni Mitchell.'"

Fittingly, Mitchell has been the soundtrack to some of Stevie Nicks's most formative life moments. When Buckingham Nicks made their New York City live debut in early 1974, the duo covered the single "Raised on Robbery." Later, when Nicks was reeling over the failure of the *Buckingham Nicks* LP and realizing that she and Lindsey Buckingham were on the precipice of a breakup, she took solace in repeat spins of Mitchell's classic LP *Court and Spark*.

To this day, Mitchell's piercing observations inspire Nicks. Tucked away near the end of the 1972 LP *For the Roses*, the lilting piano ballad "Blonde in the Bleachers" chronicles the ups and downs of dating a rock 'n' roll star. At first, the girl at the heart of the song seems to have found her perfect match. However, the bliss is short-lived: Her rocker beau thinks that settling down will rob him of his wild creativity and the pair split, leaving her heartbroken.

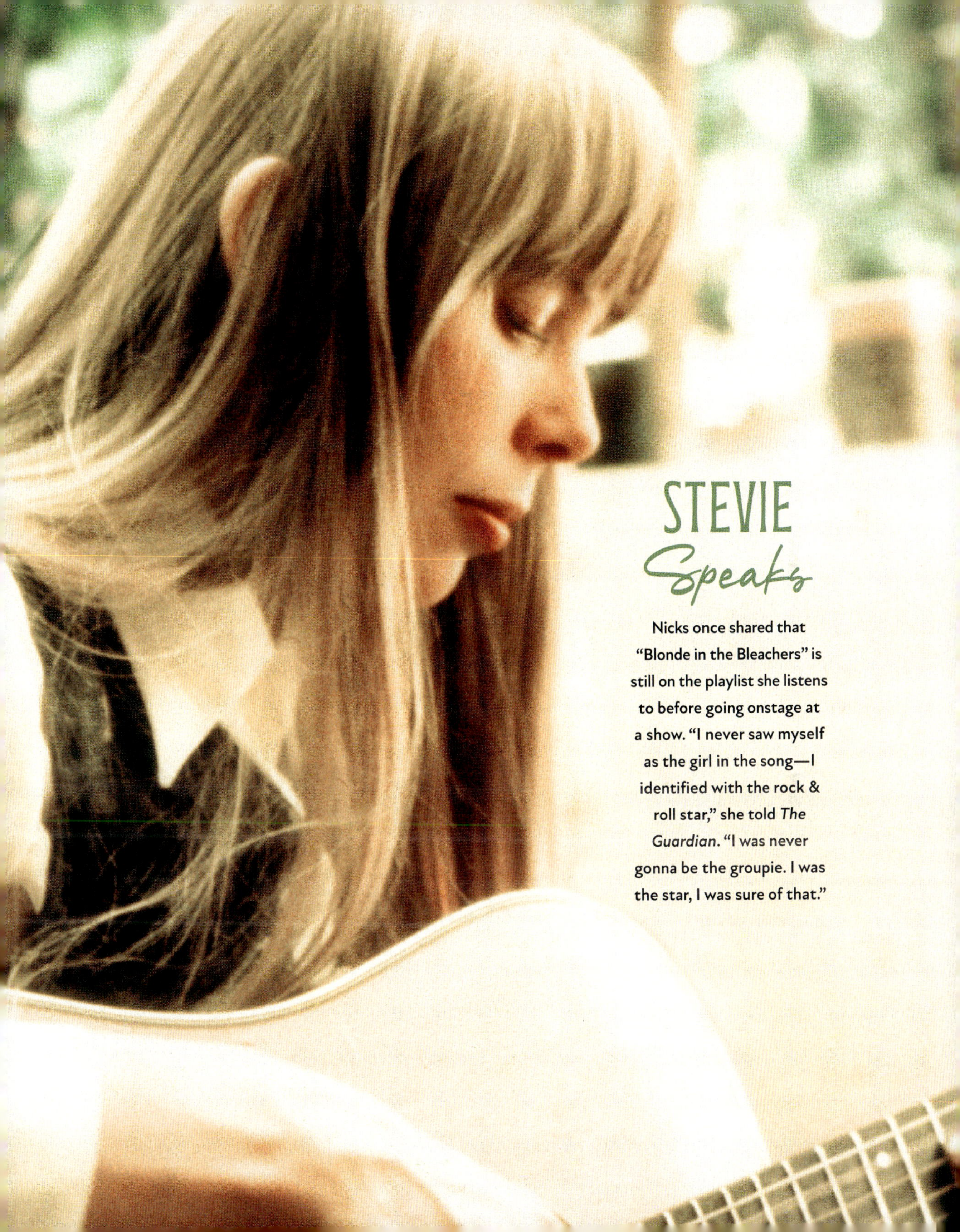

STEVIE *Speaks*

Nicks once shared that "Blonde in the Bleachers" is still on the playlist she listens to before going onstage at a show. "I never saw myself as the girl in the song—I identified with the rock & roll star," she told *The Guardian*. "I was never gonna be the groupie. I was the star, I was sure of that."

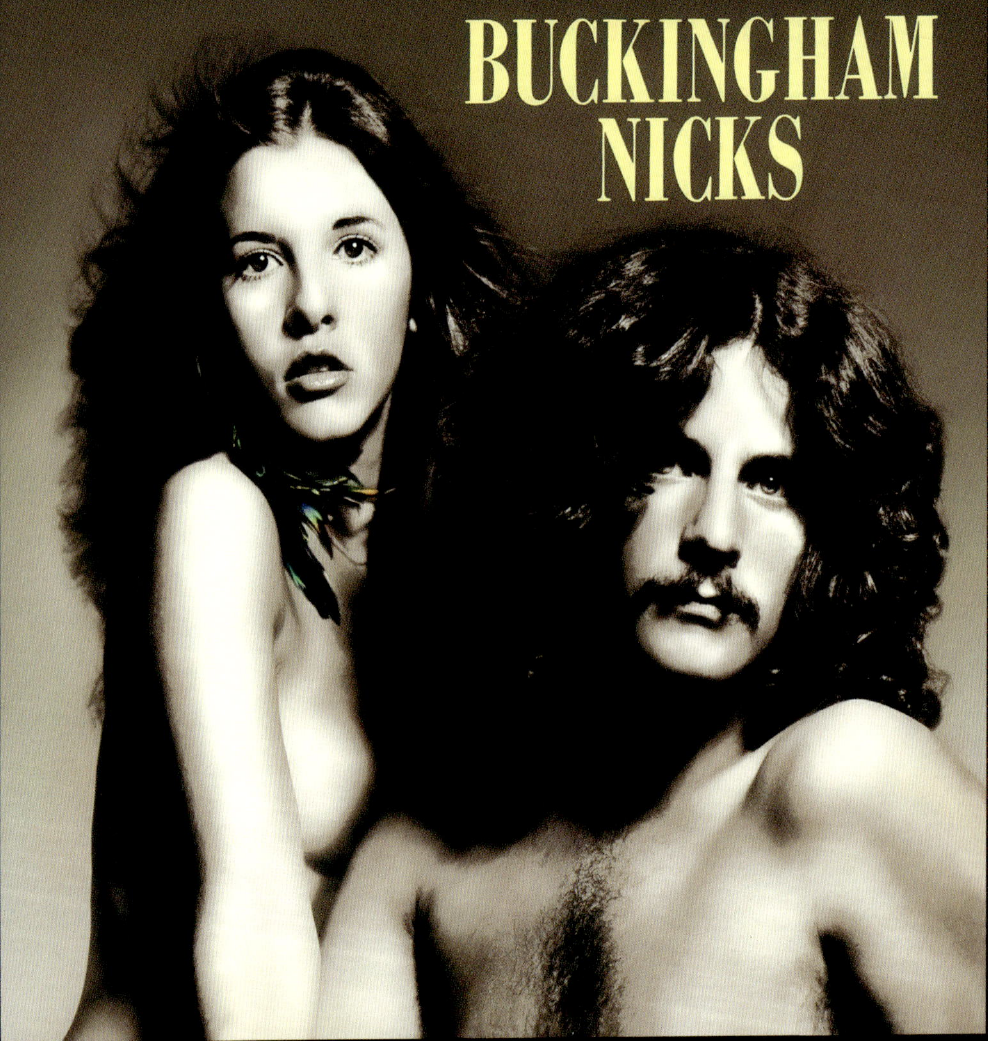
BUCKINGHAM
NICKS

In advance of the long-awaited reissue of 1973's Buckingham Nicks, *Stevie and Lindsey teased the release with an L.A. billboard and social media posts.*

6. BUCKINGHAM NICKS

"Crying in the Night" *1973*

A song from Stevie's cult favorite LP gets a second chance.

IN 2016, STEVIE NICKS DELIGHTED HARDCORE FANS BY ADDING A true rarity to her setlist: "Crying in the Night," the lead track from the 1973 LP she released with Lindsey Buckingham under the name Buckingham Nicks. Incredibly, she had never performed the song live in her solo sets, although the full-band "Crying in the Night" compares favorably with any of her classic songs, given its buoyant hook, conspiratorial tone, and freewheeling guitars.

Nicks wrote the tune about the actress Lesley Ann Warren, who "did some movie that was very a-la-Gunsmoke Kitty—you know, that type of thing," as she put it to the radio show *Rockline* in 1989. Fans speculated she was referring to Warren's character Mae in the 1972 TV movie *The Daughters of Joshua Cabe*, although the lyrics could refer to any devious, unreliable woman who's not to be trusted.

Buckingham and Nicks started recording and performing as a duo after their band Fritz dissolved in 1971. At the behest of producer Keith Olsen, the pair moved to Los Angeles and inked a deal with Polydor Records; a self-titled album recorded at the legendary Sound City Studios followed. Unfortunately, the label was indifferent to the LP and, despite Olsen's advocacy and support from some of the nation's more open-minded radio stations, the duo unceremoniously lost their record deal. "Crying in the Night" was going to be a single, Nicks revealed, but this plan fell apart because of the LP's commercial failure; instead, it was issued in 1977 to capitalize on the success of Fleetwood Mac.

After a period of sadness and soul-searching when their LP failed to connect, Buckingham and Nicks received the offer to join Fleetwood Mac on New Year's Eve 1974. Within the month, Buckingham Nicks wrapped up their engagements by performing several concerts in Alabama, as the duo's debut LP was extremely popular in Birmingham. Incredibly enough, their setlist featured early takes on multiple future Fleetwood Mac classics, including a primitive "Monday Morning" and a stomping version of "Rhiannon."

Over the years, the *Buckingham Nicks* LP became a heavily bootlegged cult classic that fetched hefty prices on the resale market, owing to the fact it was out of print and wasn't on streaming services. But in September 2025, the improbable finally happened: Rhino Records reissued the album everywhere (including on CD and LP), ensuring it was no longer a beloved (and unfairly obscure) curio in Nicks's cabinet.

STAYING AFLOAT

The failure of the *Buckingham Nicks* LP was a bitter pill to swallow. Nicks thought about going back to school—to the chagrin of her parents, she had spent five years studying speech communication at San José State University before dropping out to move to Los Angeles—but decided to soldier on toward a creative path.

Buckingham focused on music and Nicks worked to keep them afloat by cleaning producer Keith Olsen's house and waitressing at restaurants like Bob's Big Boy. "It was the only way we could do it," she told *BAM* magazine. "Lindsey couldn't be a waitress. He didn't know how to do anything but play the guitar and I did, so it was obvious I was going to be the one to do the work if we were going to live." The couple didn't have a lot of money and times were very tough.

But Nicks kept the faith that bigger things were in the cards. "Somewhere in my heart I knew that it would work out," she told *BAM*, "and that if I kept making enough money to pay the rent, that Lindsey would hang in there and get better and better on guitar and keep learning about the business."

"It was horrifying to Lindsey and I because we had a taste of the big time, we recorded in a big studio, we met famous people, we made what we consider to be a brilliant record and nobody liked it."

—STEVIE NICKS TO *PERFORMING SONGWRITER* ON *BUCKINGHAM NICKS*

7. BUCKINGHAM NICKS + FLEETWOOD MAC

"Crystal"

1973/1975/1998

The mystical song that made Fleetwood Mac a powerhouse.

THE UNASSUMING "CRYSTAL" PLAYED A PIVOTAL ROLE IN STEVIE Nicks and Lindsey Buckingham joining Fleetwood Mac. In late 1974, drummer Mick Fleetwood was on the hunt for a recording space and met Keith Olsen at the famed Sound City Studios. To show off the studio's capabilities, Olsen cued up a few tracks from the *Buckingham Nicks* LP, including the Nicks-penned "Crystal," a mystical folk song with oboe woven throughout and a sensitive Buckingham lead vocal. "He truly does a better job on it," Nicks told *Arizona Living*, explaining why she didn't sing it. "That song was a lot about my father and grandfather."

Duly impressed, Fleetwood asked what the duo were up to. "And Keith said, 'Actually, they're starving,'" Nicks said on a 1981 radio special. "And so [Mick] called us up, and he just said, 'You want to be in my band?' Which is exactly what Lindsey said to me years before. And we said, 'Absolutely.'"

Years later, Fleetwood still remembered hearing "Crystal" for the very first time. "That song had so much connective power to our story," he told *Mojo* in 2014. "It is a signpost that needs to be read in this band's story." Fittingly, Fleetwood Mac cut a confident version on their 1975 self-titled album that incorporated stronger backing vocals and delicate synthesizer curlicues from Christine McVie.

Incredibly enough, however, Nicks was reluctant to re-record the song with Fleetwood Mac, for a very simple reason. "It took the place of a new song," she said on a 1981 radio special. "Since I write so much, I don't need to keep putting [out] old songs that take places of new songs."

For good measure, Nicks finally did the song her way decades later, re-recording "Crystal" as a solo song for the 1998 film *Practical Magic,* which starred Sandra Bullock and Nicole Kidman as sisters who also happen to be witches. This take was folky soft rock, with lovely string flourishes and a warm, empathetic lead—you might say sparkling with witchy wonder.

Stevie brought a delicate, witchy vibe to her 1977 stage look.

"That song had so much connective power to our story."

— MICK FLEETWOOD ON "CRYSTAL" TO *MOJO*

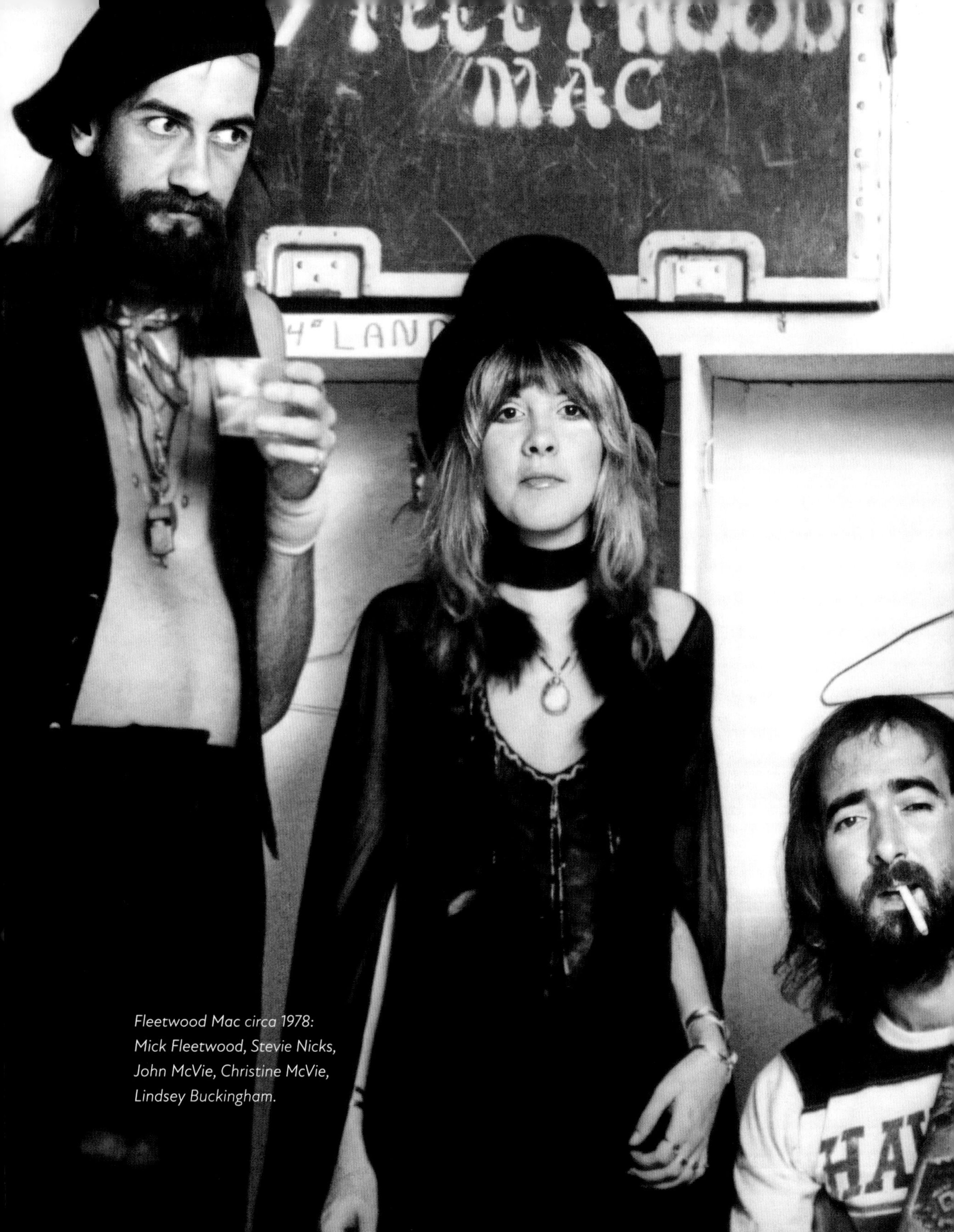

Fleetwood Mac circa 1978: Mick Fleetwood, Stevie Nicks, John McVie, Christine McVie, Lindsey Buckingham.

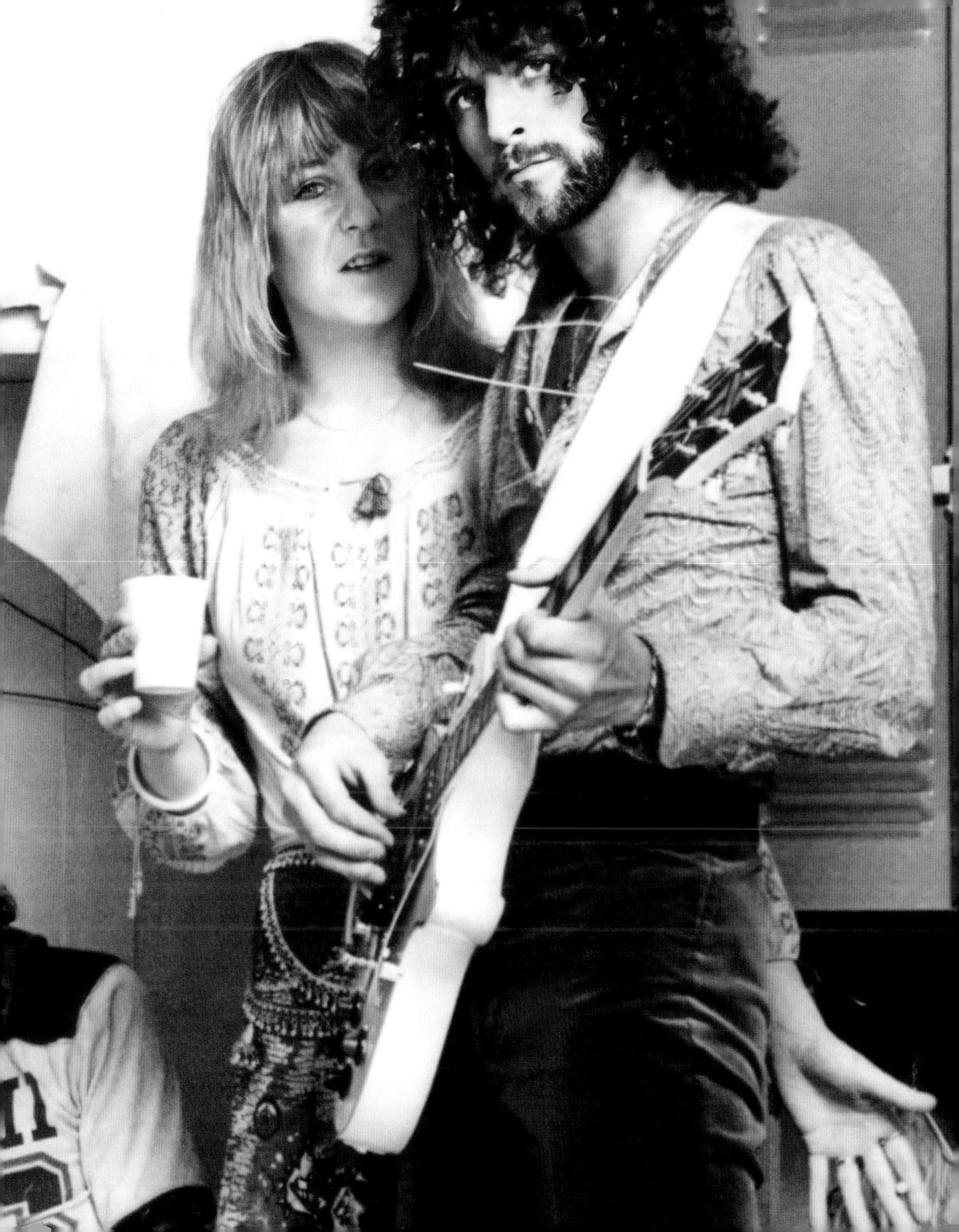

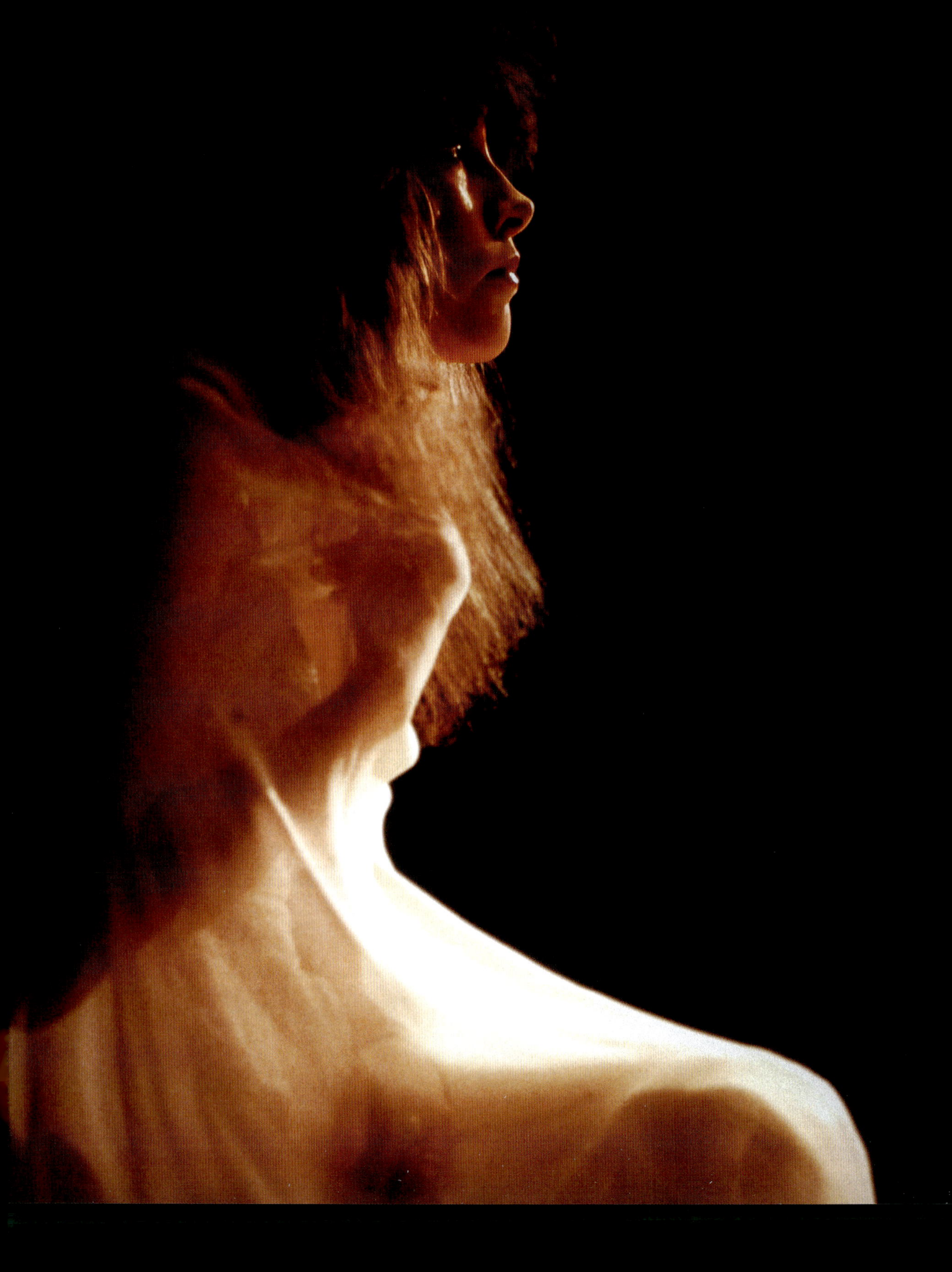

Stevie created classic, folk-leaning anthems like "Landslide" with Fleetwood Mac.

8. FLEETWOOD MAC

"Landslide" 1975

A moment of doubt turned into magic.

THE DELICATE FOLK-POP BEAUTY "LANDSLIDE" IS ONE OF NICKS'S best and most meaningful songs. Written on guitar, the tune grapples with how to cope when your life is crashing down around you and everything you *thought* you knew feels unstable. The narrator isn't sure they have the fortitude to deal with these profound changes—whether this involves a career, a relationship, or a loved one—but realizes that she is braver than she thinks and growing up means confronting your fears.

Nicks planted the seeds for "Landslide" in 1974. Her dad, Jess, who had been living with angina and was having chest pains, ended up having emergency surgery at the Mayo Clinic to prevent a heart attack. These pains didn't abate even after the procedure, and he ended up retiring from his job. Years later, Jess Nicks told *Arizona Living* that the "Landslide" lyrics "are meant to portray the relationship between a parent and child. She wrote that song because she was fearful of my dying." In 1998, Stevie Nicks acknowledged this take, telling *The Arizona Republic* that "it's about a father-daughter relationship."

But like so many Stevie Nicks songs, "Landslide" has another layer of meaning. That same year, she and Lindsey Buckingham were at a serious crossroads in their personal lives and careers. Her dad suggested she give music six more months—and if it didn't pan out and she wanted to go back and finish college, her parents would pay for it. With this offer in mind, Nicks and Buckingham relocated to Aspen, Colorado, in September 1974, because he was preparing to go on tour as a guitarist with a newly solo Don Everly of the Everly Brothers. "Our management company had the Carpenters and Jim Croce; they had some pretty big acts and weren't too interested in us," Buckingham told *Magnet*. "I knew

Warren Zevon, who had been playing with Don. There was an opening for a guitar player, and I got the gig."

For Nicks, living in Aspen did not help her downtrodden mood. She had forty dollars, her poodle Jenny, and a Toyota that wasn't working very well in the cold. "I had gotten to a point where it was like, 'I'm not happy. I am tired,'" she told *Performing Songwriter*. "'But I don't know if we can do any better than this. If nobody likes this, then what are we going to do?'" Nicks went into the living room of the house where she was staying and looked outside at the gorgeous Colorado landscape. The beautiful scenery stirred something in her, and "Landslide" came pouring out.

"During that two months [in Aspen] I made a decision to continue," Nicks said. "'Landslide' was the decision. . . . But looking up at those Rocky Mountains and going, 'Okay, we can do it. I'm sure we can do it.' In one of my journal entries, it says, 'I took Lindsey and said, "We're going to the top!"'"

It wasn't quite as easy as that, of course. The Everly tour ended up being a bust, as Don struggled with being a solo artist, Buckingham recalled: "All we would get was people yelling, 'Play "Bye Bye Love" [and] "Wake Up Little Susie."' " When Buckingham returned from the ill-fated tour, he decided to take the car and their poodle back to Los Angeles, stranding Stevie in Colorado. The bus pass she had because of her dad's job was of no use—Greyhound was on strike—and she had to call and ask her parents to get her a plane ticket.

The couple's romance persisted despite this hiccup. And in a testament to the power of manifestation and positive thinking, three months later, the couple received the fateful call from Mick Fleetwood to join Fleetwood Mac. "Landslide" appeared on the band's self-titled 1975 album and, incredibly, wasn't released as a single at the time. However, a live version from 1997's *The Dance*—complete with a simple Nicks dedication at the start, "This is for you, Daddy"—became a US adult contemporary radio hit.

ICONIC COVERS

It wasn't the first time "Landslide" became a hit—in 1994, the alt-rock band Smashing Pumpkins landed a modern rock radio smash with an acoustic take—and it wasn't the last time, either. In 2002, country trio the Chicks reached the top 10 on the Billboard Hot 100 with a harmony-rich version; Nicks has performed "Landslide" multiple times with Harry Styles [see page 185]; and Miley Cyrus, Anohni, and the Japanese House have also performed touching takes on the song.

"During that two months I made a decision to continue. 'Landslide' was the decision . . . I took Lindsey and said, 'We're going to the top!'"

—STEVIE NICKS TO *PERFORMING SONGWRITER*

Stevie poses for a portrait around 1976, as she had her first hit with Fleetwood Mac, "Rhiannon."

9. FLEETWOOD MAC

"Rhiannon" 1975

The book that inspired Stevie's first hit.

IN ONE OF THE LAST BUCKINGHAM NICKS SHOWS, WHICH TOOK place in Alabama in early 1975, the duo performed a brisk version of "Rhiannon." The lyrics were quite different in spots, but the song's folk-rock framework was in place. Written during the same Aspen stay that brought "Landslide," the song "is just about a very mystical woman that finds it very, very hard to be tied down in any kind of way—and she's uplifting all through the song," Nicks said in a 1976 interview. Fittingly, her vocals during the Buckingham Nicks performance are raw and passionate; she channels the wild, unfettered nature of the titular character with characteristic urgency.

Nicks took the name Rhiannon from a 1973 book by Mary Bartlet Leader called *Triad: A Novel of the Supernatural* that she happened to pick up. "It was all about this girl who becomes possessed by a spirit named Rhiannon," she told Classic Rock. "I was so taken with that name that I thought: 'I've got to write something about this.' So I sat down at the piano and started this song about a woman that was all involved with these birds and magic."

As it turns out, this loose concept evolved to encompass lyrics and themes drawing from the stories of the Welsh *Mabinogion*. Rhiannon is "goddess of steeds and maker of birds and her song is a song that takes away pain," Nicks said in a 1994 interview. "When you hear her song, you close your eyes and you fall asleep, and when you wake up your pain or the danger is gone and you see her three birds flying above. That's the legend behind it—and that's what I think about when I'm singing that song."

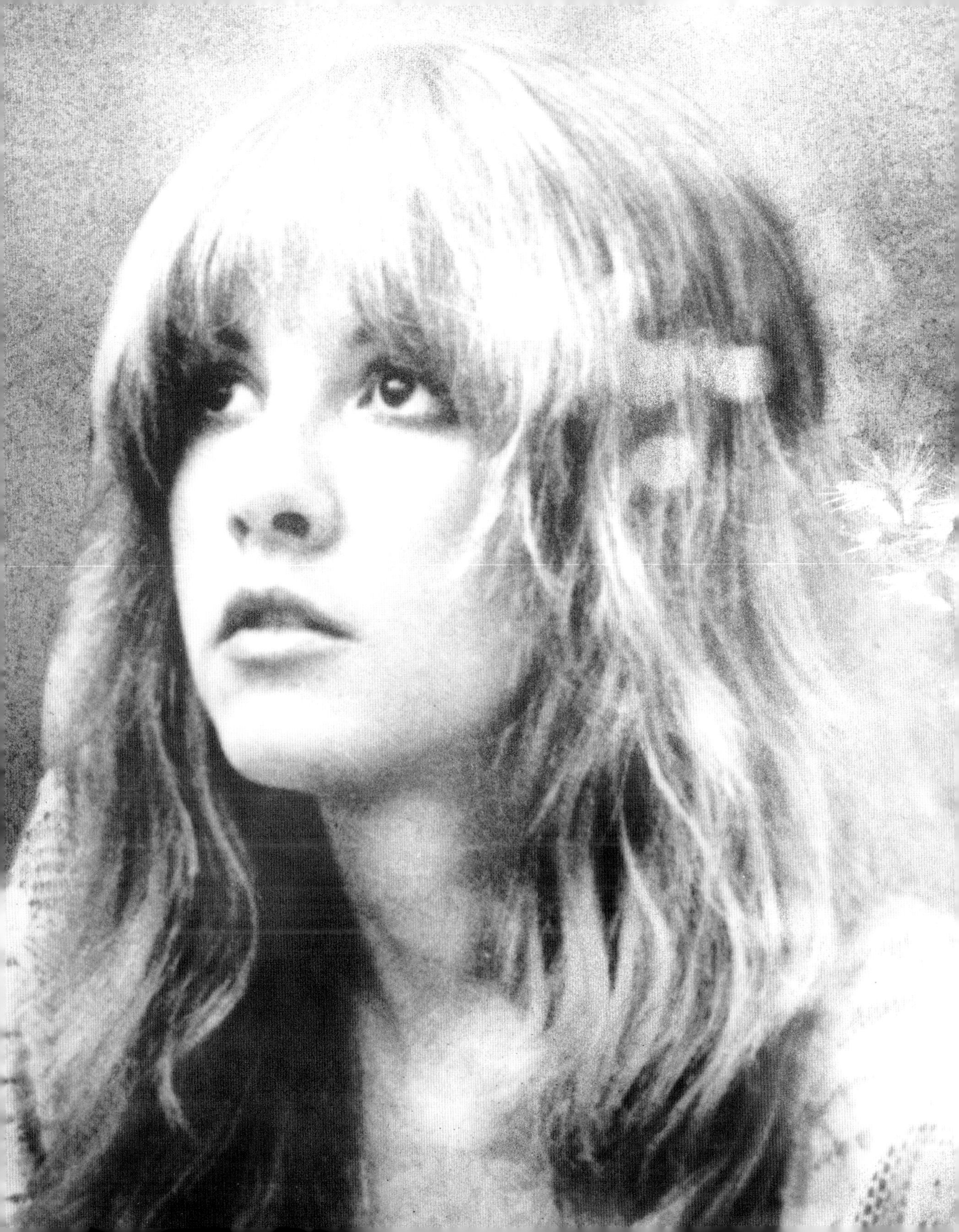

"People come up to me every place we play and tell me what an effect 'Rhiannon' has had on their lives, as if it has some spiritual power over them."

—STEVIE NICKS TO *MELODY MAKER*

Released under the title "Rhiannon (Will You Ever Win)," the single was the first Nicks-penned hit for Fleetwood Mac, reaching No. 11 on the Billboard Hot 100. "People come up to me every place we play and tell me what an effect 'Rhiannon' has had on their lives, as if it has some spiritual power over them," Nicks told *Melody Maker* in 1976. That's no doubt also because of the full-band Fleetwood Mac live version, which was a revelation during this era: The musicians throttled their instruments with ferocious intensity, as Nicks belted out the song like she was infused by the mythological Rhiannon's spirit.

In addition to the song, a film version of "Rhiannon" has always loomed large in Nicks's mythology. In fact, when she announced a solo record deal in February 1979, press reports at the time noted her first album was going to be the soundtrack to a United Artists film adaptation of the song that Nicks planned to shoot in Wales in the fall. The proposed movie even had a screenwriter (Paul Mayersberg, who also penned *The Man Who Fell to Earth*) and producer (*The Wiz*'s Rob Cohen) attached. "Of course [Nicks will] star in it, and write all the music too," noted the syndicated Rock Talk newspaper column. "*Rhiannon* will be a fantasy that takes place in ancient times, with gods, goddesses, magic, the whole bit."

As it turns out, a fan had recently sent Nicks four paperbacks by author Evangeline Walton that retold the Welsh *Mabinogion* stories, and the musician had bought the rights to these books. The first volume had actually been published in 1936 under the title *The Virgin and the Swine*; however, this book (and Walton herself) only received wider praise after the novel was reissued as *The Island of the Mighty* in 1970. Three more books in the series soon followed, led by 1971's *The Children of Llyr* and (appropriately enough) 1972's *The Song of Rhiannon*. Incredibly, Nicks said she hadn't seen the latter book before naming the song.

Of course, neither the Rhiannon film nor soundtrack happened in 1979; instead, Fleetwood Mac released *Tusk* and went on tour that fall. But Nicks never gave up on her beloved idea. By 2020, the thought of a film had evolved into a TV miniseries; in fact, Nicks told the *Los Angeles Times* she linked up with a studio for filming and still had ten unreleased songs held back for the eventual release.

That same year, she decided to dig into yet another Rhiannon-related project. "I have some Rhiannon poetry that I have written over the last 30 years that I've kept very quiet," she told *Rolling Stone*. "I'm thinking, 'Well, here I have all this time and I have a recording setup.' . . . I'm going to start putting some of these really beautiful poems to music." Neither these poems nor the TV miniseries had surfaced as of 2025—but no doubt whenever they do emerge, they will be worth the wait.

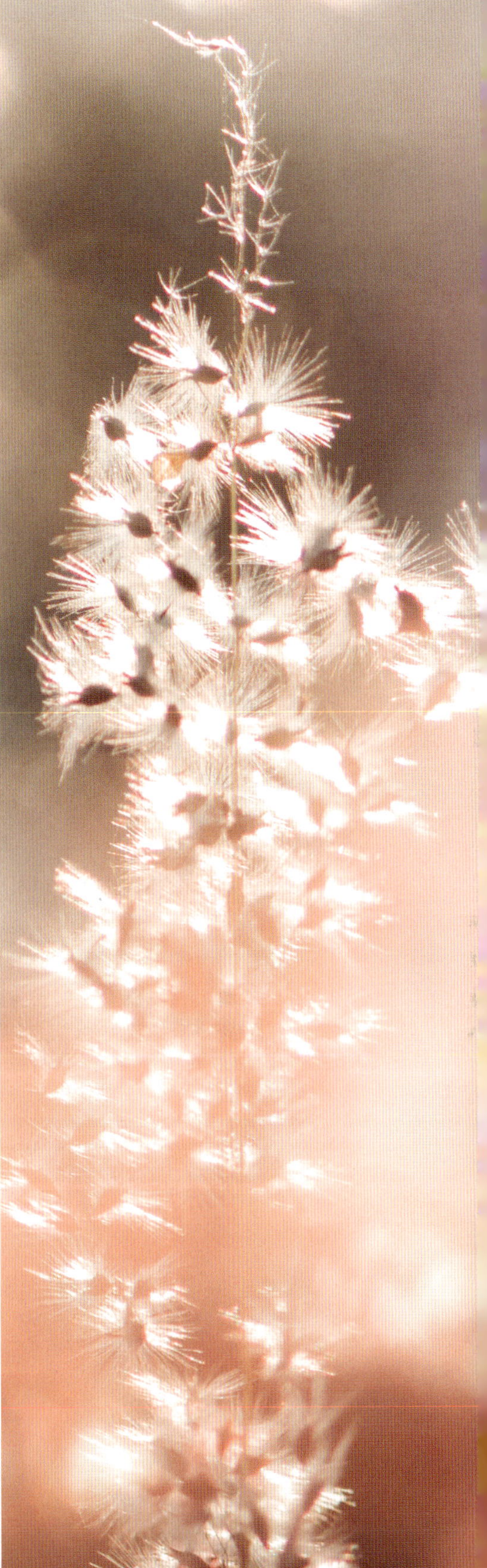

Witchy WOMAN

The release of "Rhiannon" also kicked off one of the most enduring misconceptions about Stevie Nicks: that she's a witch. "Somehow the press turned me into the Great Dark Witch of the North because of that song," she said in a 1994 interview, "I don't think about all that satanic black arts thing that a lot of people wanted to put on me, because it's really not true at all."

In a 1984 MTV interview, she addressed one potential source of this rumor: the fact that she apparently once told an interviewer she was a witch. "I lied," she said lightly. "Or just in the funny sense . . . like the silly witch that crashes into your window on the broom." Indeed, Nicks seemed rather unbothered by the witch chatter, telling MTV in 1987 that she has "more important things that I could worry about . . . All you have to do is come by my house, drop in. There's no owls up there." Nicks adds that she does collect "crystal stuff" and "some beautiful things that people would say, 'Well, it's very kind of mystical,'" but noted that's just who she is. "I'd say, 'But even if I wasn't Stevie Nicks and even if I wasn't in Fleetwood Mac I would still have these things.'"

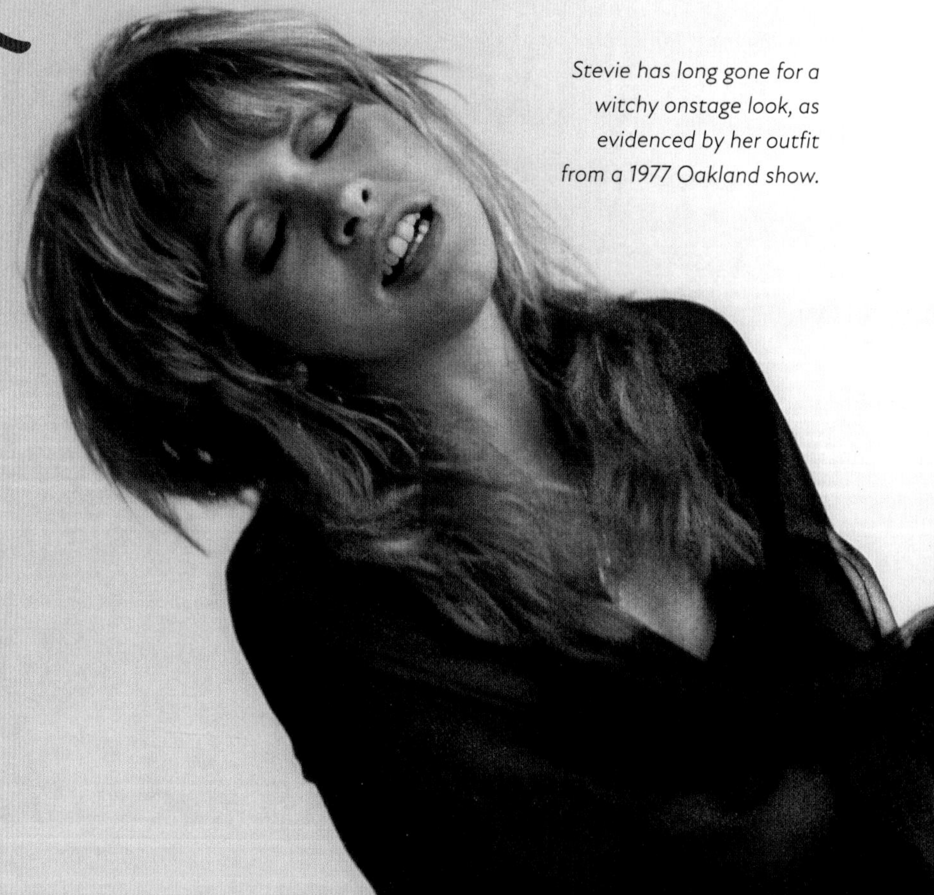

Stevie has long gone for a witchy onstage look, as evidenced by her outfit from a 1977 Oakland show.

Still, the witchy woman rumors continued to have real-world implications. In 1998, Alabama high school students were barred from singing Fleetwood Mac's "Landslide" at a baccalaureate service because "the music minister said the leader of Fleetwood Mac is a witch and a Satan worshipper," vocalist Emily McDowell, who subsequently didn't stay for the service, told a newspaper. "I can't believe people are still telling me I'm a witch because I wear black," Nicks said in response.

In fact, she told MTV her sartorial choices were a matter of taste: "And the dripping black sleeves and everything and the hats—this was a style I thought was just absolutely great." Speaking to the *Los Angeles Times*, she clarified another factor going into her clothing choices, saying that she told the witch hunters, "I just wear black because it makes me look thinner, you idiots."

Years later, however, Nicks admitted that these accusations got under her skin. "I got freaked out at one point," she told *Rolling Stone* in 2024. "People were writing about me being a witch, and I stopped wearing black and I made the girls stop wearing black, too. [Designer] Margi [Kent] made us all-new pale-pastel outfits; it was the '80s." Footage from a 1981 *Bella Donna*–era show indeed shows her wearing a pale pink shawl during "Gold Dust Woman." But then they all came to their senses, Nicks said: "And then we all looked at each other one day and said, 'Why are we wearing these Easter egg dresses? This is not us.'"

"I thought that being a witch was the absolute most fun thing you could be on Halloween. I didn't want to go as a hot dog or a box of Kleenex."

—STEVIE NICKS TO *DAILY MAIL*

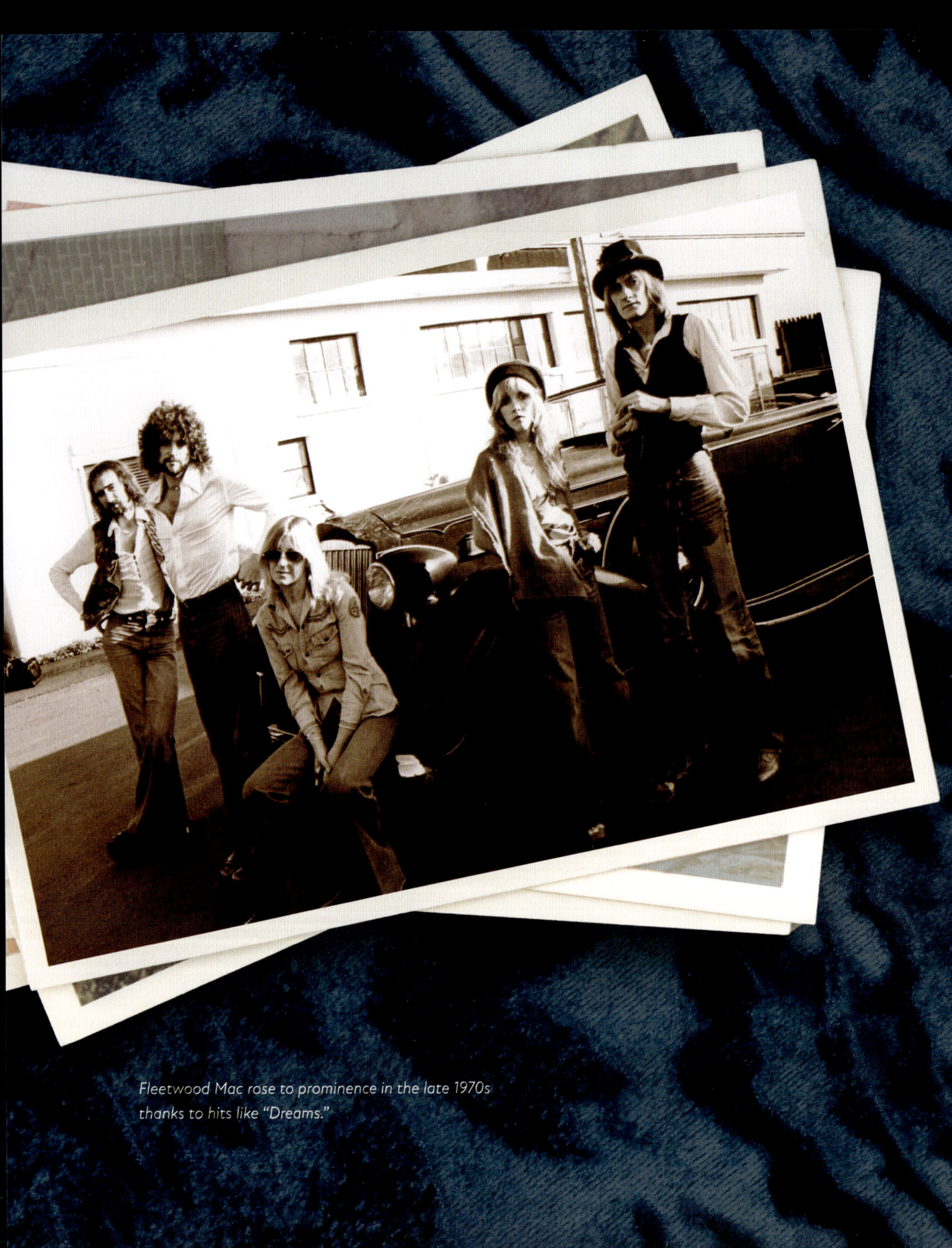

Fleetwood Mac rose to prominence in the late 1970s thanks to hits like "Dreams."

10. FLEETWOOD MAC

"Dreams" 1977

The tumultuous roots of Fleetwood Mac's only US number one.

FLEETWOOD MAC'S *RUMOURS* IS NOTORIOUS FOR BEING A CHRONICLE of intra-band drama. During this era, Christine McVie had divorced John McVie in 1976 and was having an affair with the band's lighting director; Nicks and Lindsey Buckingham were on the romantic rocks; and Mick Fleetwood was splitting from his wife, Jenny. "Everybody was pretty weirded out," Christine McVie told *Rolling Stone* in 1977. "Somehow Mick was there, the figurehead: 'We must carry on . . . let's be mature about this, sort it out.' Somehow we waded through it."

Given that all the bandmates were songwriters, the quintet poured their emotional tumult into music. For example, Nicks wrote the cautionary tale "Dreams" about her and Lindsey Buckingham's breakup. The narrator warns a restless partner who wants to leave to be careful what they wish for: The grass isn't always greener on the other side, and it's very likely they'll encounter loneliness and regret rather than bliss. Nicks assumes a conspiratorial vocal tone throughout, ensuring she sounds equal parts wistful and resigned, as slipshod guitar parts, a dewy bassline, and laid-back drums give "Dreams" a liminal, hazy vibe.

Buckingham's musical response to the couple's breakup, "Go Your Own Way," markedly possesses a tougher, harder-edged sound. "I write philosophically; he writes angry," Nicks observed in a 1998 BBC Radio 2 special, noting that she would get upset by some things he wrote. "However, as a songwriter, I have to respect that he's gonna write about what's happening to him, and so am I. I could never say to him, you know, 'Back off, stop writing songs about me,' because that was his life then, and that's when the best songs are written.

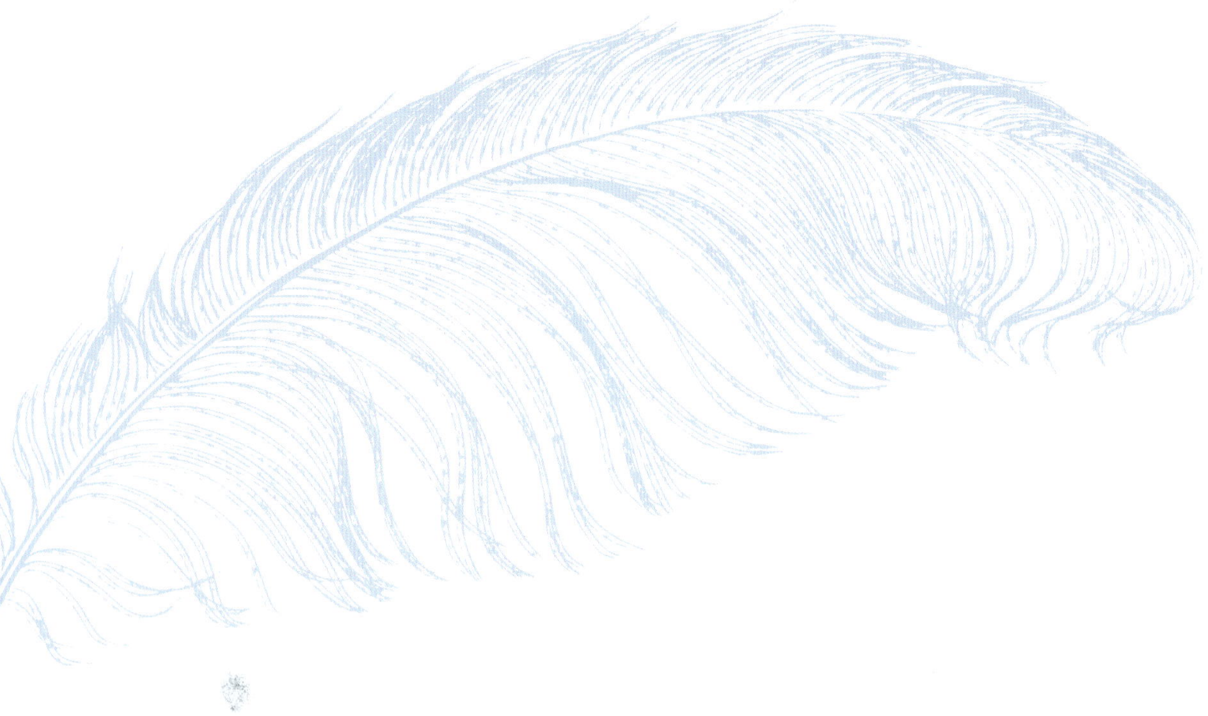

And it doesn't really matter who breaks up with who at that point; that's when everybody writes the best songs."

"Dreams" came together while Fleetwood Mac were hunkered down at the Record Plant in Sausalito, California, recording *Rumours*. Sly Stone happened to have a studio on the premises, a "black and red room" with "a stairway that went down into this, like, kind of tunnel thing where people would set up and play around this lighthouse sort of setup," Nicks said during her *VH1 Storytellers* episode. Fender Rhodes piano in tow, she retreated to this space and wrote "Dreams" in "about an hour," she added. "And then I went back in to Fleetwood Mac and actually was brave enough to play it for them, 'cause I really thought it was good."

In a later interview, she recalled that Buckingham especially was pleased with the song, which aligned with Christine McVie's remembrance of how "Dreams" evolved from this solo demo to a full-band masterpiece. "When Stevie first played it for me on the piano it was just three chords and one note in the left hand," she told *Record Hunter* magazine. "I thought, 'This is really boring.' But the Lindsey genius came into play, and he fashioned three sections out of identical chords, making each section sound completely different. He created the impression that there's a thread running through the whole thing."

> "We were couples who couldn't make it through. But, as musicians, we still respected each other—and we got some brilliant songs out of it."

— STEVIE NICKS TO THE *DAILY MAIL* ON FLEETWOOD MAC

"Dreams" topped the Billboard Hot 100 for one week in June 1977, becoming Fleetwood Mac's first and only US No. 1 single. The song has had tremendous staying power: Irish group the Corrs had a massive hit with a 1998 cover, while a breezy dance remix by Jolyon Petch that featured the vocalist Reigan topped Australia's ARIA Top 50 Club Tracks chart in 2021.

In 2020, "Dreams" became a viral sensation after Nathan Apodaca (who went by the username 420doggface208 on TikTok) filmed himself skateboarding and swigging Ocean Spray cranberry juice from the bottle while vibing to the song. The members of Fleetwood Mac loved the trend. Mick Fleetwood re-created the video, while Buckingham posted a video of himself drinking cranberry juice while riding a horse. And Nicks one-upped them all by posting a video of herself sitting at her piano while lacing up roller skates and singing along to "Dreams." Next to her? A bottle of cranberry juice.

Thanks to this attention, "Dreams" leapt back into the Billboard Hot 100, peaking at No. 12, and also made inroads on the Hot Rock & Alternative Songs chart. It's clear the song's sentiments transcended generations. "What was going on between us was sad," Nicks told the *Daily Mail* about her and Buckingham and the rest of Fleetwood Mac. "We were couples who couldn't make it through. But, as musicians, we still respected each other—and we got some brilliant songs out of it."

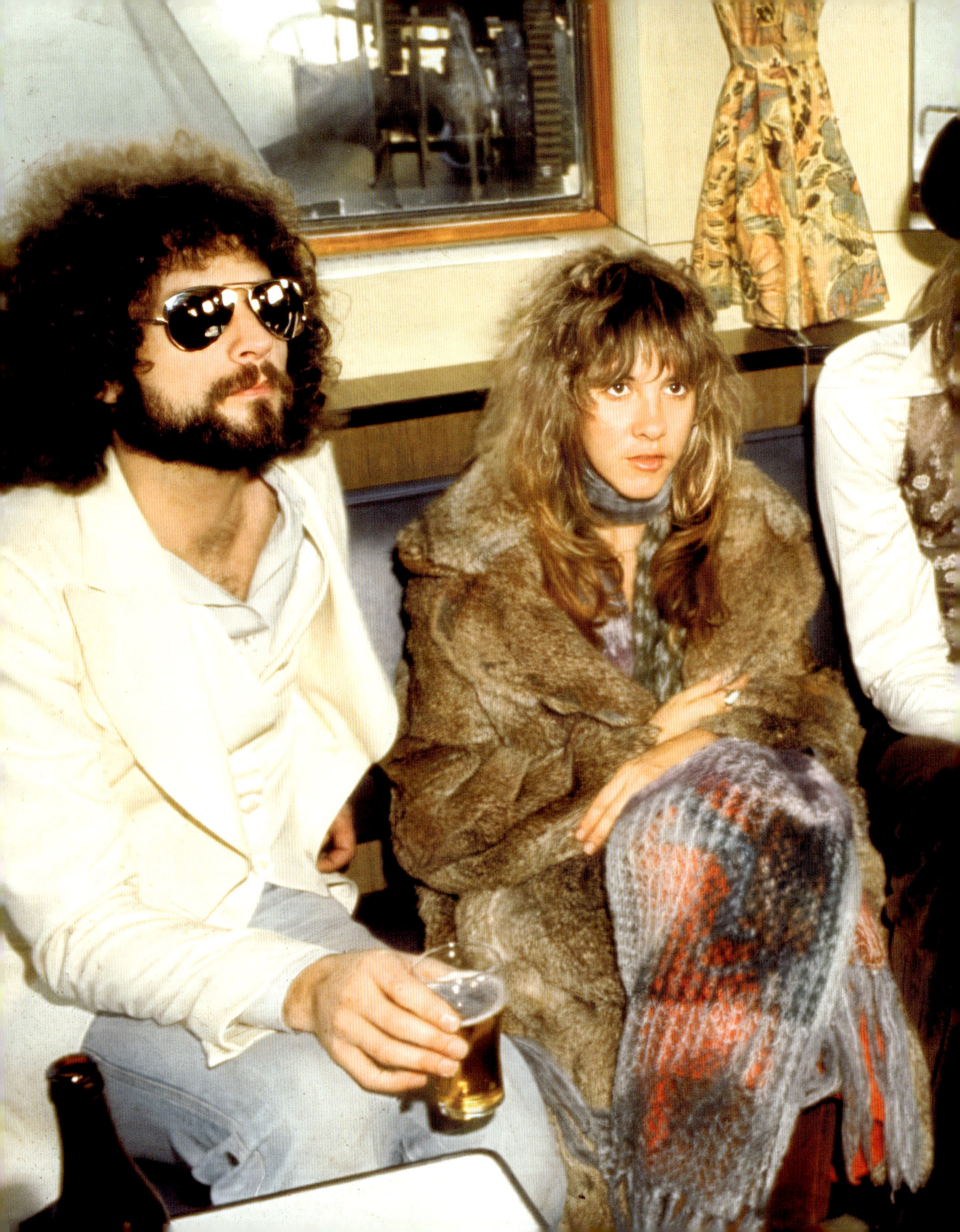

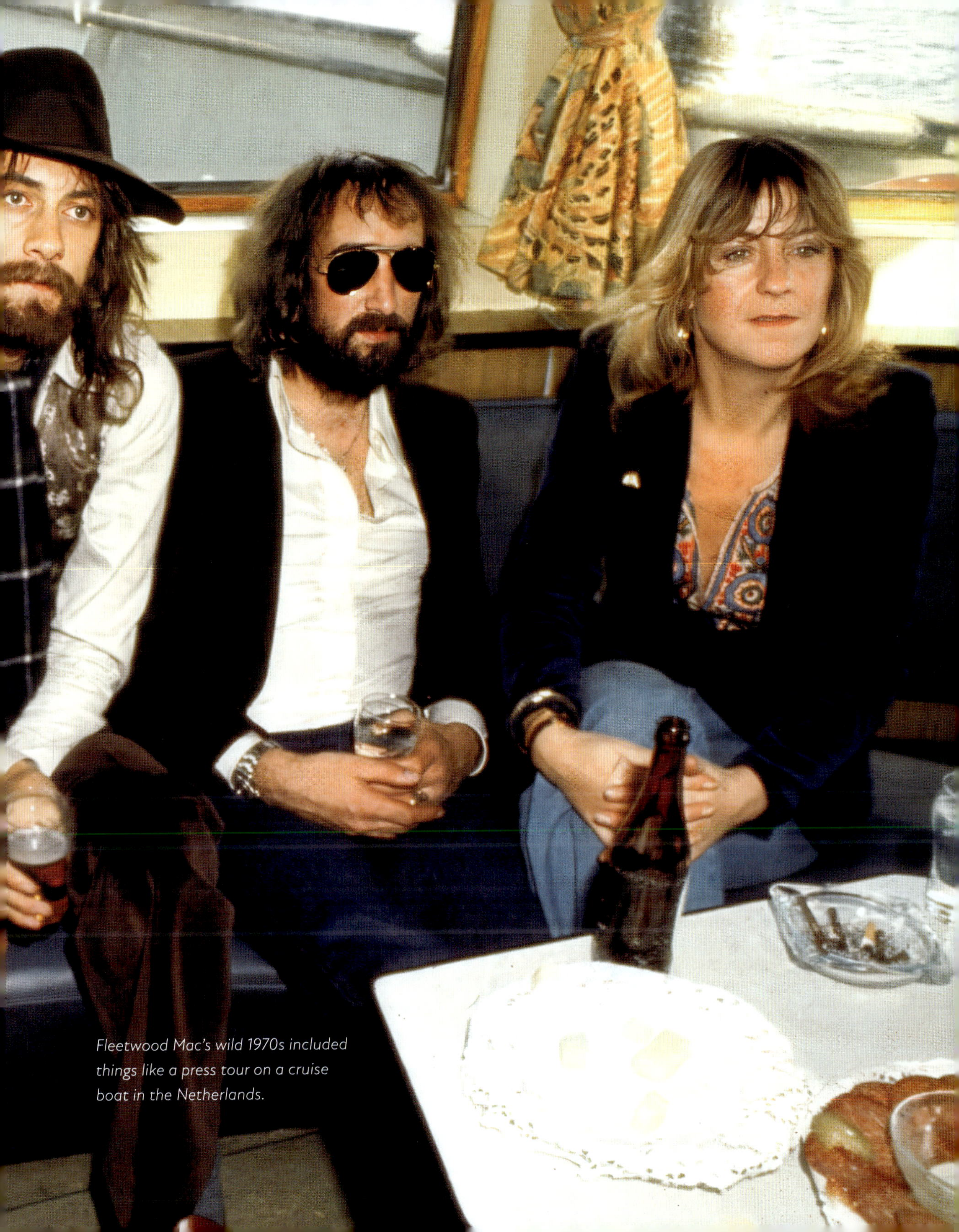

Fleetwood Mac's wild 1970s included things like a press tour on a cruise boat in the Netherlands.

STEVIE GETS A *Barbie*

During her October 2023 Madison Square Garden concert, Nicks gave the crowd a thrilling surprise: She announced that Mattel had approached her about having her own Barbie doll. Nicks initially found the prospect slightly overwhelming, she admitted: "Of course I questioned, 'Would she look like me? Would she have my spirit? Would she have my heart?'"

She definitely had no need to worry. The final version of the doll clutched a tambourine while sporting miniature versions of Nicks's flowing black *Rumours* outfit, her signature 1977 Di Fabrizio boots, and a moon necklace. After sharing photos of the doll on the arena's big screens, Nicks excitedly showed the Madison Square Garden audience the actual doll, pretended to make it sing "Edge of Seventeen," and remarked on what this meant to her.

"When I look at her, I see my twenty-seven-year-old self," she said. "All the memories of walking out on a big stage in that black outfit and those fabulous black boots come rushing back to me. And then I see myself now in her face, what we have been through since 1975: the battles that we have fought, the lessons that we have learned together. I am her and she is me. She absolutely has my heart."

Naturally, the doll sold out everywhere almost immediately once it went on sale for fifty-five dollars. But fans weren't the only ones who

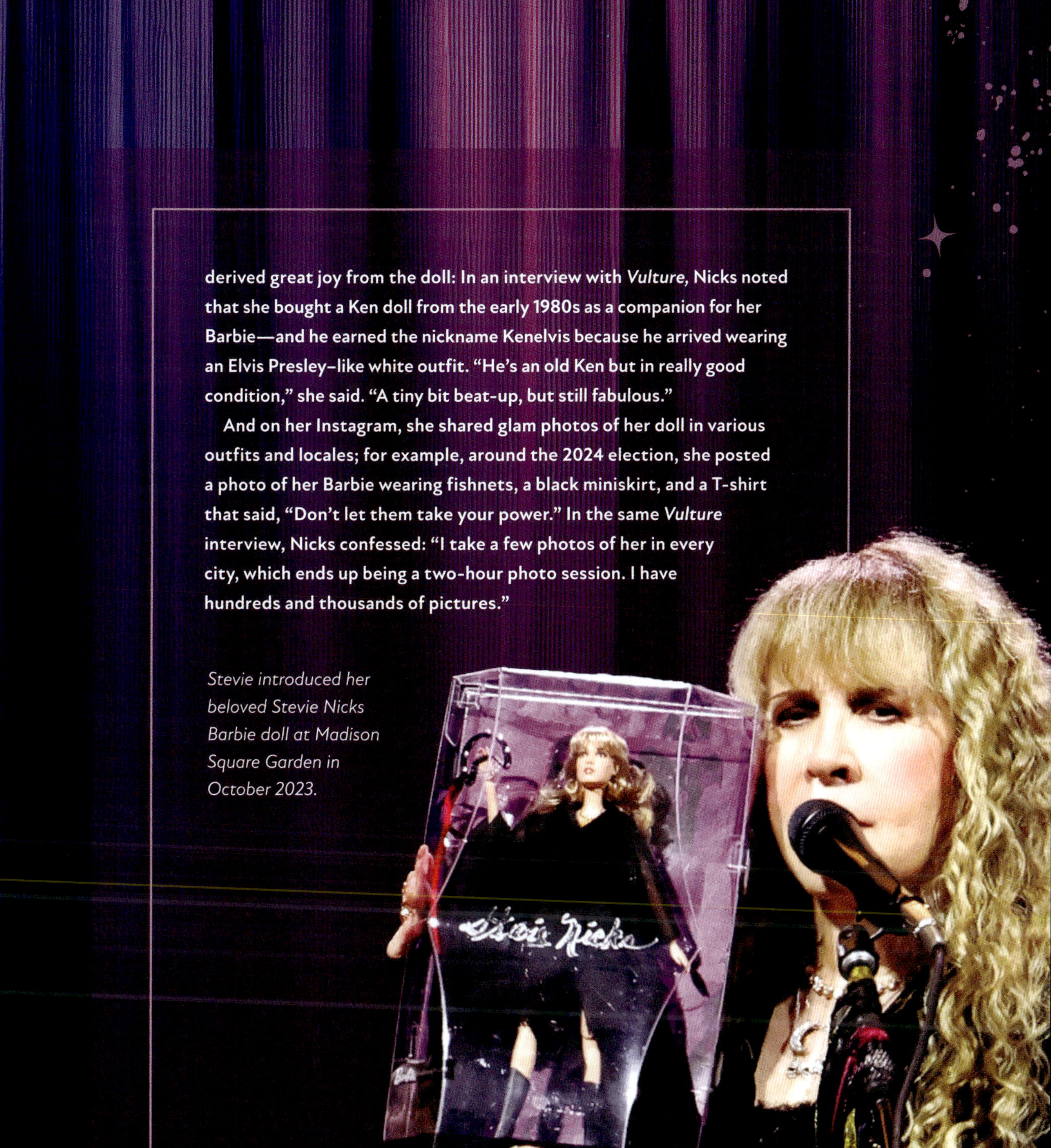

derived great joy from the doll: In an interview with *Vulture*, Nicks noted that she bought a Ken doll from the early 1980s as a companion for her Barbie—and he earned the nickname Kenelvis because he arrived wearing an Elvis Presley–like white outfit. "He's an old Ken but in really good condition," she said. "A tiny bit beat-up, but still fabulous."

And on her Instagram, she shared glam photos of her doll in various outfits and locales; for example, around the 2024 election, she posted a photo of her Barbie wearing fishnets, a black miniskirt, and a T-shirt that said, "Don't let them take your power." In the same *Vulture* interview, Nicks confessed: "I take a few photos of her in every city, which ends up being a two-hour photo session. I have hundreds and thousands of pictures."

Stevie introduced her beloved Stevie Nicks Barbie doll at Madison Square Garden in October 2023.

Fleetwood Mac poses together circa 1976.

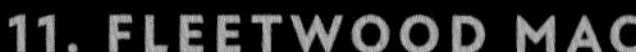

11. FLEETWOOD MAC

“The Chain” 1977

The Rumours *classic grew out of a Stevie demo.*

“THE CHAIN” IS ONE OF THE FEW FLEETWOOD MAC SONGS on *Rumours* where every band member has a songwriting credit. The reason is simple: The tune, which opens side two, was Frankensteined together from multiple separate songs. “We ended up calling it ‘The Chain’ because it was a bunch of pieces,” Lindsey Buckingham once told *Rolling Stone*.

This was no exaggeration. For starters, Buckngham borrowed lilting guitars from “Lola (My Love),” a song from the 1973 *Buckingham Nicks* LP. Separately, Fleetwood Mac were also kicking around a sinewy, psychedelic-glossed demo called “Keep Me There” with Christine McVie on lead vocals *and* a John McVie bass solo that rumbled like a powerful thunderstorm.

The band decided to build a song around the latter part, but needed better musical connective tissue. Buckingham recalled that Stevie Nicks had a sparse, folk-leaning demo that might work, and asked if she'd be willing to give it to the band. “And I thought to myself, ‘Well, okay. I will take one for the team here,’” Nicks told *Variety* in 2020.

Incredibly enough, this demo also had elements of “If You Ever Did Believe,” which later ended up as a Nicks solo song on the soundtrack of 1998's *Practical Magic*. When Nicks re-listened to this demo back in 2020, the links between these eras were quite strong.

“I thought, ‘Wow, I had full-on plans for the original “Chain” song before I gave it to Fleetwood Mac,’” she told *Variety*. “I'm really glad that I gave it to Fleetwood Mac because it turned into one of the best songs. But it was holding its own before they recorded it.”

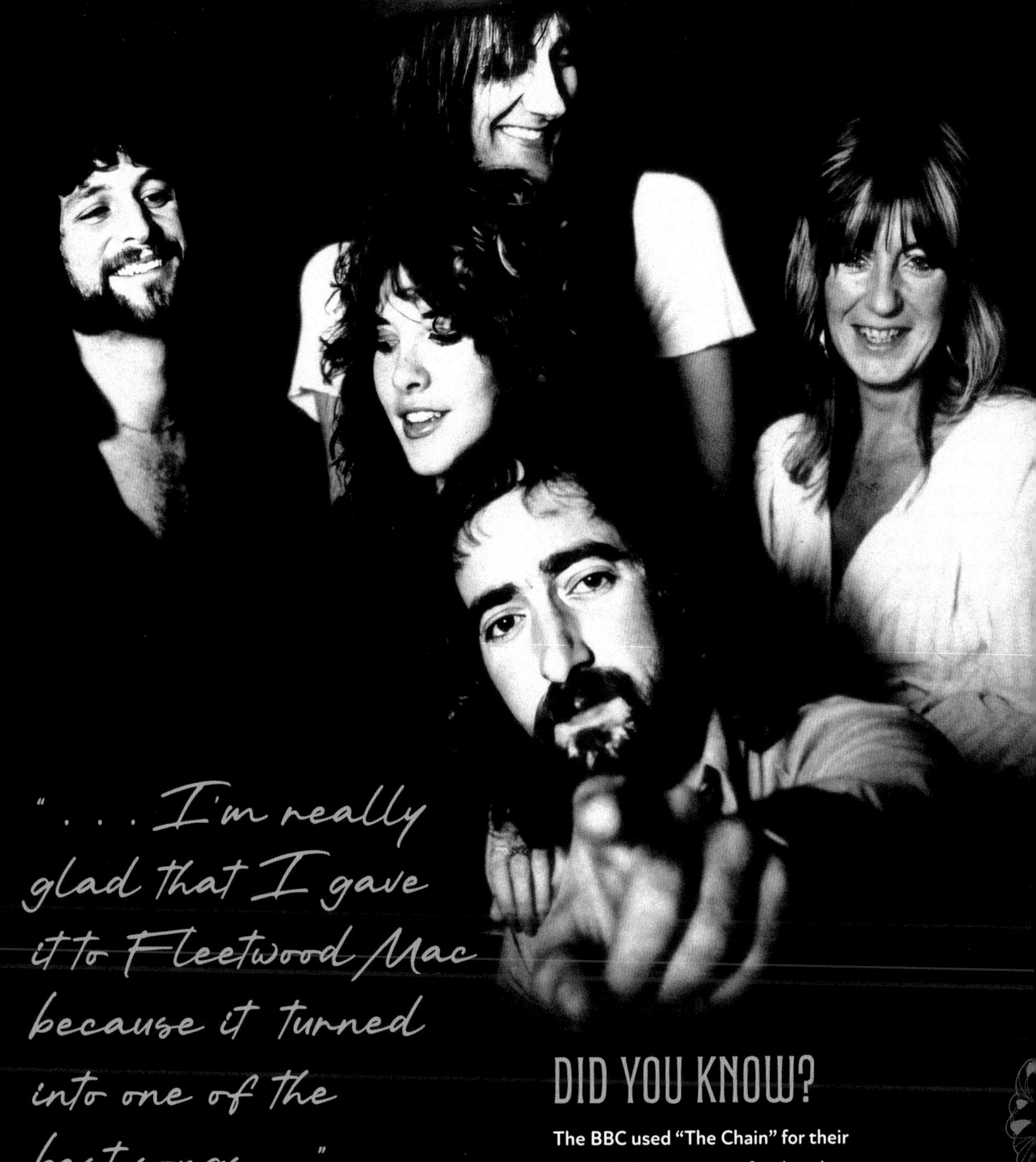

"... I'm really glad that I gave it to Fleetwood Mac because it turned into one of the best songs ..."

—STEVIE NICKS TO *VARIETY* ON "THE CHAIN"

DID YOU KNOW?

The BBC used "The Chain" for their Formula One coverage for decades, causing the song to re-enter the UK singles charts several times.

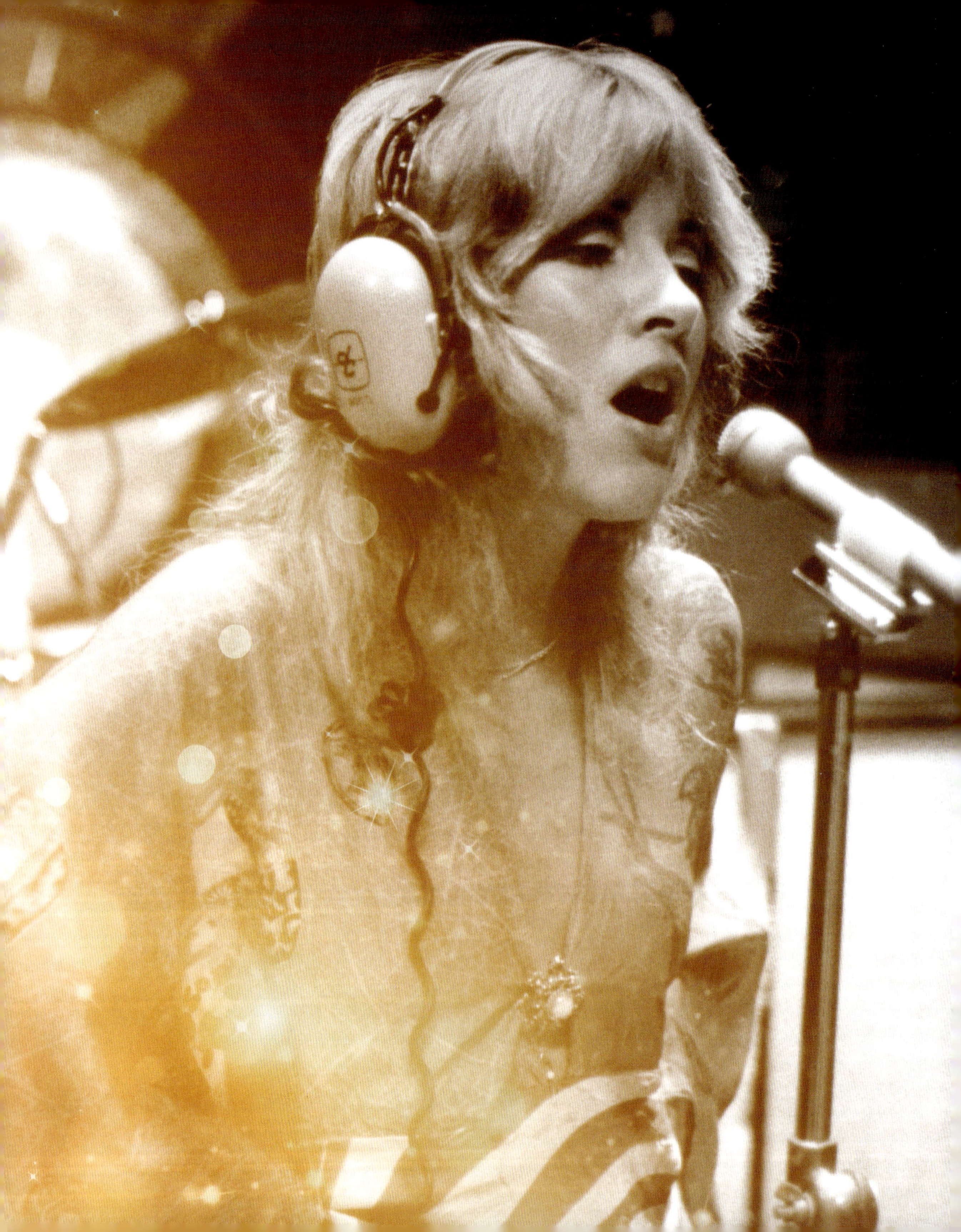

Stevie lays down vocals in the studio in 1975.

12. FLEETWOOD MAC

"Gold Dust Woman" 1977

An ominous cautionary tale about a powerful, shadowy figure.

WHEN NICKS PERFORMS THE THUNDERING ROCK EPIC "GOLD Dust Woman" live, she very deliberately puts on a shimmering gold-colored shawl. The accessory helps her become the song's titular character: a powerful, destructive force who wields emotions like a sharp sword. Run into the gold dust woman and you'll end up in tears, disillusioned by life—or worse.

At least part of Nicks's inspiration for the song is "groupie-type ladies," she told *Crawdaddy* in 1976. "About women who stand around and give me and Christine [McVie] dirty looks but as soon as a guy comes in the room are overcome with smiles." However, she also viewed the gold dust in the title as a euphemism for cocaine.

"But it's not completely about that, because there wasn't that much cocaine around then," Nicks confessed in a 1997 *SPIN* magazine conversation with Hole front woman Courtney Love. "Everybody was doing a little bit—you know, we never bought it or anything, it was just around—and I think I had a real serious flask of what this stuff could be, of what it could do to you." Even still, she recalls writing "Gold Dust Woman" as an ominous warning: "I really imagined that it could overtake everything, never thinking a million years that it would overtake me."

> "[Stevie] had become this witch she was always writing about."
>
> —KEN CAILLAT TO GRAMMY.COM

"Gold Dust Woman" is the perfect end to *Rumours*, as its psychedelic folk vibe and slow-burning arrangement create maximum menace. "It evolved slowly," *Rumours* coproducer Ken Caillat told Grammy.com. "The basic track was very simple, kind of like a folk song. Stevie wanted it to grow. It just kind of snuck up on you. The next thing I knew it was getting kind of creepy." Credit for that vibe goes to the song's use of electric harpsichord and a Dobro, as well as guitar zaps that feel like prickly needles.

Nicks, meanwhile, sounds positively haunted—some might say possessed—as she sings. Mick Fleetwood recalls that the singer's first crack at "Gold Dust Woman" was in a "fully lit studio, and as take followed take, she began withdrawing into herself." They made the space darker and brought her amenities such as tissues, a Vicks inhaler, lozenges, and mineral water. It did the trick. "And on the eighth take, at four in the morning," Fleetwood says, "she sang the lyric straight through to perfection."

Caillat recalls a similar transformation, noting that Nicks "had a lot of Courvoisier in her, and she did this incredible coyote-like howling at the end. She had become this witch she was always writing about." Fleetwood augmented this wild vibe by breaking sheets of glass in another studio area. "He was wearing goggles and coveralls—it was pretty funny," Caillat says. "He just went mad, bashing glass with this big hammer."

"Gold Dust Woman" wasn't a single, but it was released as the B side to "You Make Loving Fun." In 1996, Hole covered "Gold Dust Woman" for *The Crow: City of Angels* soundtrack. "I thought it was great," Nicks told *Us Weekly*. "It's a little raucous for me, but she's so very true to my song." She also liked Courtney Love after meeting the rocker at a Smashing Pumpkins concert. "Everyone wanted us to really like each other," Nicks said. "And I really did like her. She's really a lot of fun for me, because I get to share stuff with her like maybe I would if I had a daughter."

Shawls & CAPES

Nicks is known for her extensive collection of luxurious shawls and capes. Of particular note is that she still owns (and tours with) a dark blue cape she bought circa *Bella Donna*; it appears within the album artwork. "Love your cape and it will love you back," she said during a show, after demonstrating how it's in pristine condition. Naturally, it helps that Nicks has her own shawl vault to store these treasured articles of clothing. "They're all in temperature-controlled storage," she told *Rolling Stone*. "I have these huge red cases Fleetwood Mac bought, all the way back in 1975—my clothes are saved in these cases. . . . I'm trying to give my shawls away—but there's thousands of them. If I ever write my life story, maybe that should be the name of my book: There's Enough Shawls to Go Around." Still, it's clear she always has room for more. In 2014, Utah designer Celeste Meyeres won a contest to design a shawl for Nicks after creating a black-and-silver knitted piece named "NAY-TIV RAY-VIN," which the *Cedar City News* noted "was a nod to her own Cherokee heritage and her love of the mercurial and mischievous ravens endemic to the American Southwest."

Stevie stores her gorgeous shawl collection in a temperature-controlled vault.

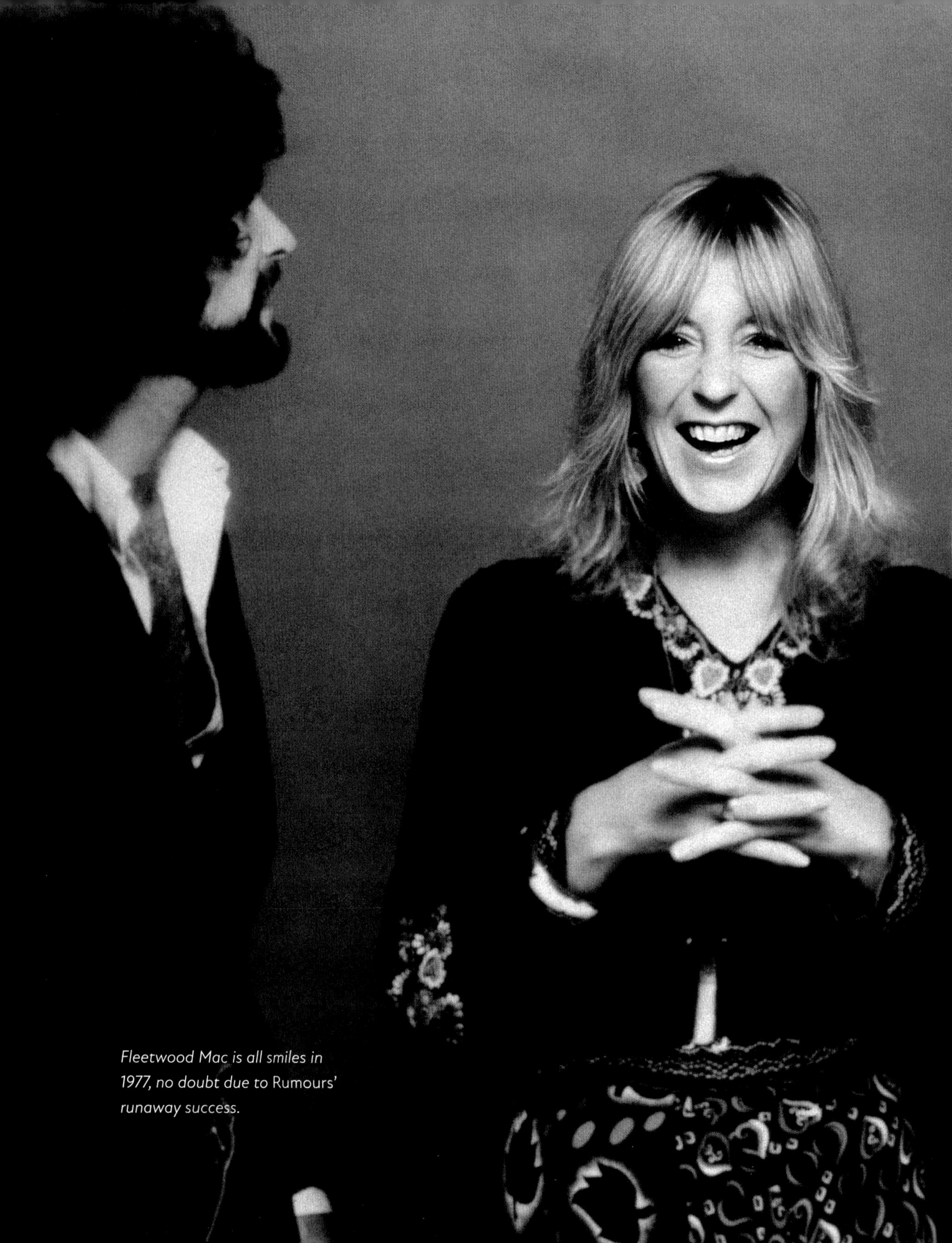

Fleetwood Mac is all smiles in 1977, no doubt due to Rumours' runaway success.

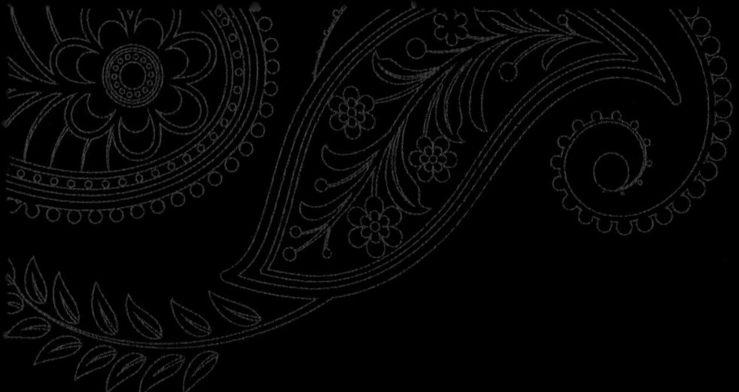

13. FLEETWOOD MAC

"Silver Springs" 1977

A beloved song that finally received its due.

IT WAS THE LOOK SEEN AROUND THE WORLD. DURING FLEETWOOD Mac's 1997 TV special *The Dance*, Nicks stared intensely at Lindsey Buckingham while singing "Silver Springs" like she was shooting fireballs from her eyes. It's an absolutely mesmerizing performance that's since become the stuff of legend, spawning T-shirts with lighthearted slogans ("Sorry, I can't talk. I'm thinking about the 1997 performance of 'Silver Springs' where Stevie Nicks stares a hole through Lindsey Buckingham."), lively YouTube comments sections, and internet memes.

Nicks told *The Arizona Republic* that the band captured this performance on the Friday night of taping several shows for the special. "In six weeks of rehearsal, it was never like that," she said. "Only on Friday night did we let it go into something deeper. . . . The other shows were really, really good, but they weren't the show I wanted to leave behind. This show was. I wanted people to stand back and really watch and understand what [the relationship] was."

In that same interview, Nicks also detailed her thought process when she wrote the pristine folk-pop song: "I'm so angry with you. You will listen to me on the radio for the rest of your life, and it will bug you. I hope it bugs you." Fittingly, the narrator is finally done with an emotionally unavailable romantic partner—among other things, he's apparently found someone else—but says she has plans to haunt him for the rest of his days. "Silver Springs" was slated to appear on *Rumours*, but didn't end up on the final version. When asked in 1977 why the song wasn't there, Buckingham told the *Fort Worth Star-Telegram* that "It was a tough decision. We simply had one too many songs. So it was a toss-up as to what to leave off." According to Nicks, Mick Fleetwood told her "Silver Springs" was too long, and they wanted to put another Nicks tune, "I Don't Wanna Know," on *Rumours* instead.

Nicks told the *Arizona Daily Star* that she didn't take this decision lightly: "I was so upset I almost had a nervous breakdown." *Rolling Stone* reported that producers explored potential options, like shortening "Gold Dust Woman" or removing another song, to squeeze "Silver Springs" onto the LP. As a result, however, Nicks would've also then had three slower songs on the album. In the end, "Silver Springs" ended up as the B-side of "Go Your Own Way"; in a small measure of vindication, the *New York Times* encouraged people to buy the single specifically for its flip side, noting, "It's as lovely as one might expect from this fine composer and singer, if not necessarily superior to her other songs on the LP."

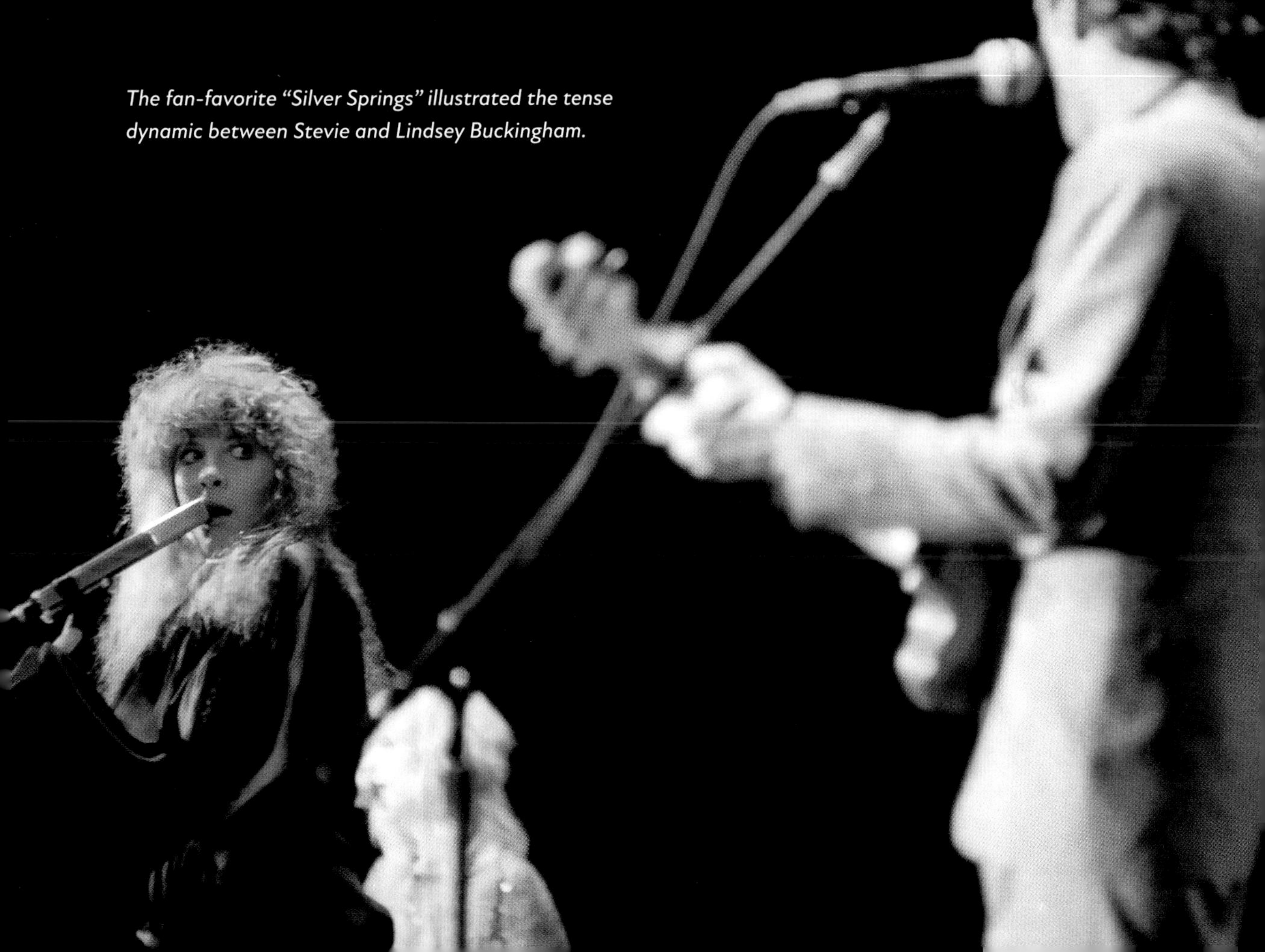

The fan-favorite "Silver Springs" illustrated the tense dynamic between Stevie and Lindsey Buckingham.

"I'm so angry with you. You will listen to me on the radio for the rest of your life, and it will bug you. I hope it bugs you."

—STEVIE NICKS DESCRIBES HER "SILVER SPRINGS" INSPIRATION TO THE *ARIZONA REPUBLIC*

It's quite understandable that Nicks was so upset over the song's omission: She had decided to give the songwriting and publishing royalties of "Silver Springs" to her mom, Barbara. "My mother would never take a penny from me, so I figured the only way I could actually give her some money would be to give her a song," Nicks said in a 2001 radio interview. "'Silver Springs' was her favorite song; she named her antique store The Silver Springs Emporium. Then they took it off the record, so it was very much of a dud gift."

And unsurprisingly, Nicks held a grudge over the way the band treated "Silver Springs." In fact, she left Fleetwood Mac in 1990 because she wasn't allowed to include it on her 1991 compilation *Timespace*. "When *Timespace* came around, it didn't occur to me that they wouldn't let me have it back," she told the BBC. She had reached out to Mick Fleetwood (to no avail) to discuss "Silver Springs" and then contacted his manager. "I said, 'You find Mick, and you tell him that if I don't have those tapes by Monday, I am no longer a member of Fleetwood Mac.'" Fleetwood's manager did get an answer from the drummer, though it wasn't what Nicks wanted to hear: "Mick had said, 'Over my dead body will I ever give her that song back.'"

Thanks to its inclusion on *The Dance*, "Silver Springs" has become one of Fleetwood Mac's most popular songs; the band's live performance was also nominated for a Grammy for Best Pop Performance by a Duo or Group with Vocals. But what the song means to Nicks matters above all, she noted in a 2015 *Maclean's* magazine interview. "When I finish [performing] 'Silver Springs' [live], Christine waits for me and takes my hand. We walk off and we never let go of each other until we get to our tent. In that 30 seconds, it's like my heart just comes out of my body."

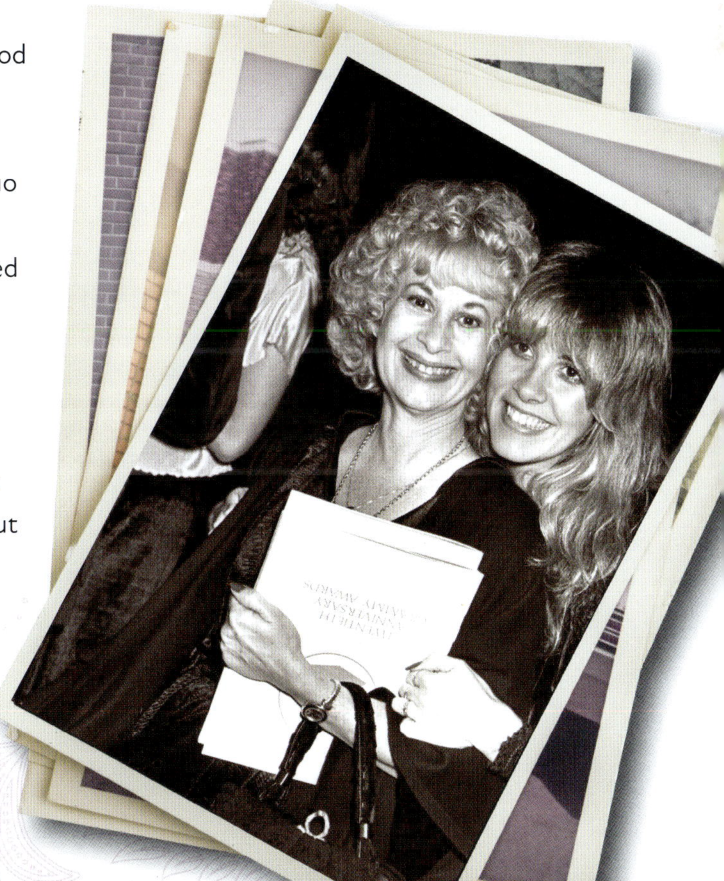

Stevie and her mom Barbara attend the Grammy Awards together in 1978.

Christine McVie and Stevie were best friends as well as musical collaborators.

14. FLEETWOOD MAC

"Don't Stop" 1977

Christine McVie's hopeful hit with hidden sting.

IN 1993, THE UNTHINKABLE HAPPENED: NICKS AND THE REST of the *Rumours*-era lineup of Fleetwood Mac reunited. The occasion was the inaugural gala of incoming US President Bill Clinton, who had used the Christine McVie–penned "Don't Stop" as his campaign song. "It perfectly captured the mood of a nation eager for better days," Clinton said in 2022. "I'm grateful to Christine and Fleetwood Mac for entrusting us with such a meaningful song."

The appearance didn't lead to a full-blown band reunion just yet; in fact, Fleetwood Mac played just that one tune. But the tune's sentiments—don't dwell on the past, turn the page, and have hope for the future—certainly planted the seeds for a future victory lap. Paradoxically, Christine McVie wrote "Don't Stop" about a painful ending: her split from John McVie. (Hilariously, the bassist never realized the song was about him. "I never put that together," he told *Mojo* in 2015. "I've been playing it for years and it wasn't until someone told me, 'Chris wrote that about you' [that I figured it out].") Christine ended up singing the song as a duet alongside Buckingham, reinforcing the song's unified front. "Don't Stop" was a major hit in 1977, reaching No. 3 on the Billboard Hot 100, and over time also came to represent Fleetwood Mac's internal resilience in the face of turbulence.

DID YOU KNOW? **After they reunited for *The Dance*, the band also performed "Don't Stop" as part of a medley at the Grammy Awards in February 1998.**

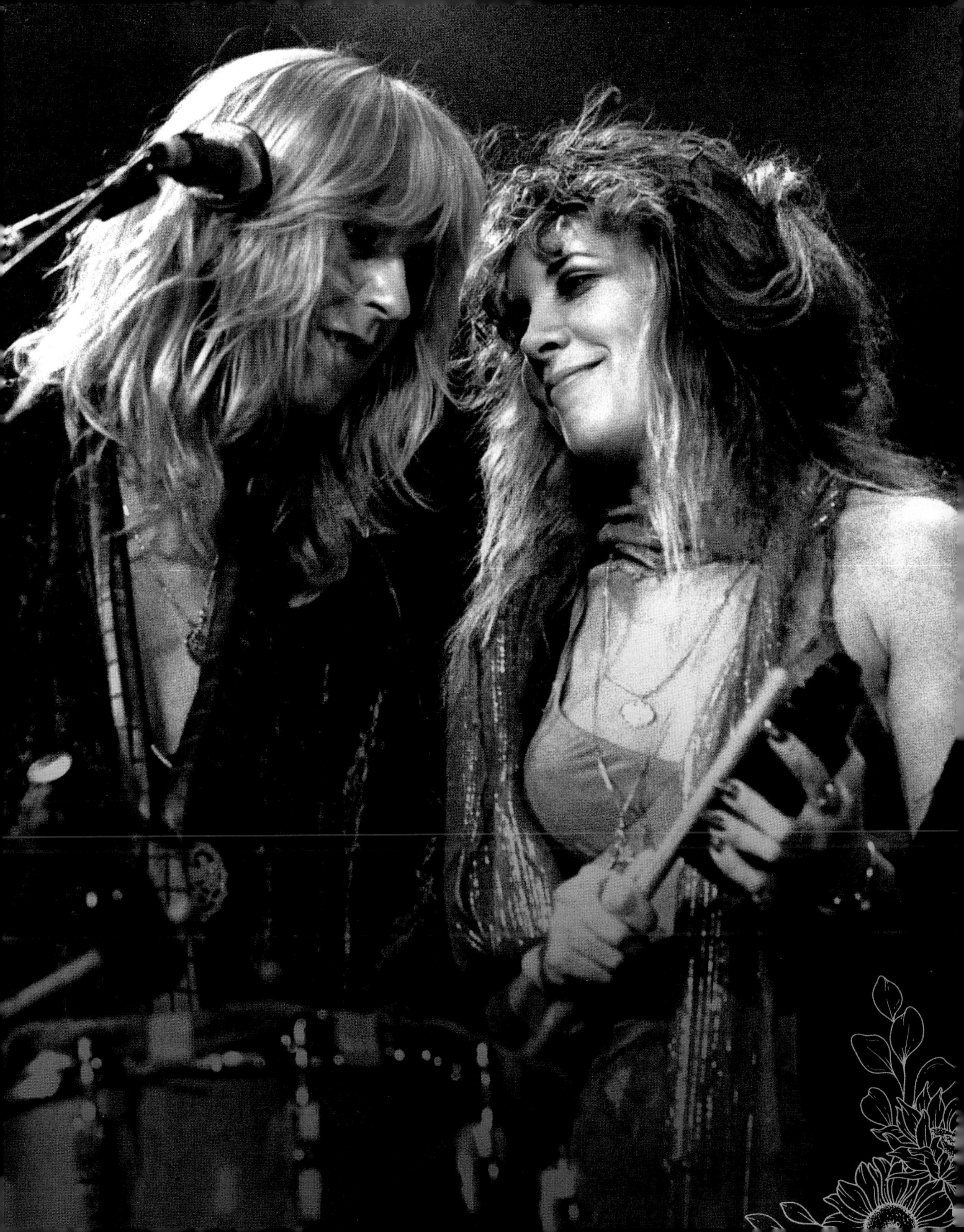

Fashion

"I love long dresses. I love velvet. I love high boots. I never change. I love the same eye make-up, I'm not a fad person. I still have everything I had then." In a testament to Nicks's fashion consistency, it's nearly impossible to tell when she said this. (For the record, it was 1982!) In tandem with designer Margi Kent, she cultivated a feminine style that included gauzy materials, dramatic cuts of clothing, and stalwart brands (for example, her boots were by Di Fabrizio). Once she settled on a look she liked, she didn't change.

"The outfit that's on the *Rumours* cover is exactly the same outfit that's on the *[Trouble in] Shangri-La* cover. It's the same outfit that's on the *Bella Donna* cover. It's timeless . . . it's a timeless outfit, and it has made my life much easier because I don't ever have to think about it."

Nicks developed her fashion sense in response to several formative experiences. Before taking photographs for the cover of the *Buckingham Nicks* LP, she bought herself "a really beautiful, very sexy blouse" with the last money she had. "And they agreed to do half of the session in the blouse," she said in 1990. "And I thought, 'Oh, I'll win. They'll love this blouse, and they're gonna love the way I look.'"

Much to her chagrin, the photographer still told her to take the shirt off. "That cover is about as close to selling the music on sex as you'll ever get, and I was crying when we took that picture," Nicks revealed. "And Lindsey was mad at me. He said, 'You know, you're just being a child. This is art.' And I'm going, 'This is not art. This is taking a nude photograph with you, and I don't dig it.'"

From then on, she decided to do fashion her own way. "I said, 'All right, that's it. We're gonna work this out so that I still have an image and a vibe, but instead of going in the direction that a lot of the women singers are going in now, I'll be very, very sexy under 18 pounds of chiffon and lace and velvet. And nobody will know what I really am. I will have a mystique.'"

> ". . . I'll be very, very sexy under 18 pounds of chiffon and lace and velvet . . ."
>
> —STEVIE NICKS

It took some time to get there; for example, she discovered after doing her first tour with Fleetwood Mac that she needed to up her fashion game. Very quickly, she developed her "English Dickensian waif in a shabby, raggedy black chiffony skirt and heavy boots" look, she told *The Independent*. "I thought, if I'm going to take this really seriously I'm going to plan this all out. I had my hair a certain way, my make-up a certain way. I wanted it to be a complete package."

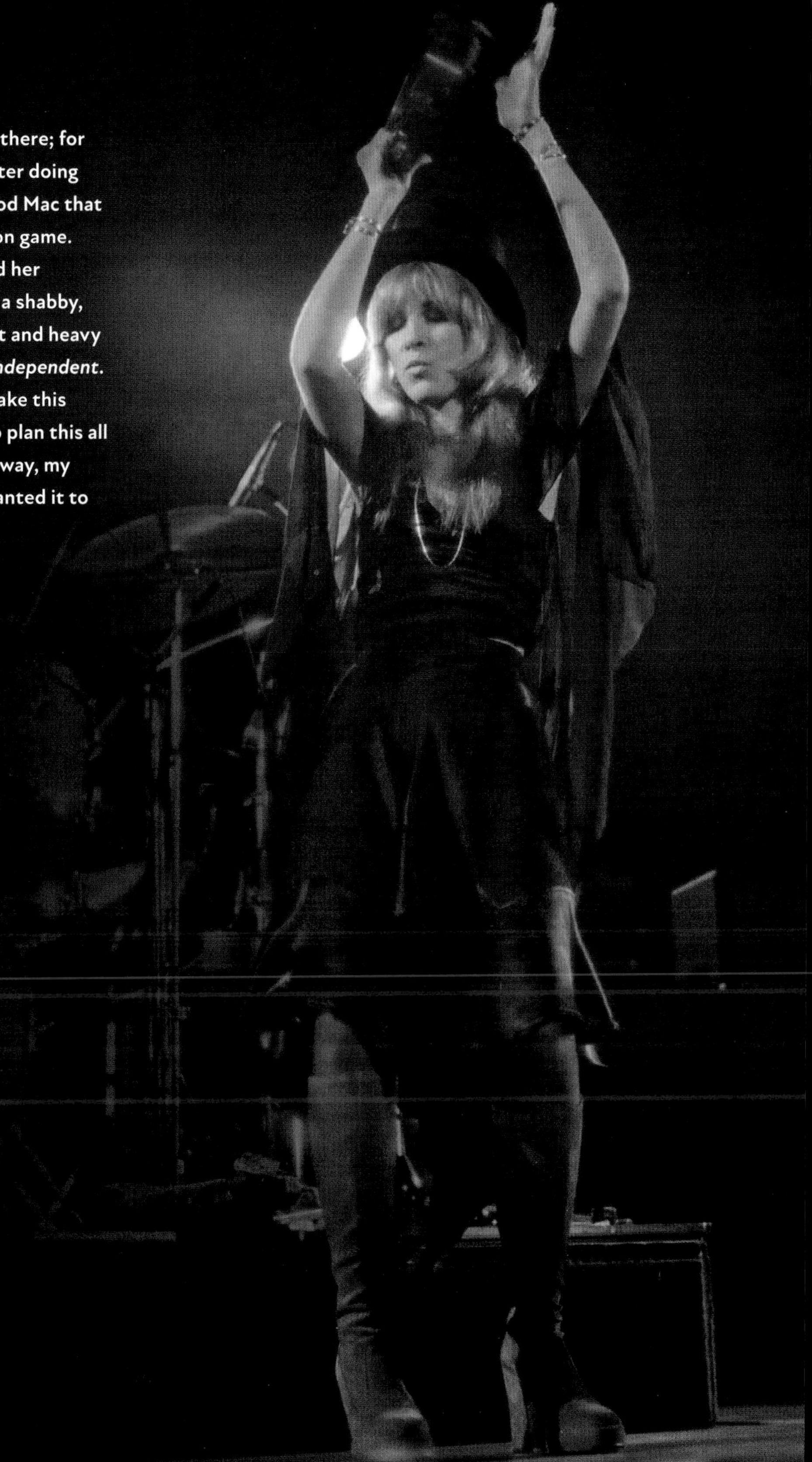

Stevie is a fashion icon thanks to her signature looks, which can include a top hat, flowing skirts, and bespoke boots.

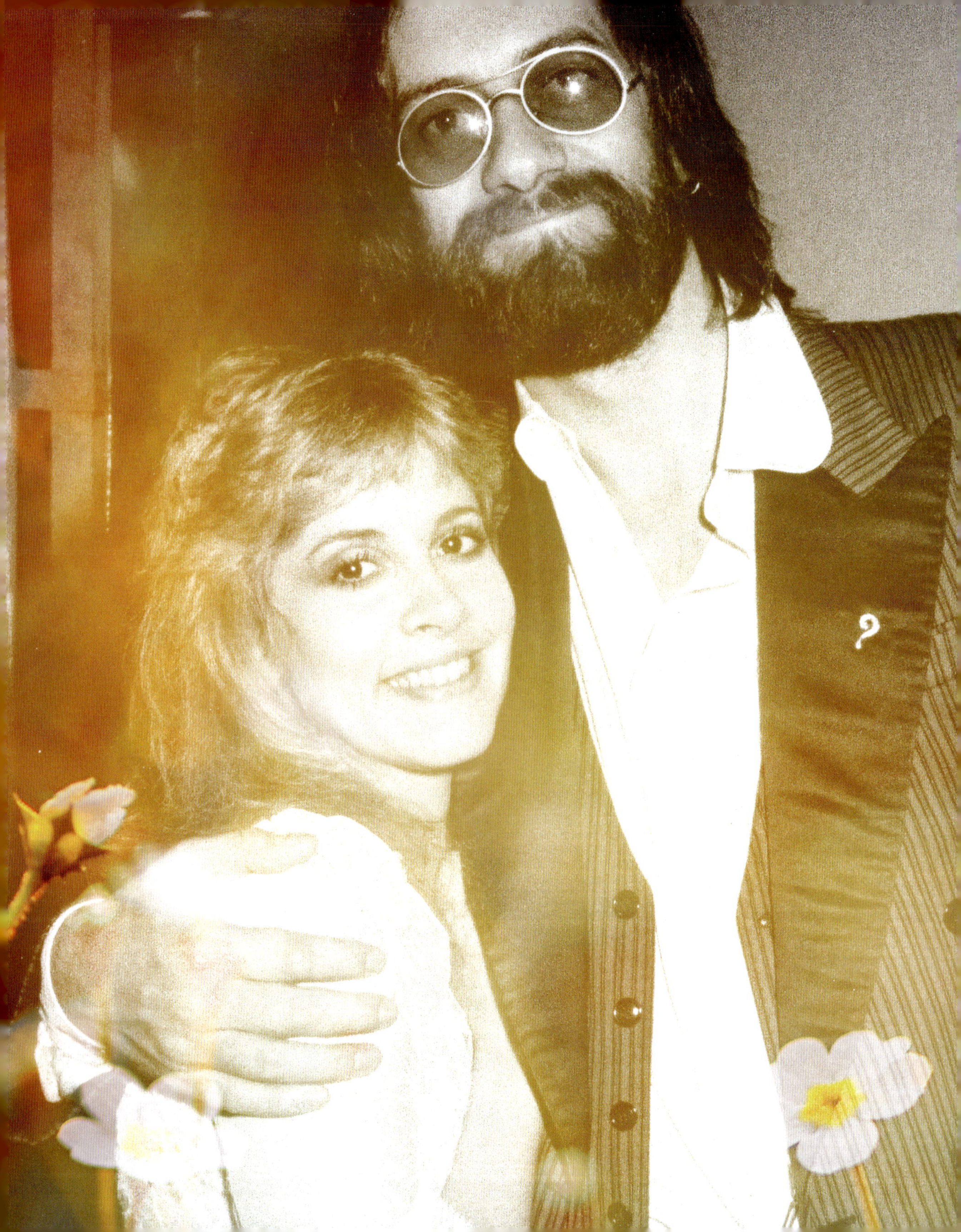

Stevie and Mick Fleetwood appear together at the 1983 American Music Awards.

15. FLEETWOOD MAC

"Sara" 1979

The tangled relationships behind a masterpiece.

"ALL TOO WELL" BECAME ONE OF TAYLOR SWIFT'S MOST POPULAR songs after the icon released an extended ten-minute version that described, in excruciating detail, the emotional wreckage of a relationship. Consider the gauzy "Sara" to be Nicks's own "All Too Well." Written on the piano, the song was originally sixteen minutes long, with nine additional verses covering many different people in Nicks's universe. She managed to cut it down to a six-and-half-minute album version, but the shorter length didn't diminish the ornate music or elegant, confessional lyrics about love and loss.

"I played it for J.D. [Souther] and Don Henley and they both said, 'You know what, it's almost not too long. It's good in its full 16 minuteness—it's got all these great verses and it just kinda travels through the world of your relationships,'" Nicks said in the liner notes of a 2015 deluxe reissue of *Tusk*.

Nicks spent a "long, long night" recording the "Sara" demo alongside her friend Sara Recor. "She kept the coffee going and kept the cassettes coming and made sure we didn't run out of batteries," Nicks said in the liner notes. "She was a great songwriter helper."

Sara also started seeing (and later married) Mick Fleetwood, which caused some tension since Nicks also had a fling with her bandmate. Much later, Nicks made it clear that "Sara" was about Fleetwood—but stressed that, like Swift's "All Too Well," the song's meaning was also open to interpretation. "It's about me, about [Sara], about Mick, about Fleetwood Mac," she said in 1994. "It's about all of us at that point. There's little bits about each one of us in that song."

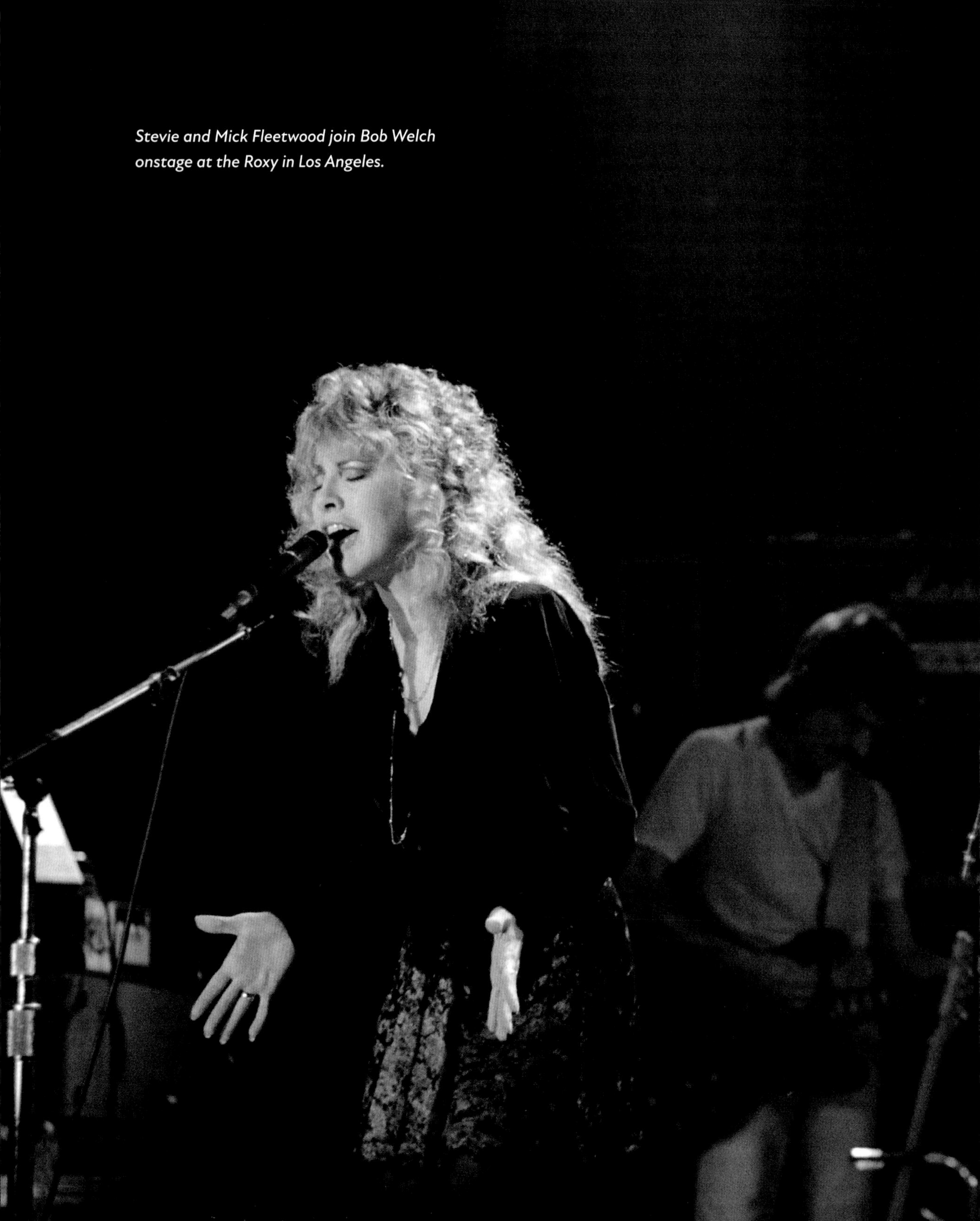

Stevie and Mick Fleetwood join Bob Welch onstage at the Roxy in Los Angeles.

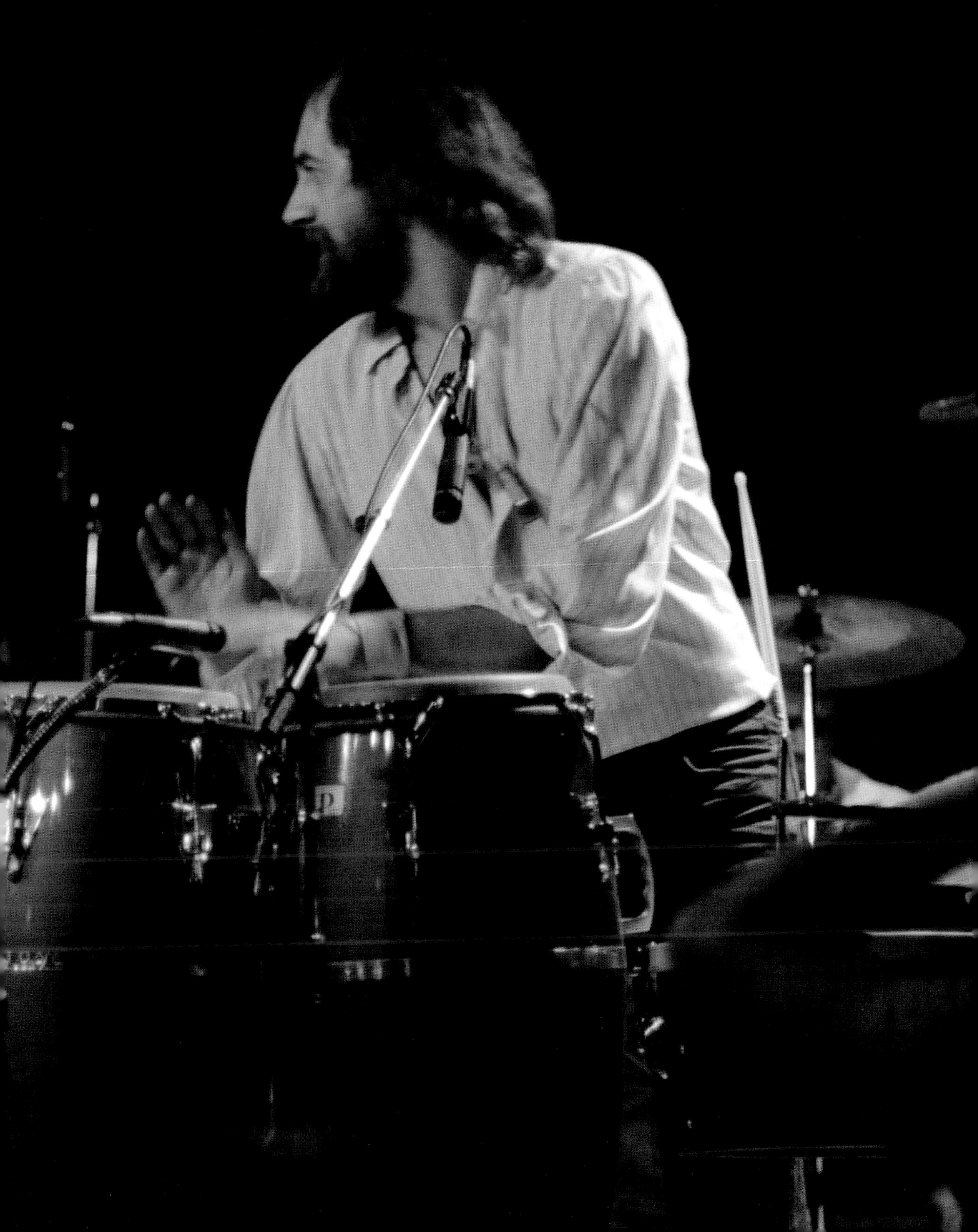

The ever-stylish Mick Fleetwood poses for a portait in 1984.

16. FLEETWOOD MAC

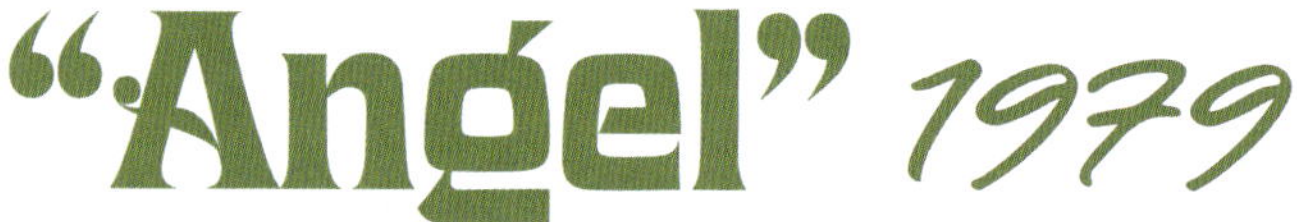

An ode to Mick Fleetwood's sartorial flair.

FLEETWOOD MAC'S *TUSK* IS NOTORIOUS FOR BEING AN ECLECTIC mix of Lindsey Buckingham's new-wave experiments. But Nicks also started exploring new avenues with her songwriting—like on "Angel," a country-rock song with a loping bassline, twangy guitars, and a lead vocal in which she displays tough but tender grit. In hindsight, it feels very much like a preview of the sonic directions she would go on *Bella Donna*.

Nicks wrote the song about Mick Fleetwood—but not in the way you might think. Instead of chronicling their star-crossed affair, she decided to fete his dashing sense of style. "It's all about him and his crazy fob watch and his really beautiful clothes," she said in the liner notes of a 2015 deluxe reissue of *Tusk*. "He's a very stylish individual and I was just this little California girl who'd never really known anybody like him."

In a documentary about the making of *Tusk*, Nicks explained that she wrote "Angel" to be a rock 'n' roll song. "It started out being much sillier than it came out. It didn't end up being silly at all. It ended up being very serious, actually." Nicks didn't mind this tone, she added, since it was a nice change of pace for her. "I thought, 'This is good for me,' since I write so many, like, intense, serious, dark songs that I wanted to write something that was up. And it starts out that way, and it is up, but there's a definite eeriness that goes through that song too that I didn't even know was there."

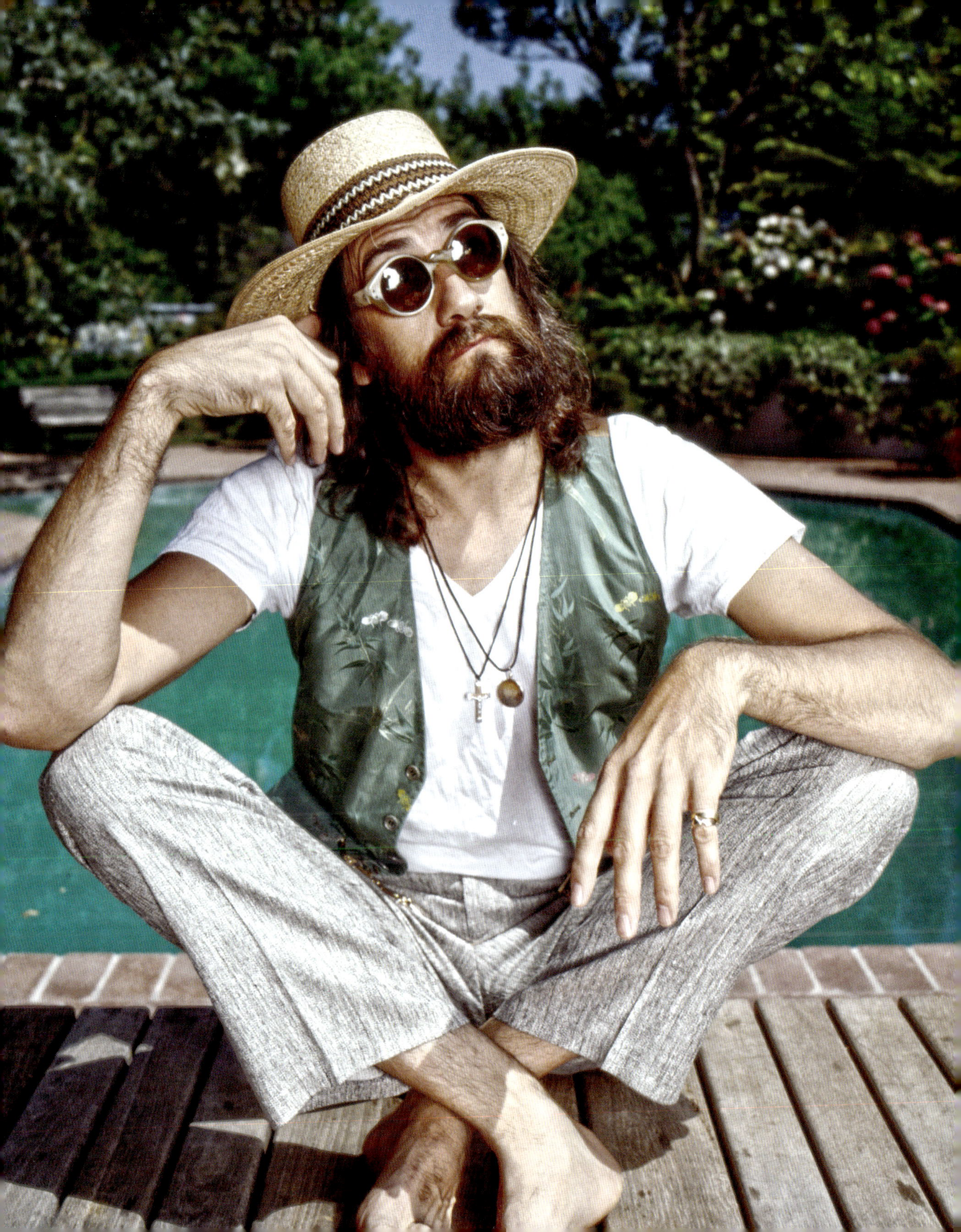

17. FLEETWOOD MAC

"Sisters of the Moon" 1979

Stevie channels mystery, magic, and moonlight.

DRIVEN BY A THRUMMING BASSLINE RESEMBLING OMINOUS footsteps and thunderstorm guitars, "Sisters of the Moon" is peak Stevie Nicks Gothic fantasia. The lyrics describe a shadowy stranger dressed in black who has murky intentions; references to black widow spiders and being wrapped in velvet only amplify the spooky factor.

As it turns out, Nicks was utterly mystified by what "Sisters of the Moon" meant. "I honestly don't know what the hell this song is about," she said in the liner notes of a 2015 deluxe reissue of *Tusk*. "I think it was me putting up an alter ego or something, the dark lady in the corner, and there's a Gemini twin thing. It wasn't a love song; it wasn't written about a man, or anything precious. It was just about a feeling I might have had over a couple days, going inward in my gnarly trollness."

In another odd twist, Fleetwood Mac actually didn't perform the song first. That honor went to Walter Egan, a songwriter with whom Nicks was acquainted in the late 1970s. She slipped him "Sisters of the Moon" in 1977 and he worked up a live version for a tour, well before Fleetwood Mac cut the song on *Tusk*. "I think it was the strength of my demo version that made them decide to record it," Egan said in a 1979 syndicated newspaper article. "At least, that's what Stevie tells me." For good measure, Egan eventually recorded his own studio version in 1985.

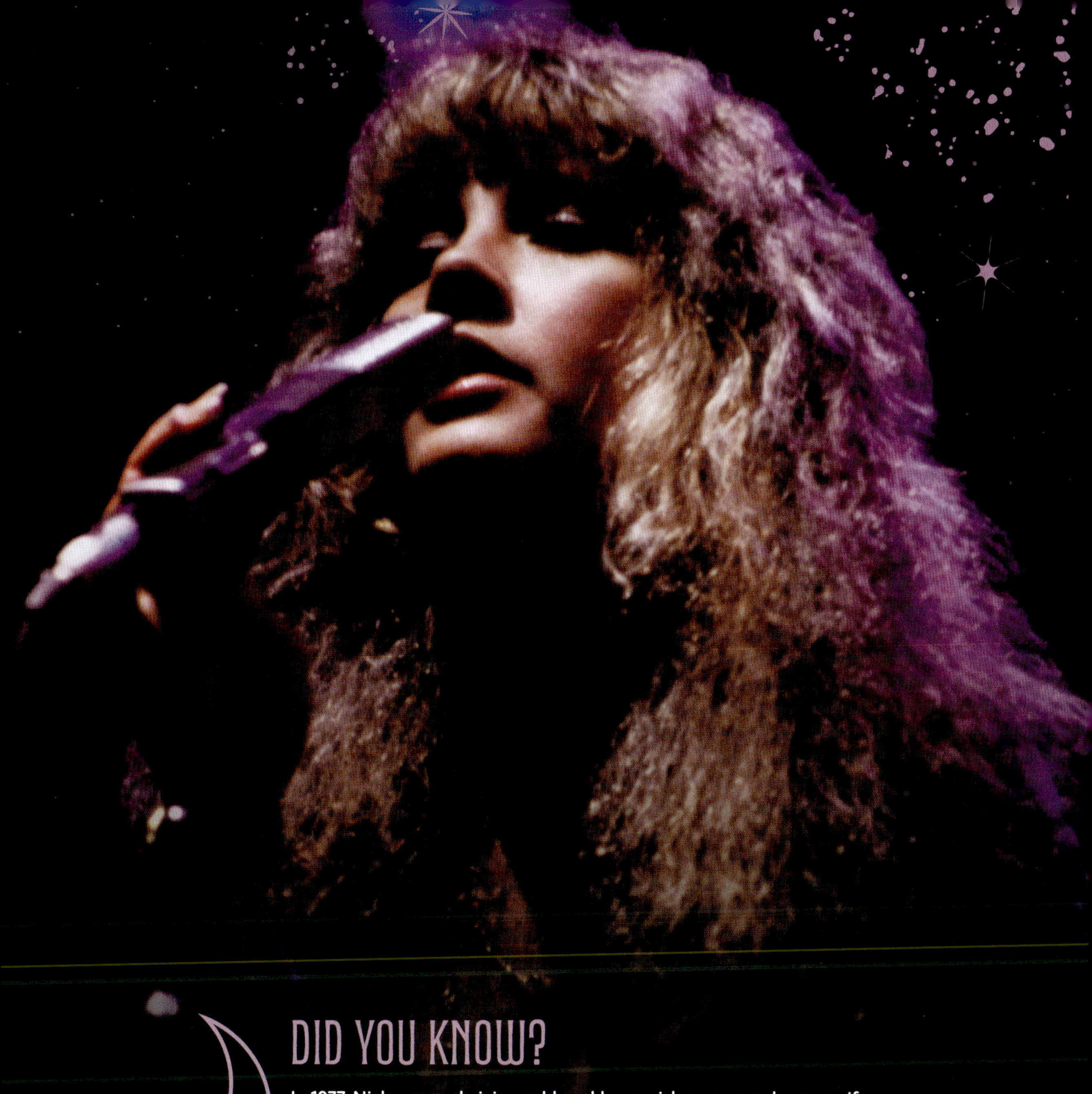

DID YOU KNOW?

In 1977, Nicks started giving gold necklaces with moon pendants as gifts. Recipients to date include Christina Applegate, Taylor Swift, Tavi Gevinson, and the members of HAIM. According to the *Los Angeles Times*, “Members of the coven—her ‘Sisters of the Moon’—are told the moons are lucky charms and to pass them along to another in need, should the moment arise.”

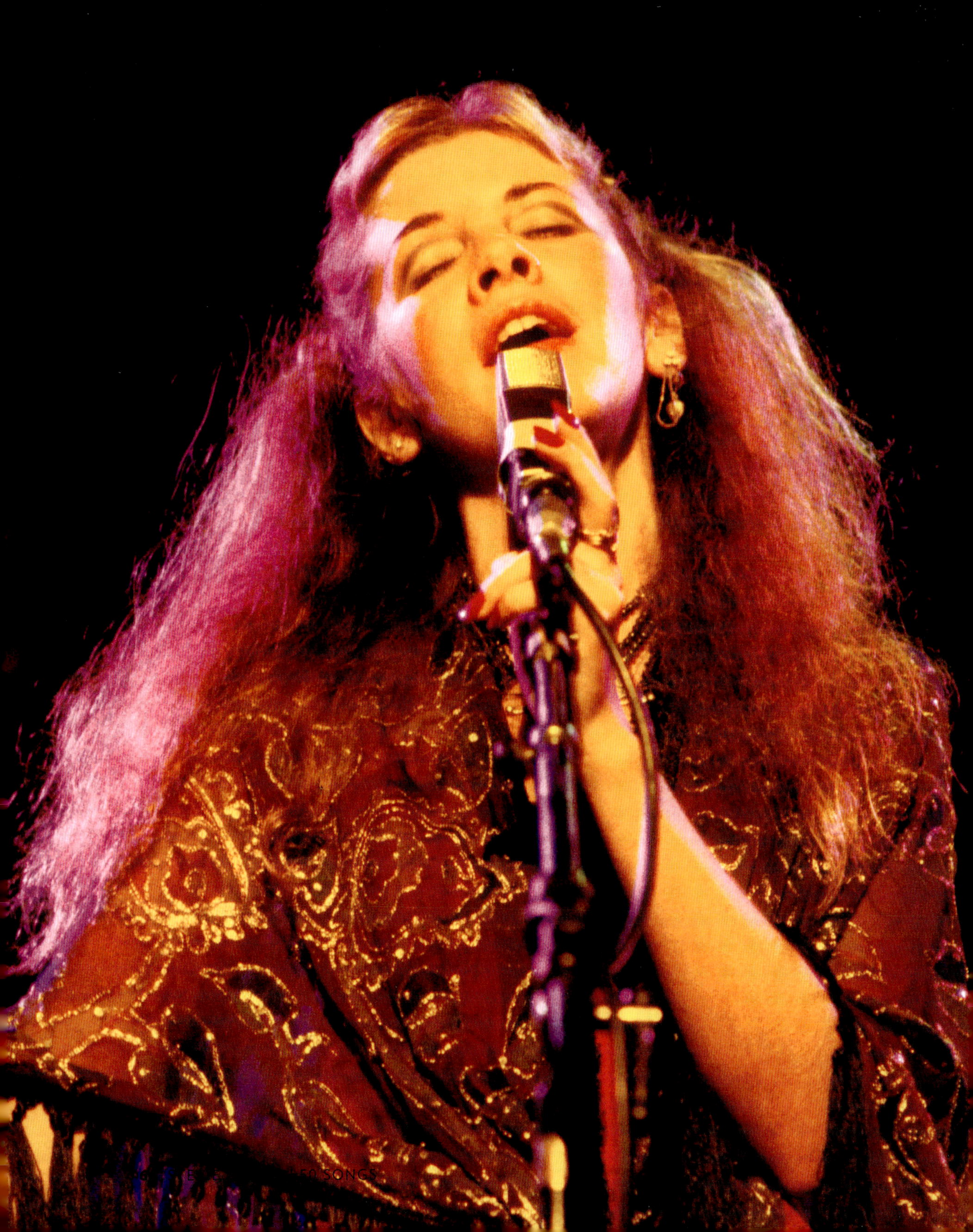

Stevie sports one of her beautiful shawls onstage in 1978.

18. FLEETWOOD MAC

"Beautiful Child" 1979

A bittersweet lullaby about what Stevie calls "another one of my doomed relationships."

IN JANUARY 1979, SOME OF MUSIC'S BIGGEST NAMES JOINED FORCES to raise money for UNICEF, an organization dedicated to helping children in need. Participants included the Bee Gees, Rod Stewart, Donna Summer, ABBA, and Fleetwood Mac; the latter vowed to donate the publishing of their then-unreleased "Beautiful Child" to the campaign.

Nicks wrote the song in 1977 "on a Sunday night sometime after midnight, and finished before dawn," she told *Circus* magazine. "It is my most special song . . . from Fleetwood Mac to the children, with love." Musically, "Beautiful Child" was a fitting choice for UNICEF, as it was a sparse lullaby driven by brittle piano and hushed harmonies. However, the melancholy lyrics came from a more sophisticated place: The protagonist, who's lamenting a breakup with an older man, notes she's no longer a child and are capable of dreaming big without him.

"Beautiful Child" is about her brief romance with Derek Taylor, who was best known as the road manager of the Beatles. "It didn't last very long, because he was married," Nicks said in a 2013 Q&A, "but it affected me very much, because he told me so many stories about the Beatles."

She also fondly remembered him reading poetry to her, although "Beautiful Child" itself focused on more bittersweet times. "The song is like a straight retelling of the last night of that relationship," she said in the liner notes of a 2015 deluxe reissue of *Tusk*. "Every time I sing it I'm transported back to the Beverly Hills Hotel and walking across the grounds to get a cab after saying goodbye."

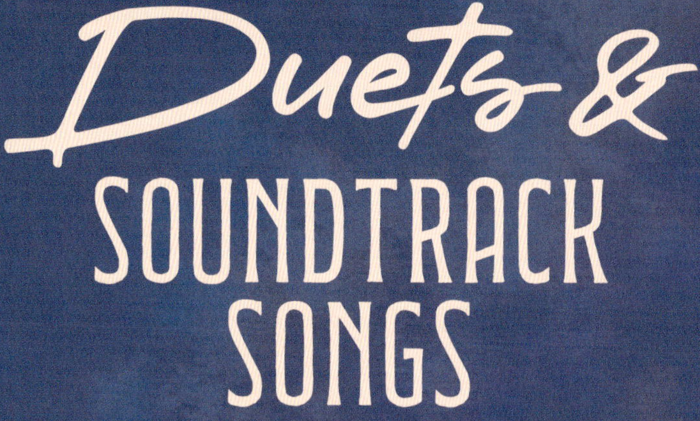

Duets & SOUNDTRACK SONGS

In a 1983 interview, Nicks explained why she's done so many duets. "I just love singing with people and they know it. So when people call me up they know I'll come down." Even before releasing *Bella Donna*, she stepped out on her own for a soft-pop collaboration with Kenny Loggins (the 1978 top 5 hit "Whenever I Call You 'Friend'"), and rollicking duets with Walter Egan (1977's Fleetwood Mac-esque "Only the Lucky"), and former Kingston Trio member John Stewart (the top 40 hits "Lost Her in the Sun" and "Midnight Wind").

"I just love singing with people and they know it."

—STEVIE NICKS

Once she became a solo star, Nicks continued to carve out time for duets, including with onetime Fleetwood Mac opening act Robbie Patton (the smooth-as-silk 1982 adult contemporary hit "Smiling Islands") and band member Rick Vito (1992's swinging rocker "Desireé"). She also joined forces with Cheap Trick vocalist Robin Zander (1993's underrated "Secret"), old pal Don Henley (2015's "It Don't Matter to the Sun"), and protégés like Lana Del Rey (2017's "Beautiful People Beautiful Problems").

But as her career progressed, Nicks has become less beholden to genre, leading to some surprising (and delightful) collaborations. This includes a "Gold Dust Woman"–esque Foo Fighters duet (2013's "You Can't Fix This"), a surging Elton John collaboration (2021's "Stolen Car"), and a tranquil indie-electro jam with Gorillaz (2023's "Oil"). In 2024, she even teamed up with former NFL star Jason Kelce for a lovely, low-lit take on Ron Sexsmith's "Maybe This Christmas."

In addition to duets, Nicks has placed songs on multiple film soundtracks. The kicky retro rocker "Violet and Blue," an outtake from 1983's *The Wild Heart*, appeared on the soundtrack to 1984's *Against All Odds*, while the moody "Battle of the Dragon" landed in the little-remembered 1986 film *American Anthem*. Nicks teamed up with Buckingham for the song "Twisted" for the 1996 blockbuster *Twister*—appropriately, it was a gnarled rock tune—while her folky "Touched by an Angel" appeared in 2001's Keanu Reeves and Charlize Theron movie *Sweet November*.

Recorded with Sheryl Crow, "If You Ever Did Believe" was the theme song of 1998's *Practical Magic*. (If the song sounds familiar, there's a good reason for that: It shares musical DNA with a demo of "Gold Dust Woman"—and Louise Goffin covered the song in 1981.) The cinematic "Your Hand I Will Never Let It Go" came from 2017's Naomi Watts vehicle *The Book of Henry*. And Nicks contributed some of her rare covers to movies and TV shows, taking a crack at Tom Petty's "Free Fallin'" for the soapy drama *Party of Five* and teaming up with Chris Isaak for a noirish "Cotton Candy Land" in the 2022 Elvis Presley biopic *Elvis*.

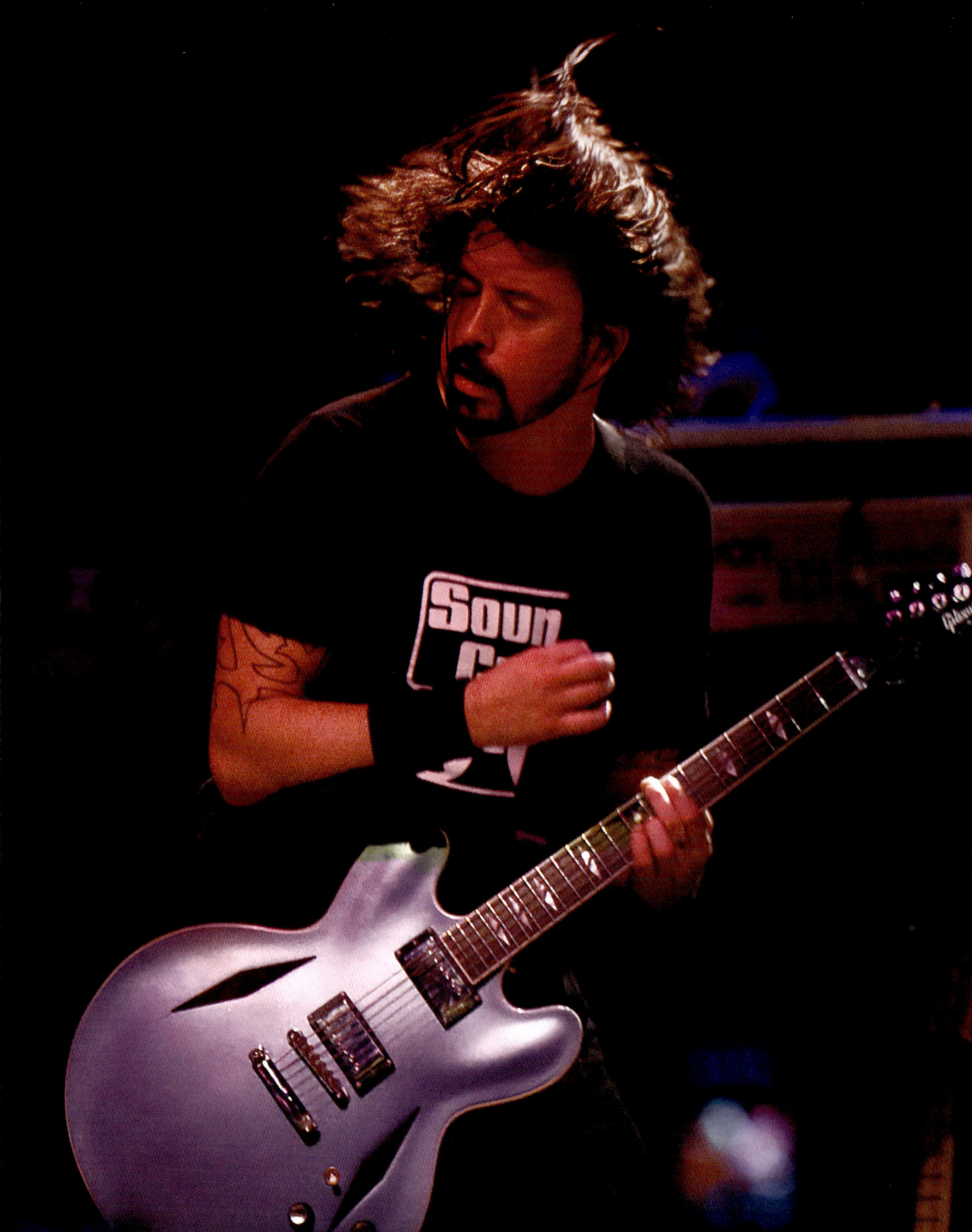

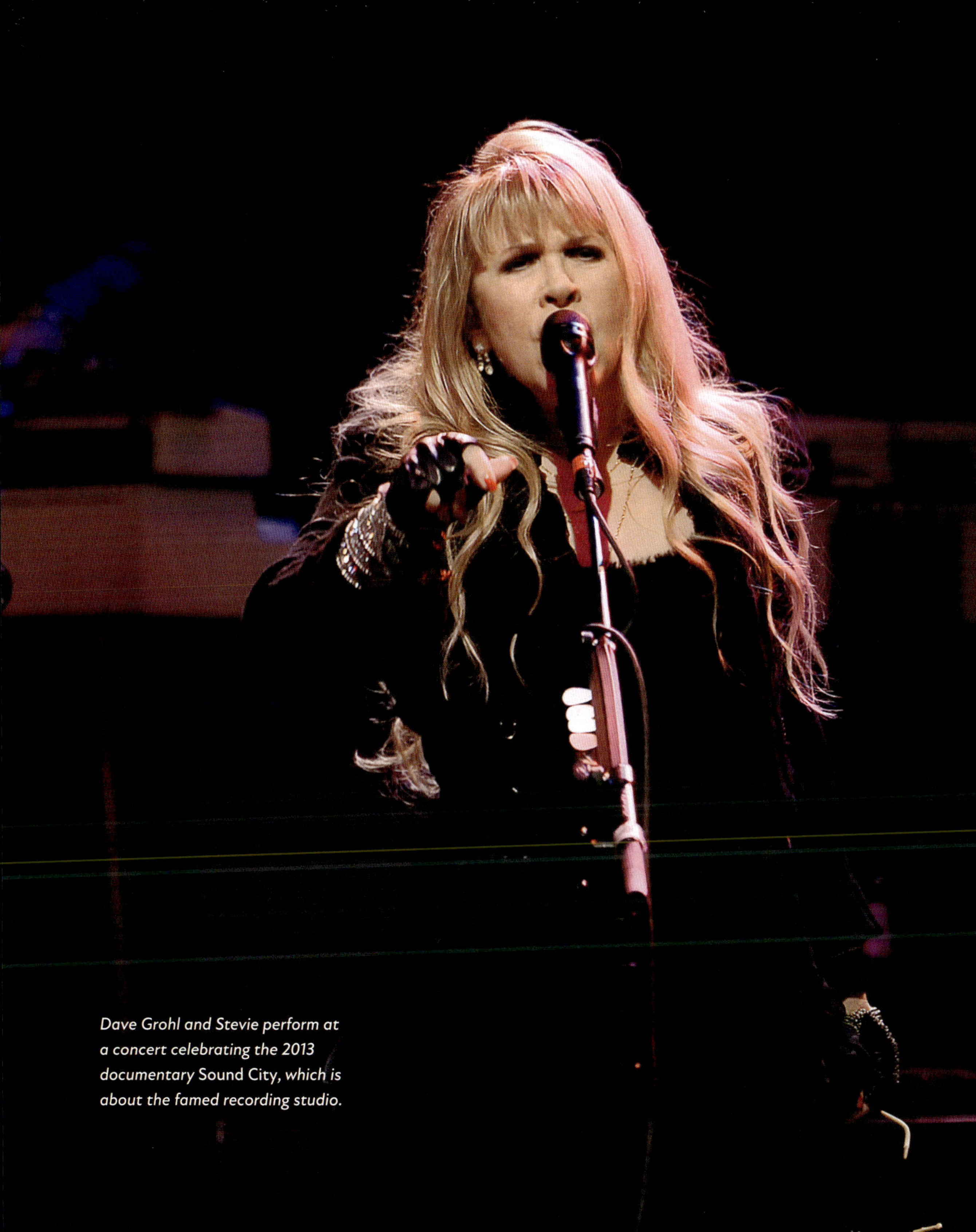

Dave Grohl and Stevie perform at a concert celebrating the 2013 documentary Sound City, *which is about the famed recording studio.*

The cover of "After the Glitter Fades" shows Stevie's treasured blue lamp.

19. STEVIE NICKS

"Blue Lamp" 1981

A beacon of light for Stevie.

AS IN MANY OF NICKS'S COMPOSITIONS, THE BLUE LAMP AT the heart of this song is both literal and metaphorical. Just after she joined Fleetwood Mac, her mom gave her a dark blue leaded glass Tiffany lamp that she absolutely treasured. "They didn't want to let me on [the plane] with this blue lamp," she said on *VH1 Storytellers*, recounting how she hauled it to Los Angeles from Phoenix. "And I said, 'Well then you're gonna have to run over me, 'cause we're not going without the lamp.'"

The lamp earned a place of honor in Nicks's house, in no small part because of what it represented: a beacon of hope during tough times. "When Fleetwood Mac—we found them or they found us—it was a definite light at the end of the tunnel for both Lindsey and I," Nicks said in 1981. "And this blue lamp really became that light . . . I keep it on all the time."

"Blue Lamp" appeared on the soundtrack to the 1981 cult sci-fi and fantasy film *Heavy Metal*; fittingly, the song sounds edgier than other Nicks songs, with darker melodies and alternative rock–leaning guitar riffs. But Nicks viewed the tune as the start of something rather momentous.

"It was very important that it found a place for itself," Nicks told *BAM* magazine. "It was really the beginning of *Bella Donna* because it was the first thing I'd ever recorded with other musicians, and it was the first time I'd ever recorded by standing in a room singing at the same time that five guys were playing."

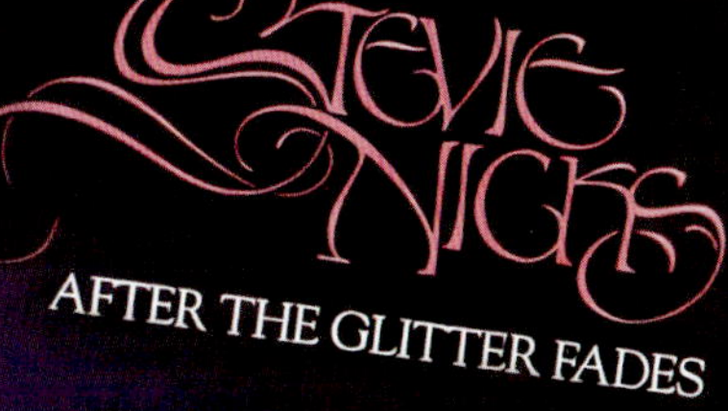

DID YOU KNOW?

A photo of the blue lamp was supposed to appear on the cover of *Bella Donna*, but Nicks went with her iconic pose on the sleeve instead.

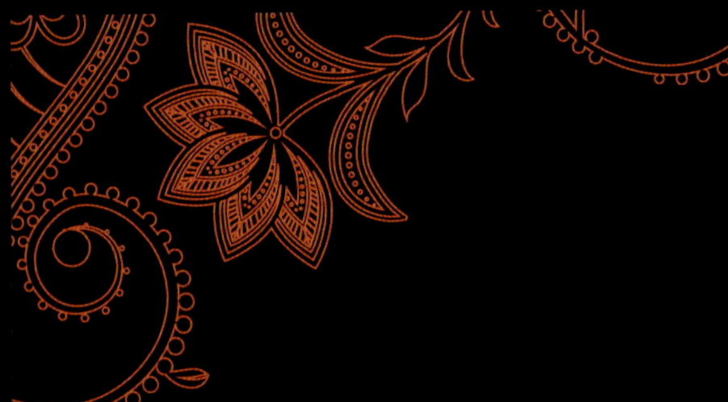

Tom Petty and Stevie perform together onstage in 1981.

20. STEVIE NICKS WITH TOM PETTY AND THE HEARTBREAKERS

"Stop Draggin' My Heart Around" 1981

A gift from Tom Petty that brought huge dividends.

WHEN STEVIE NICKS PUTS HER MIND TO SOMETHING—*WATCH OUT*. Once she decided to launch a solo career, she cofounded her own label, Modern Records, with Paul Fishkin and Danny Goldberg. Fishkin used to be president of Bearsville Records, home of Todd Rundgren; Goldberg worked with Led Zeppelin and later managed Nirvana. Then Nicks approached her "hero," Atlantic Records head Doug Morris, about a record deal.

"I said, 'So, Doug, what I want to do is I want to make a Tom Petty album, straight-up rock and roll,'" Nicks shared in her 2019 Rock & Roll Hall of Fame induction speech. "I have two great girl singers, Lori and Sharon, that are amazing, and we're going to be Crosby, Stills & Nash. I'm going to be Stills and they're going to be Nash and Crosby.'"

It took a few years, but in 1981 Nicks emerged with *Bella Donna*. Produced by Jimmy Iovine—which was no accident, as Nicks specifically wanted to work with him because he was Petty's producer—the album featured multiple musical ties to the Heartbreakers. Keyboardist Benmont Tench cowrote "Kind of Woman" and contributed organ to much of the album, while drummer Stan Lynch and guitarist Mike Campbell both appeared on "Outside the Rain," which Petty produced.

However, the band members have the most prominent presence on the album's first single, "Stop Draggin' My Heart Around"—no doubt because it was originally conceived as

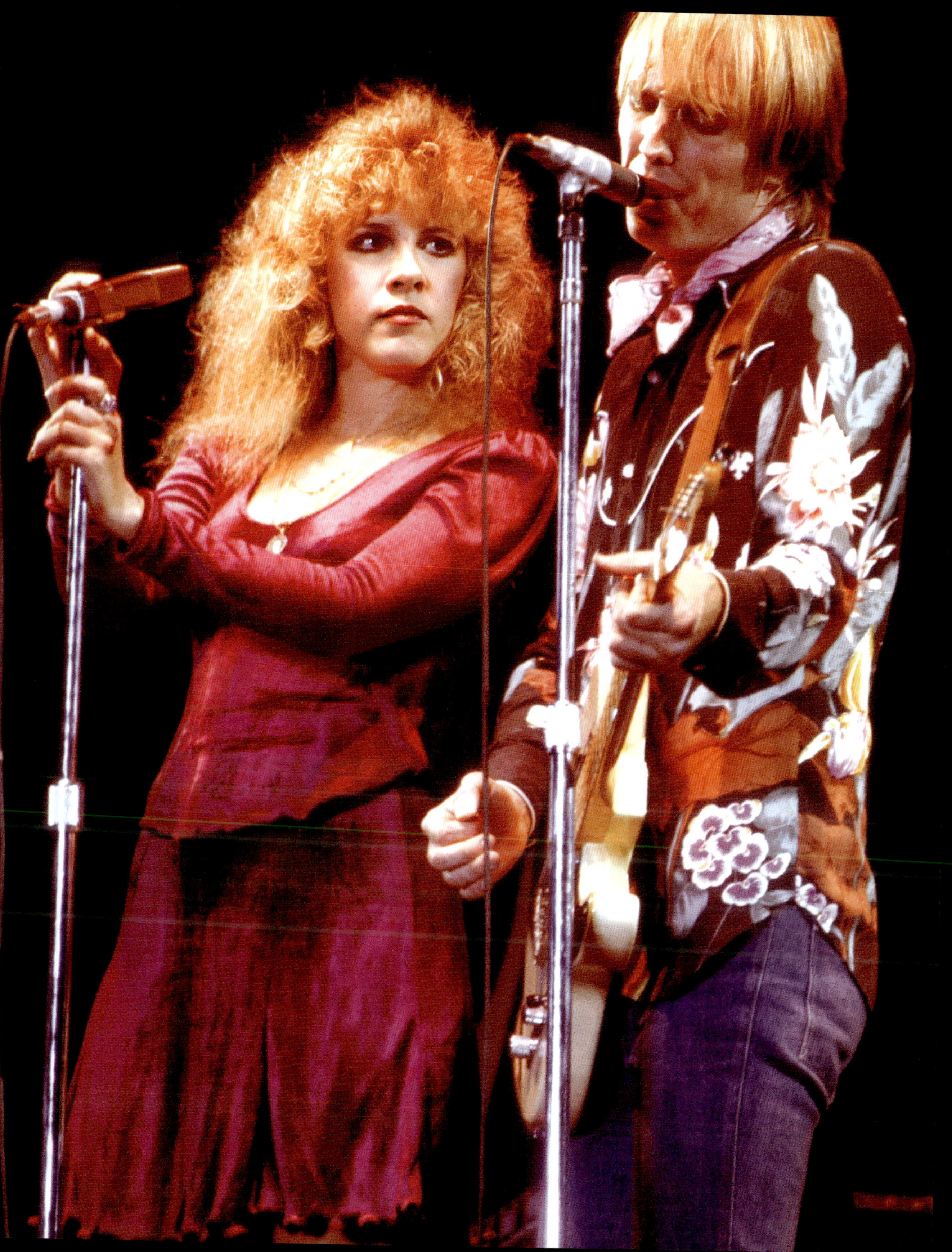

"... If a woman sings an aggressive guy's lyric, it can't miss..."

—JIMMY IOVINE ON *THE HOWARD STERN SHOW*

DID YOU KNOW?

"Stop Draggin' My Heart Around" became a massive pop hit, reaching No. 3 on the Billboard Hot 100; to this day, it's Nicks's highest-charting solo song. She and Petty made it a point to cover "Stop Draggin' My Heart Around" together—in fact, Nicks popped up at Hyde Park in 2017 to sing a laid-back version of the tune with the Heartbreakers—but she's also covered "Stop Draggin' My Heart Around" with Chrissie Hynde, Billy Joel, and Harry Styles.

a Tom Petty and the Heartbreakers song, with music by Campbell and lyrics about a relationship tug-of-war by Petty. Sonically, it's very reminiscent of the band's work in the late 1970s and early 1980s, between Campbell's trademark slide-guitar blues riffing, Tench's jazzy organ burbles, and Lynch's steady beat keeping. For added heft, legendary Booker T. and the MG's member Donald "Duck" Dunn contributed strolling bass.

How "Stop Draggin' My Heart Around" ended up on *Bella Donna* is a somewhat convoluted story. "The Heartbreakers had recorded a version of it with Jimmy Iovine, and Jimmy being the entrepreneur that he was, he was working with Stevie," Campbell told Songfacts. "And I guess he asked Tom if she could try it, and it just developed from there." In a 2017 chat with Howard Stern, Iovine was blunt about his mindset: In his eyes, Nicks needed a single on *Bella Donna* and "if a woman sings an aggressive guy's lyric, it can't miss." He wasn't necessarily wrong: Nicks's voice possesses smoky grit and determination as she stands her ground in the face of a wishy-washy partner.

Petty, however, had a slightly different recollection of how Nicks recorded "Stop Draggin' My Heart Around." He had written a song called "Insider" for her and she started singing harmonies to the main track when recording it. "When it was over, I just sat there, in awe," he told *Musician*. "She walked back in and said, 'How was it?' I said, 'It's amazing.' She said, 'I can tell by the look on your face, you don't wanna give me this song. I'm giving it back to you right now.' I really thought a lot of her for that."

"Insider" ended up on Tom Petty and the Heartbreakers' 1981 album Hard Promises. But Petty felt guilty for not giving Nicks the intended song and said he'd "trade" her "Stop Draggin' My Heart Around" to compensate. "She says, 'Wow! That's why I wanted you to write me a song—it's rock 'n' roll, that's what you do,'" he told Musician. "'The Insider' sounds like what I do.' And I thought, how dumb of me, to think that she'd want me to write like her." Campbell notes the band didn't even end up re-recording it for *Bella Donna*; Nicks just added her vocals to the existing Heartbreakers track. "It became a duet," he added. "It's basically all the Heartbreakers on that record."

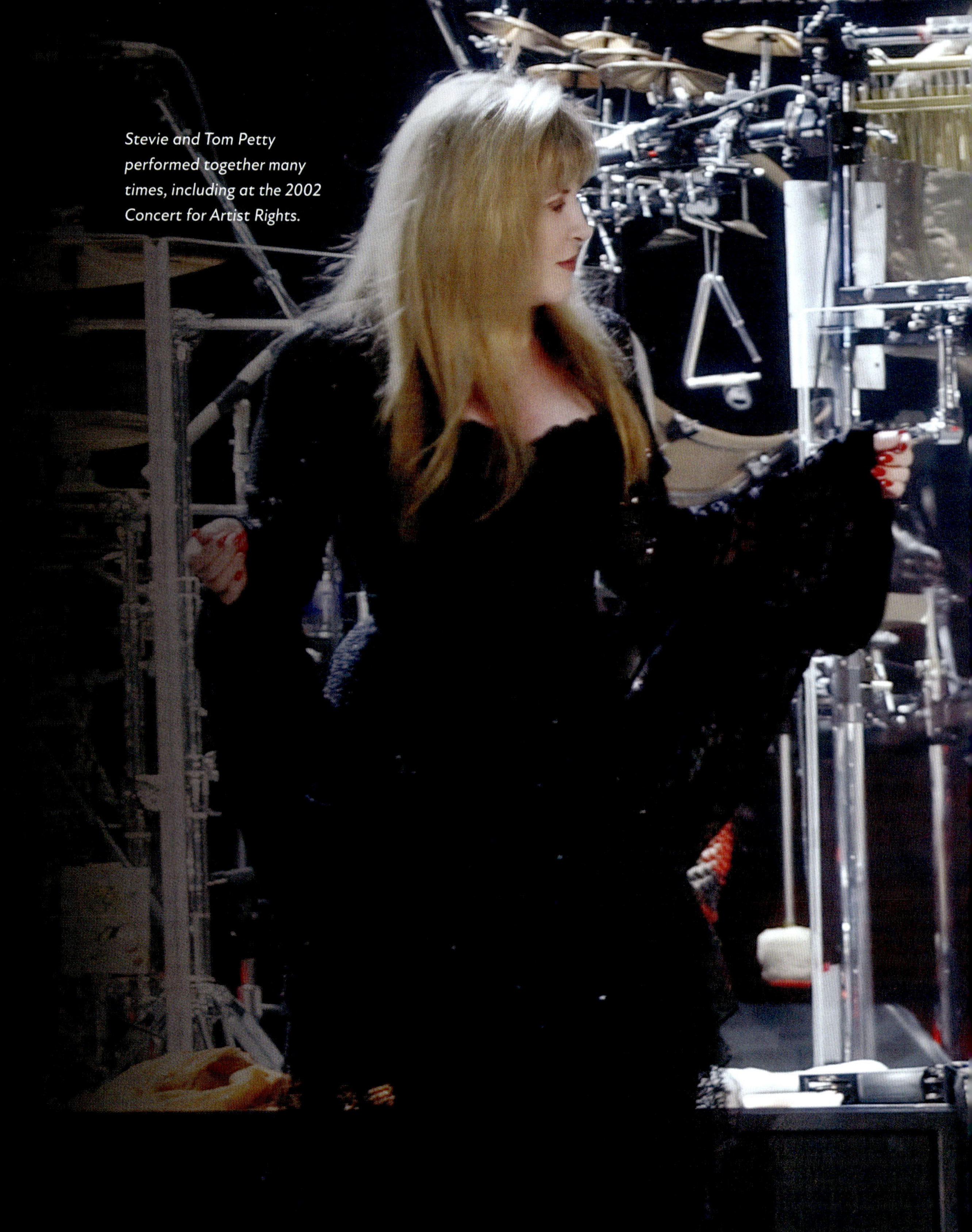

Stevie and Tom Petty performed together many times, including at the 2002 Concert for Artist Rights.

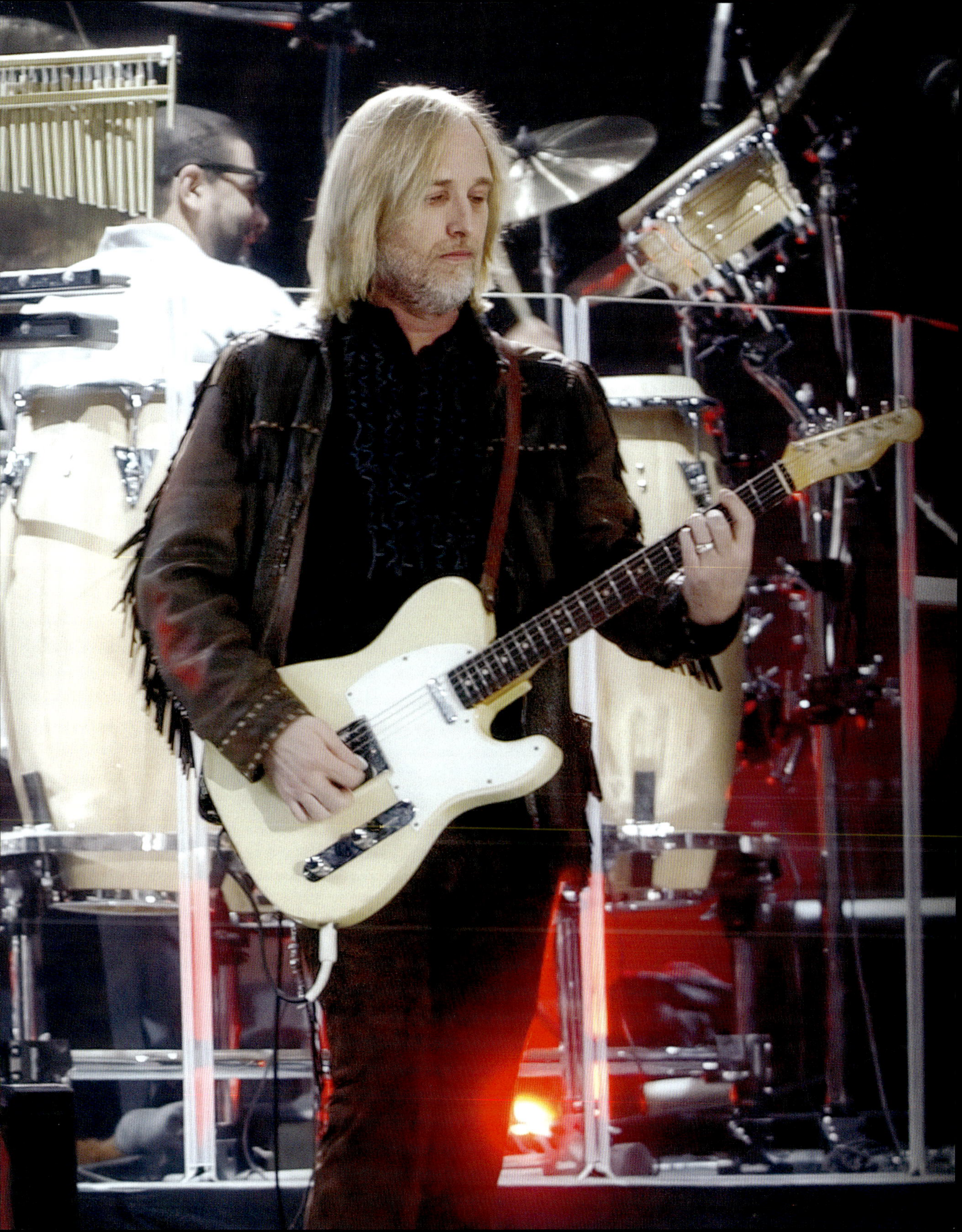

The HONORARY HEARTBREAKER

If you happened to buy a ticket to see Tom Petty and the Heartbreakers in 2006, you might have seen a familiar face unexpectedly pop up onstage: Stevie Nicks, who jumped on the band's tour for a string of dates. She sang "Stop Draggin' My Heart Around" and "Insider" with the band (of course) but also took lead on a barn-burning cover of the band's 1978 tune "I Need to Know."

These appearances were hardly novel, as Nicks is an integral part of the Heartbreakers family who appreciated the group from their very first albums. "Tom is such a great singer and so charismatic onstage," she wrote in a 2010 *Rolling Stone* essay. "I became such a fan that if I hadn't been in a band myself, I would have joined that one." That's no exaggeration: Petty once recalled from the stage that Nicks had started calling him after the Heartbreakers released their second LP, *You're Gonna Get It!* "[She was] someone I had never met before, but she was really nice."

Nicks eventually spent the subsequent decades collaborating with the band (and the band's members) both live and in the studio. For example, in 1981, she joined the group in Los Angeles at the Forum for a cover of the Searchers' "Needles and Pins." (This live version eventually surfaced on the Heartbreakers' 1985 effort *Pack Up the Plantation: Live!*) Tench played in her solo band on 1983's The Wild Heart Tour; he and Mike Campbell have played on her solo albums in addition to *Bella Donna*, with Campbell also contributing music.

On a personal level, Nicks also valued Petty's honesty. When she was fresh out of rehab for a Klonopin addiction in 1994, she asked Petty if he'd help her write songs for a new record. "I didn't really expect the reaction I got, which was, 'No, I won't.

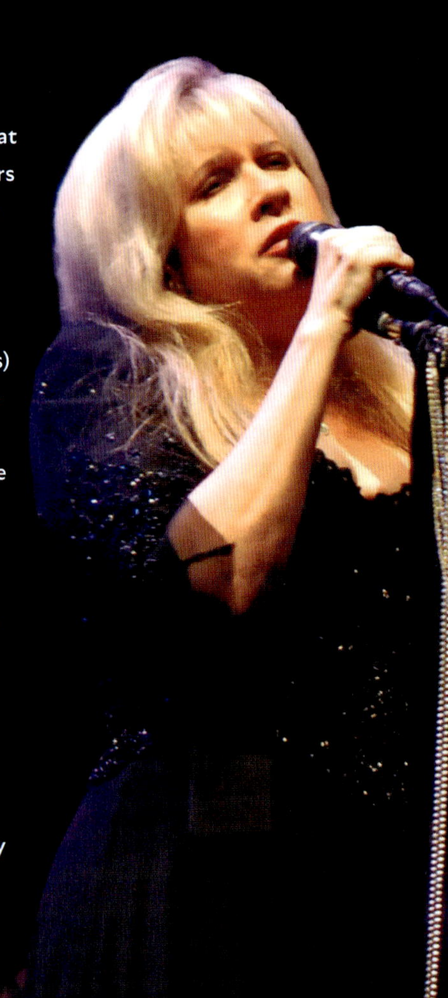

You are one of the premier songwriters in this business. Go home and turn off the radio. Don't be influenced by anything. Just write some great songs—that's what you do,'" she recalled in a 2010 *Rolling Stone* piece. "He reinforced that I was still Stevie Nicks."

And after that 2006 Heartbreakers tour, Petty gave Nicks the ultimate honor: She was named an honorary Heartbreaker. "Tom made me a little platinum sheriff's badge that had 24-karat gold and diamonds across the top and said, 'To Our Honorary Heartbreaker, Stevie Nicks,'" she wrote in *Rolling Stone*. "On the back, it says, 'To the Only Girl in Our Band.' I keep it on my black velvet top hat. It goes with me everywhere."

When Buckingham parted ways with Fleetwood Mac for what became their final tour, Campbell ended up joining the band. It was less than a year after Petty's sudden death at the age of sixty-six. "It really pulled me out of my grief, helped me to focus and process what I was going through," Campbell told *Rolling Stone*. "I owe them a debt of gratitude for that." In another touching gesture, Nicks took lead vocals on a cover of Petty's "Free Fallin'" during these sets—a cover she'd also repeat on subsequent solo tours.

"'. . . You are one of the premier songwriters in this business. Go home and turn off the radio.

Don't be influenced by anything. Just write some great songs—that's what you do' . . ."

—TOM PETTY TO STEVIE NICKS, AS RECALLED BY STEVIE NICKS IN *ROLLING STONE*

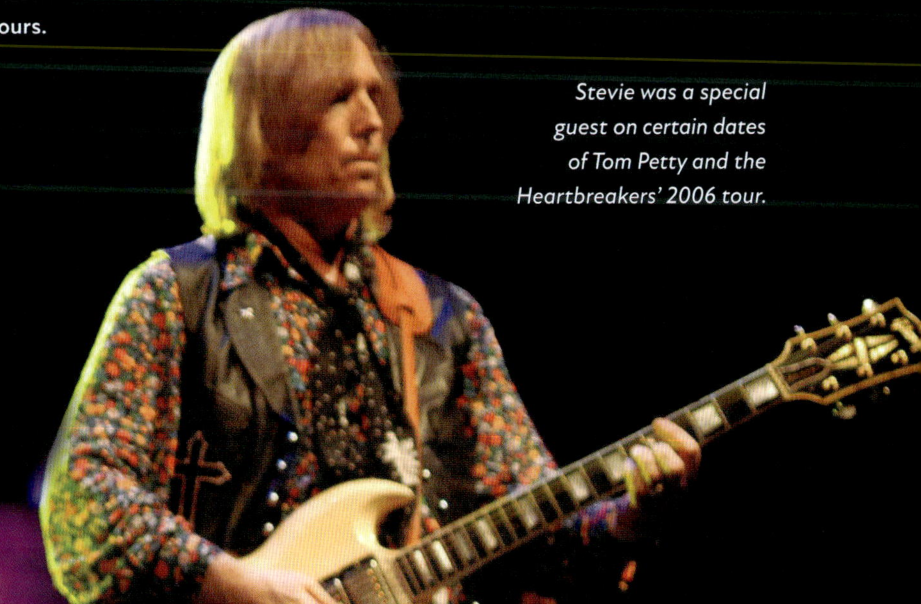

Stevie was a special guest on certain dates of Tom Petty and the Heartbreakers' 2006 tour.

Stevie performing in 1978.

21. STEVIE NICKS

"Edge of Seventeen" 1981

Brief moments come together in an enduring hit.

ALTHOUGH NICKS WROTE MANY OF HER SONGS ABOUT SPECIFIC moments or times in her life, others are more like a photo scrapbook of memories. That's certainly the case with her pop and rock radio hit "Edge of Seventeen," a galvanizing song with impressionistic lyrics and imagery drawn from multiple strands of her life which became a massive hit in 1982.

For example, the immortal white-winged dove mentioned in the song came to Nicks in a rather pedestrian way: a menu she received while on an airplane mentioned the bird being protected by a saguaro cactus. As "Edge of Seventeen" evolved, the dove came to symbolize multiple people in her orbit who had died or were sick when she wrote the song.

"It was a period of time that I just didn't know what to do, so I just sat down and wrote about it," she said in a 1981 WLIR radio interview. "I spent a lot of time thinking about how I would write this song."

"Edge of Seventeen" started coalescing in 1980, when she was living with her then-boyfriend, producer Jimmy Iovine. He was wrapping up a Tom Petty album and she was getting restless being at home. "I was starting to get very edgy to do something," she said in the *Timespace* liner notes. "I was also starting to feel very unimportant and very sorry for myself. I was ready to begin *Bella Donna*, and it seemed like it would just never happen."

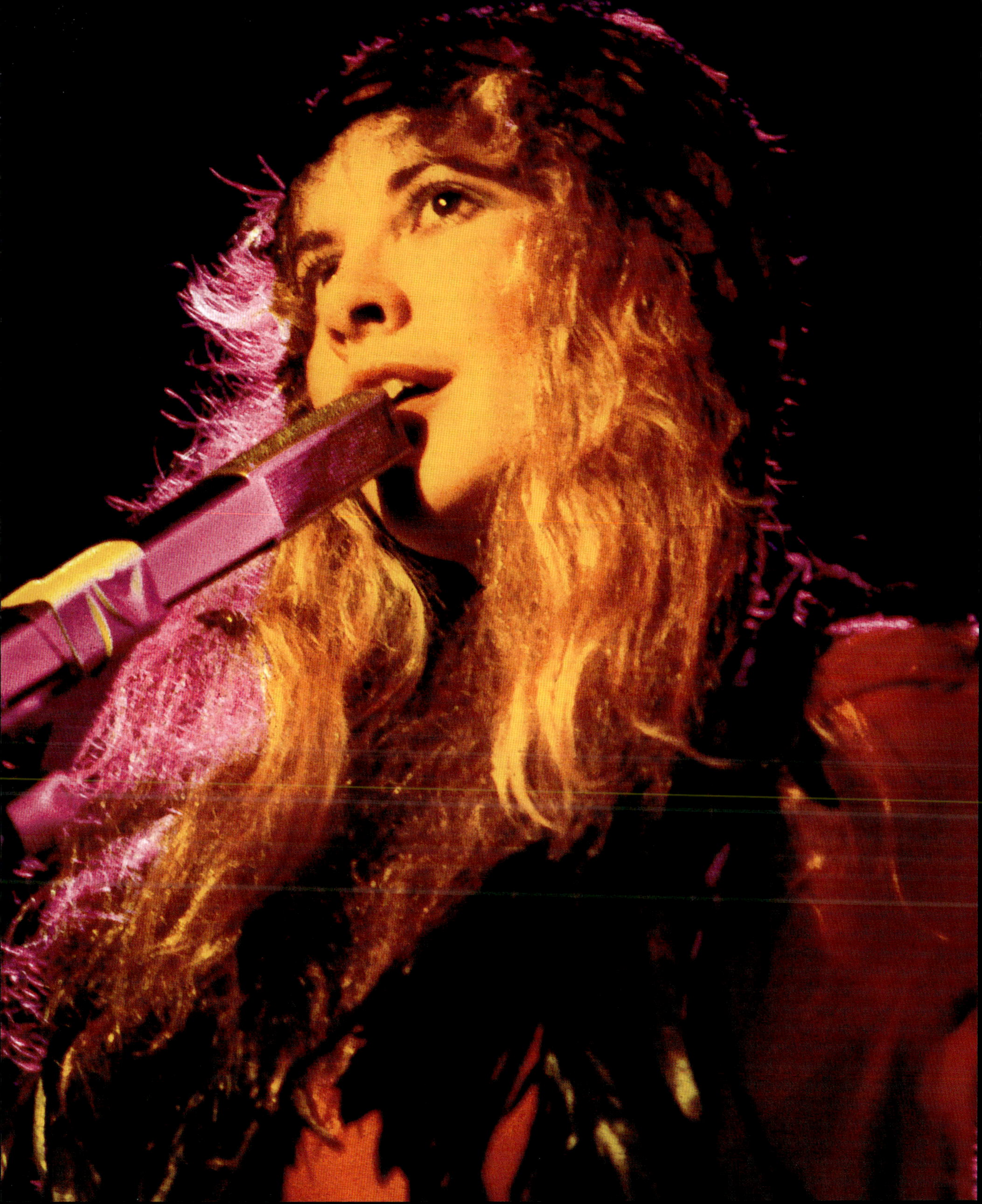

"Recording it was the most exciting thing I've ever done, because everybody felt that there was an electrical charge going through this white-winged dove all the way through that song."

—STEVIE NICKS TO *THE ARIZONA REPUBLIC* ON "EDGE OF SEVENTEEN"

Around this time, John Lennon was shot and killed. Iovine was devastated, as he and Lennon had this "incredible friendship," Nicks recalled in the same liner notes. "John had taken Jimmy in and taught him to record. He was his teacher." Less than two months later, Nicks's uncle Jonathan became very ill with colon cancer; she saw him the day before he died. "He was home, and my aunt had some music softly playing, and it was a perfect place for the spirit to go away," she told *Rolling Stone* in 1981. "The 'white-winged dove' in the song is a spirit that is leaving a body, and I felt a great loss at how both Johns were taken." Sadly, Nicks then also later came to associate "Edge of Seventeen" with her dear friend Robin Anderson, who became sick as *Bella Donna* became a success. [See page 112.]

And then there's the song's title, which came about after Nicks asked Tom Petty's first wife, Jane, when the couple met. "She said, 'I met him at some point during the age of 17,'" Nicks told *Billboard*. "But I thought she said, 'The edge of 17.' I said, 'Jane, can I use that? Can I write a song called "Edge of Seventeen"?'" Consequently, at least some of the song was "Jane talking about Tom," Nicks added. "I bet a lot of people thought I was talking about me, but I was chronicling their relationship as she told it to me."

Given this backdrop, "Edge of Seventeen" is emotionally cathartic—a feeling captured by the music, which is highlighted by glassy piano from Roy Bittan, jagged electric guitars from Waddy Wachtel, and a cascading chorus of harmonies from Nicks and her backup singers Sharon Celani and Lori Perry. Nicks herself sounds like a fire-and-brimstone preacher howling through her grief and love.

The song was also a blast to record, Nicks said. "Recording it was the most exciting thing I've ever done, because everybody felt that there was an electrical charge going through this white-winged dove all the way through that song," Nicks told WLIR in 1981. "And for the three days that we worked on recording the track of it, and we had the lady singers and myself and all 10 of the guys out in one room recording."

Years later, however, Wachtel admitted that his inimitable guitar part throughout the song was uncomfortably close to the Police's 1979 song "Bring On the Night"—and it apparently wasn't exactly an accident. "At that session they told me they were going to do this song based on this feel," he told *Musician* in 1999. "I heard something about the Police, but I didn't know what they were talking about. Then about two years ago, I had the radio on, and on comes what sounds like "Edge of Seventeen"—and all of a sudden, there's Sting's voice! I thought, 'We ripped them off completely!'"

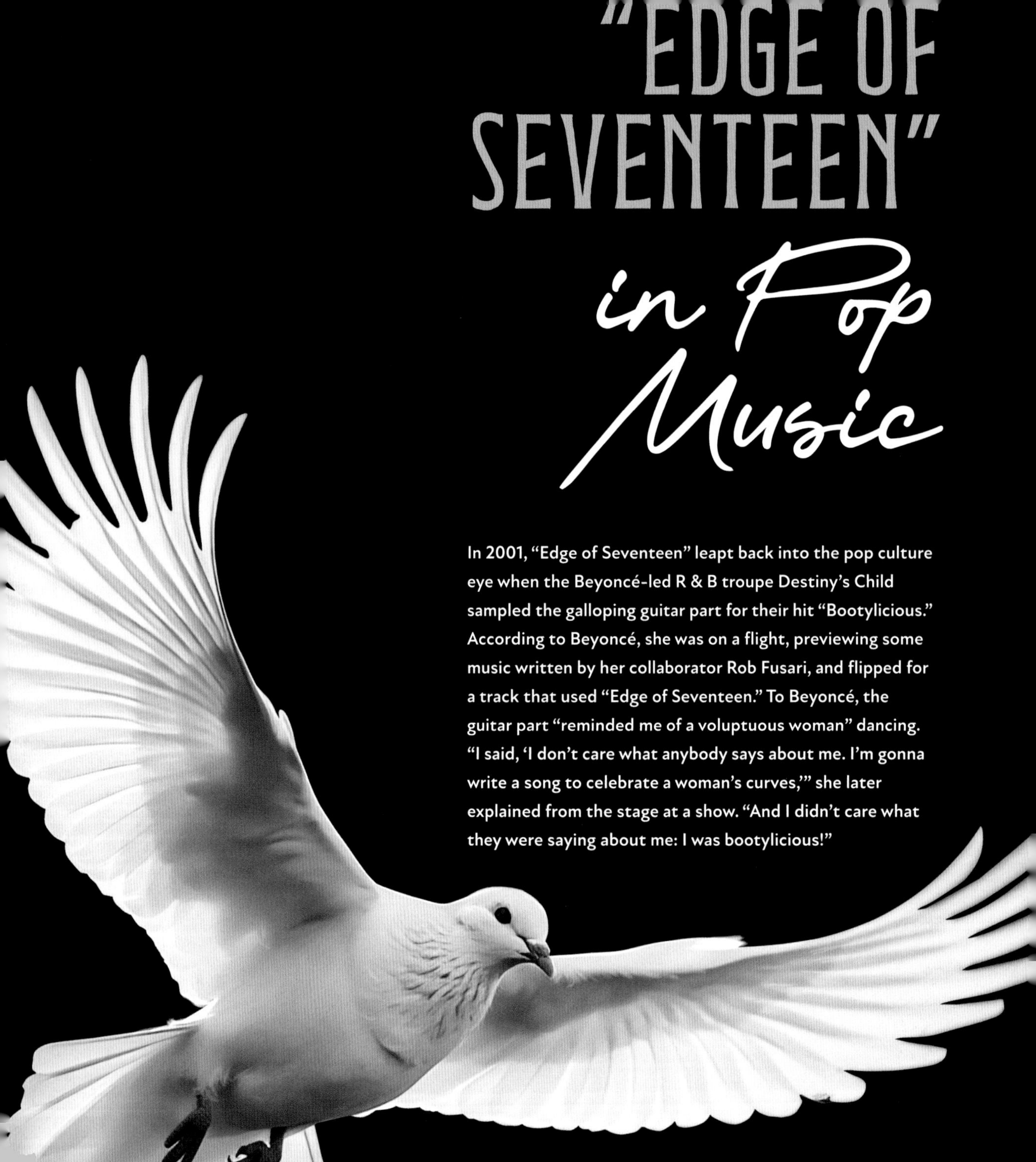

"EDGE OF SEVENTEEN" *in Pop Music*

In 2001, "Edge of Seventeen" leapt back into the pop culture eye when the Beyoncé-led R & B troupe Destiny's Child sampled the galloping guitar part for their hit "Bootylicious." According to Beyoncé, she was on a flight, previewing some music written by her collaborator Rob Fusari, and flipped for a track that used "Edge of Seventeen." To Beyoncé, the guitar part "reminded me of a voluptuous woman" dancing. "I said, 'I don't care what anybody says about me. I'm gonna write a song to celebrate a woman's curves,'" she later explained from the stage at a show. "And I didn't care what they were saying about me: I was bootylicious!"

“Bootylicious” reached No. 1 on the Billboard Hot 100. When Destiny’s Child went to film the music video, they enlisted Nicks to make a guest appearance. To her delight, she got to stretch her wings. “They gave me a chance to pretend like I was playing guitar,” she recalled in a 2020 interview. “I don’t think anybody ever gave me that chance ever again.” Beyond the miming, however, the experience was gratifying. “Without all the makeup and everything, they just looked like three really cute, little teenage girls,” Nicks says. “Then of course, they’re just like me, they put on those [things]—whatever it is that makes them—them. Whether it’s your boots or your jacket or whatever, then they became Destiny’s Child, and I saw it.”

The song remained in Beyoncé’s solo setlists for the next decade as well. But a few years later, actress Lindsay Lohan covered “Edge of Seventeen” on her solo album *A Little More Personal (Raw)*. And in 2020, Miley Cyrus fashioned a song called “Edge of Midnight (Midnight Sky Remix)” based on her song “Midnight Sky” and Nicks’s tune. This version evolved organically. “I had sampled ‘Edge of Seventeen’ and reached out to Stevie and asked her to bless it, and she said, ‘You can borrow from me anytime,’” Cyrus told Howard Stern. “And so, I’m like, ‘Shit, if you’re feeling that way, can I just borrow, like, you and your time?’”

Nicks was game and relished singing a few salacious lyrics about illicit kissing, which Cyrus loved. “And it was such a trip because I’m so used to singing Stevie Nicks lyrics, and when she started singing [my lyrics], she said, ‘I gotta say that part, it will be very controversial.’ . . . That was one of the trippier experiences of my life—having my words come out of Stevie Nicks’s mouth—because her words have come out of mine a billion times.”

“. . . That was one of the trippier experiences of my life—having my words come out of Stevie Nicks’s mouth—because her words have come out of mine a billion times.”

—MILEY CYRUS TO HOWARD STERN

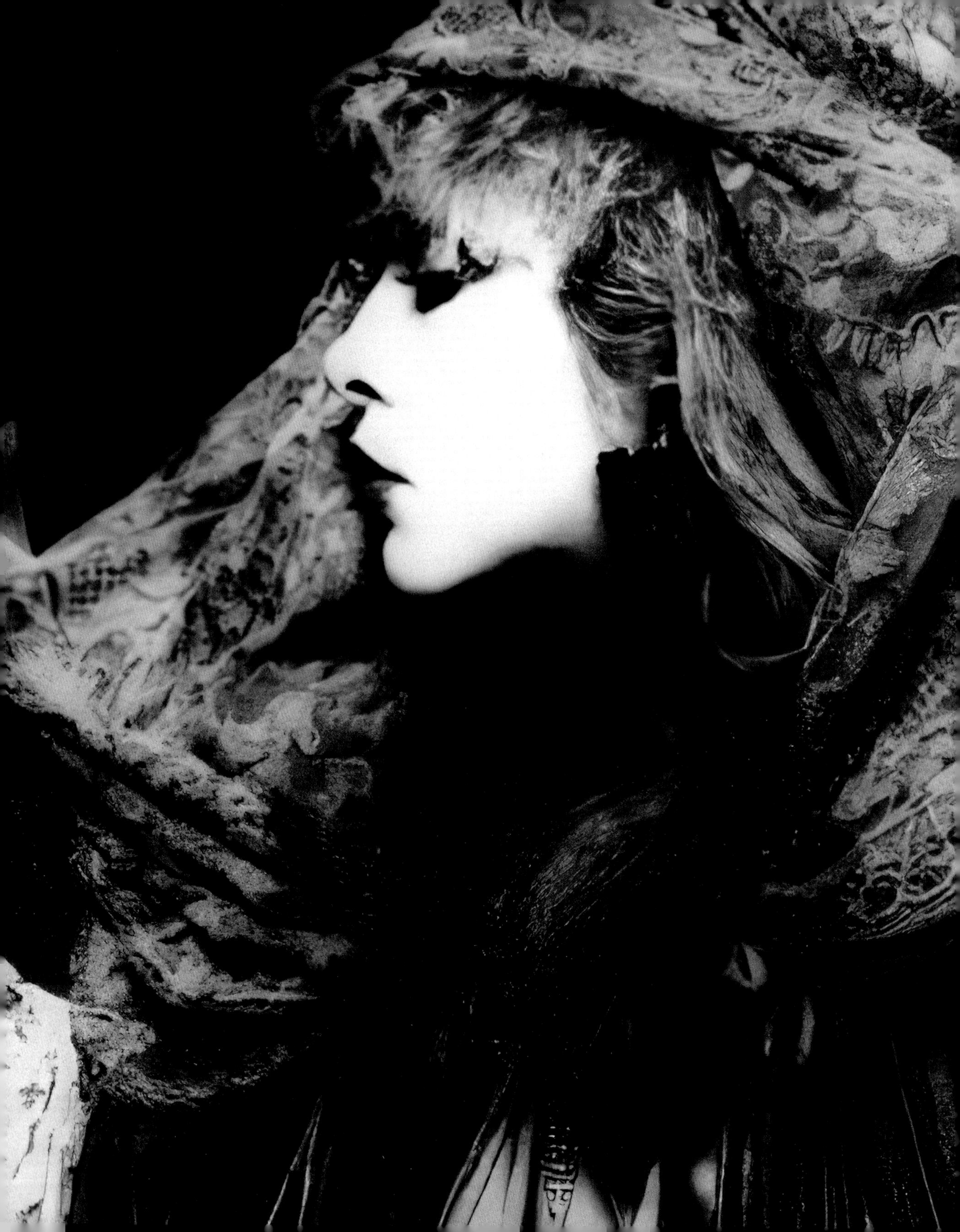

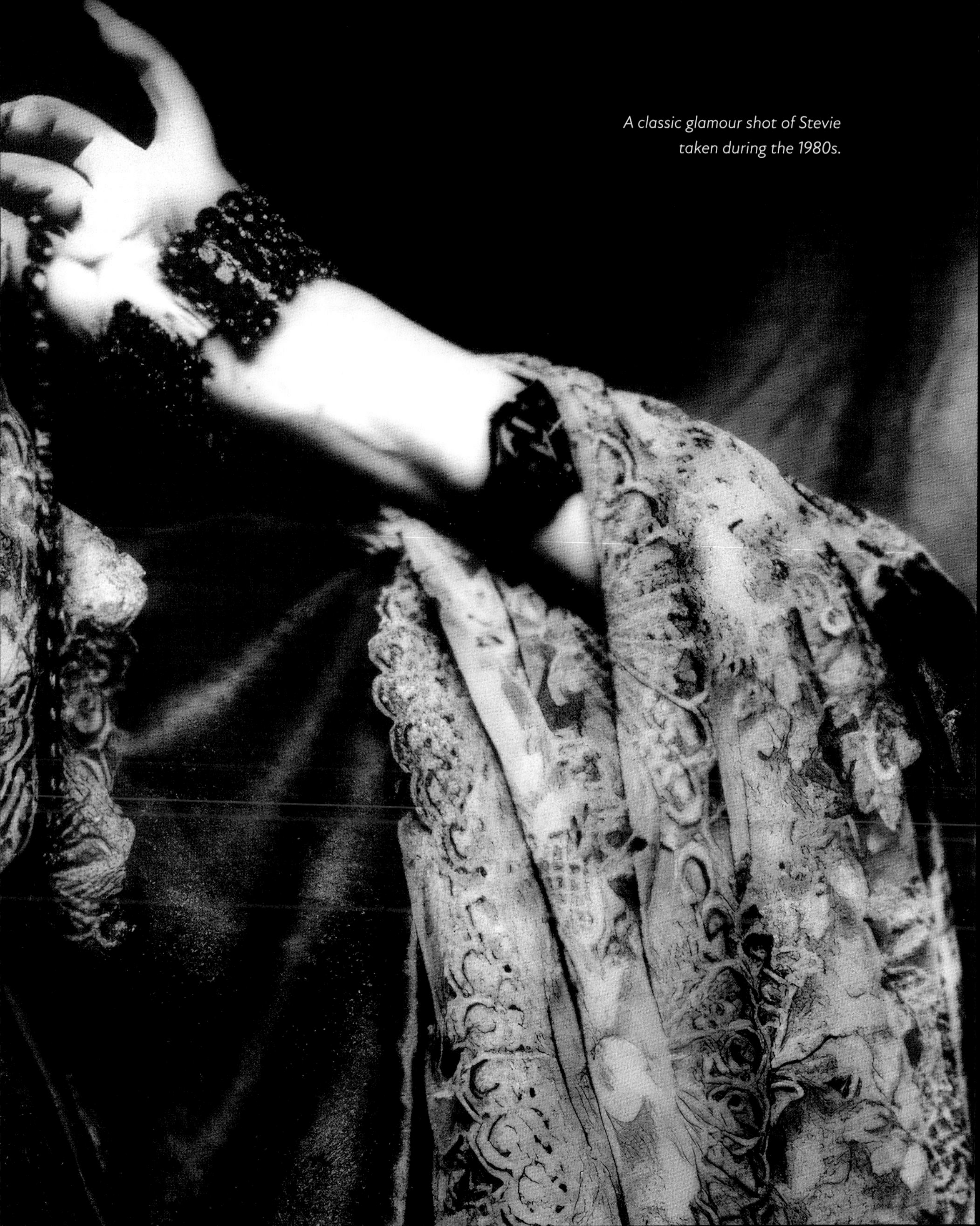

A classic glamour shot of Stevie taken during the 1980s.

22. STEVIE NICKS

"Leather and Lace" 1981

A romantic duet meant for country legends that Stevie made her own.

IN THE 1970S, OUTLAW COUNTRY STAR WAYLON JENNINGS CALLED Nicks and asked her to write a song called "Leather and Lace" for him and his wife, Jessi Colter. Nicks dug right in, to the dismay of her then-boyfriend, Eagles drummer-vocalist Don Henley. "Don did not like the idea of 'Leather and Lace' really very much," she said in a 1981 radio interview. "I had to sort of say, 'Well, I've got to write this song for Waylon, because he really wants it, and I want to write a song for him. I've been waiting for 10 years for somebody famous to ask me to write them a song.'"

As the song was coming together, Henley offered a blunt assessment of what Nicks was doing. "I would play it for Don, and he would say, 'That's terrible. Start over,'" Nicks recalled in a separate 1981 interview with WLIR, adding that she did take this advice to heart. "And I would say, 'Oh, I can't believe you said that.' And I would start over.'"

"Leather and Lace" reflects her hard work, as the lyrics portray a couple who balance each other out—he gives leather, she provides lace in return—and feel safe enough to express both strength and vulnerability. The sentiments are simple but deeply romantic. "I spent a long time on [the song]," Nicks said in 1983. "I tried to give it a little bit of Waylon, a little bit of Jessi and a little bit of what I knew it was like to be in show business, what it was like to work with your husband or your old man."

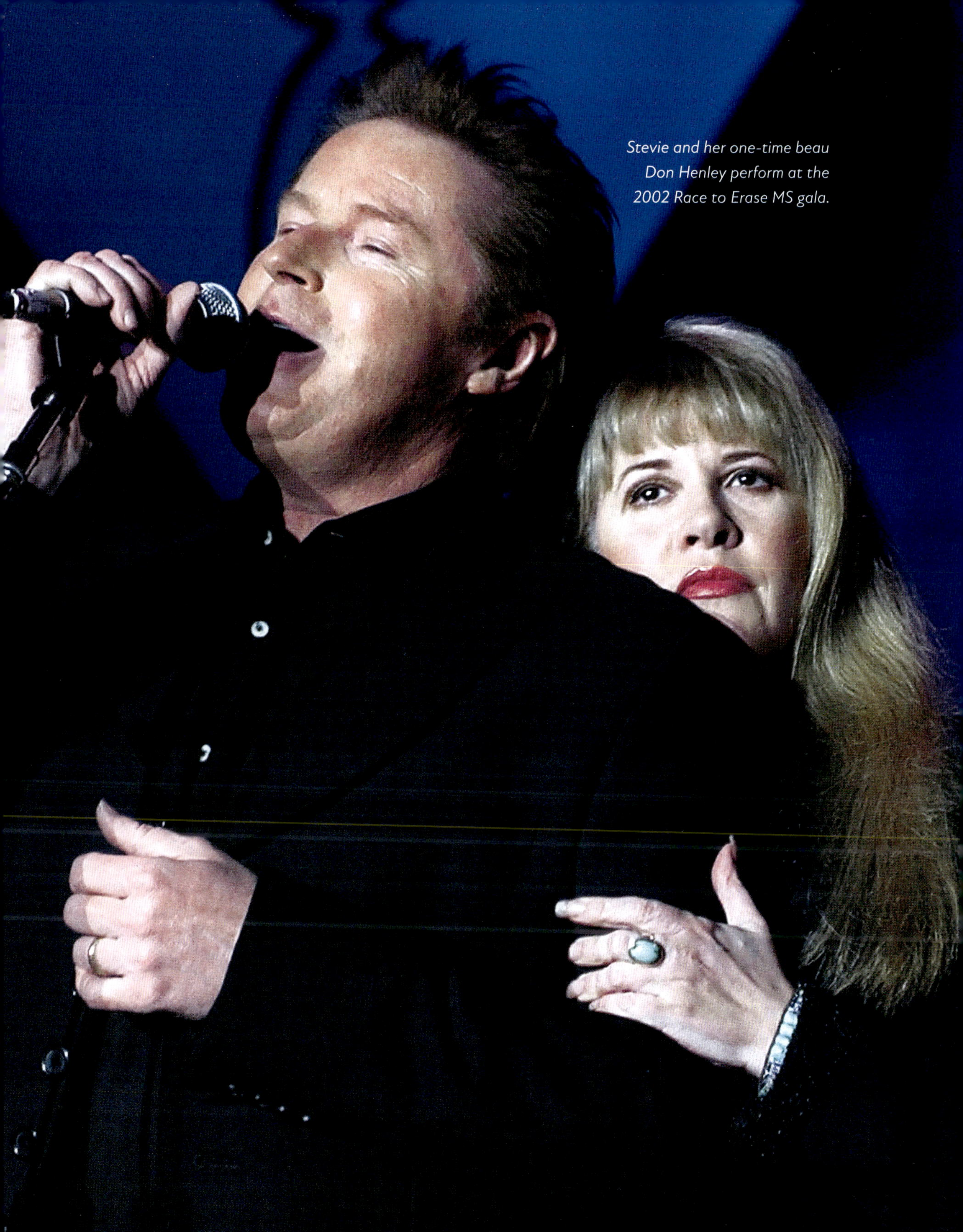

Stevie and her one-time beau Don Henley perform at the 2002 Race to Erase MS gala.

"I've been waiting for 10 years for somebody famous to ask me to write them a song." —STEVIE NICKS

Unfortunately, Jennings and Colter never recorded "Leather and Lace"—although the pair did name a 1981 duets album *Leather and Lace*—and when Waylon wanted to cut the tune anyway as a solo song, Nicks refused to let that happen, as her vision for "Leather and Lace" was always as a duet. In fact, when she dusted off the song for *Bella Donna*, she called up none other than Don Henley to be her duet partner, saying he was crucial to the song.

"[I said] 'If Waylon doesn't do it, and you don't do it, it doesn't get done because I wrote this song for a man and a woman in the music business that are trying to work out their problems together,'" she told WLIR. "'And, you know, your spirit and my spirit is greatly in it, as is Waylon's and Jessi's.'"

As usual, Nicks's vision was on point. "Leather and Lace" ended up sounding like a gentle lullaby driven by understated guitar, piano, and drums. Both Nicks and Henley turn in gorgeous vocal performances full of awe and tenderness; Nicks especially sounds like she's cracking her heart open as she admits to being a fierce individual, but is happily making room for her beloved. Given the star power of each artist, "Leather and Lace" became both a top 10 hit on the Billboard Hot 100 and one of Nicks's most beloved songs.

Relationship WITH DON HENLEY

Nicks dated Don Henley after she split from Lindsey Buckingham. The year was 1976: Fleetwood Mac were on the cusp of stardom, while the Eagles were on the brink of releasing their classic blockbuster *Hotel California*. "He found a very different kind of girl in me than in most of the women that he was used to hanging out with, and we had a very special relationship because of that," Nicks said during a TV interview filmed in the 1980s. "He always kinda treated me like we were married. In that strange sorta way, he still does, whenever I see him. I think he found in me something that he has not probably found since."

The timeline of their relationship is a little fuzzy, although Nicks later disclosed she became pregnant by him in 1979 and had an abortion. [See page 195.] But their romance ended on good terms. The pair toured together in 2005 and dueted on each other's songs, such as the Eagles' "Hotel California" and Fleetwood Mac's "Gold Dust Woman," and in a 2009 interview with *Entertainment Weekly*, Nicks called him "one of my best friends in the world."

That support extended to her biggest musical moments. When she was inducted into the Rock & Roll Hall of Fame as a solo artist in 2019, she performed "Leather and Lace" at the ceremony. Henley casually strolled onstage before the second verse to reprise his parts. In lovely recognition of the couple's shared history, he nodded vigorously after singing a lyric that mused whether a woman could love someone like him; Nicks nodded as well before laughing.

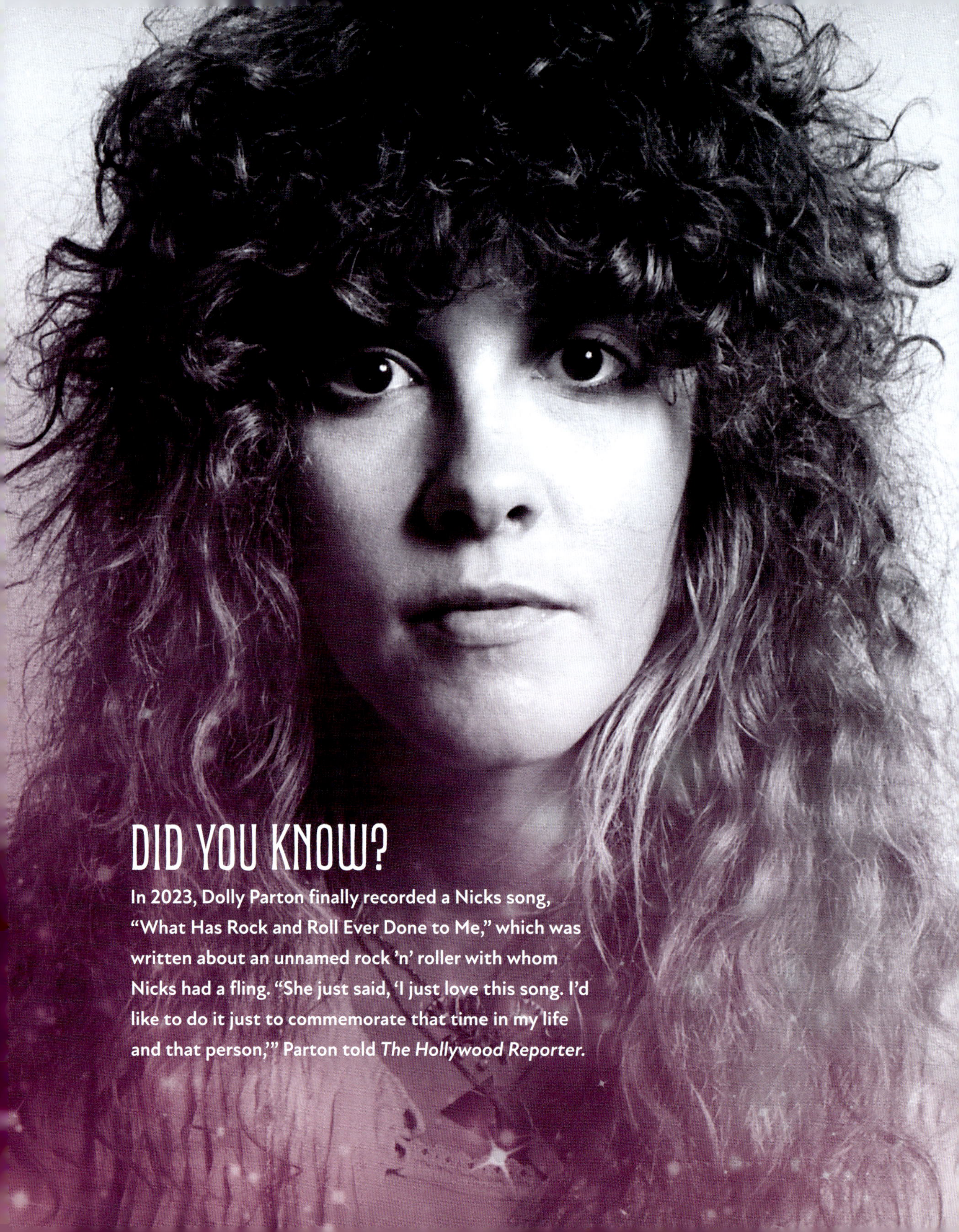

DID YOU KNOW?

In 2023, Dolly Parton finally recorded a Nicks song, "What Has Rock and Roll Ever Done to Me," which was written about an unnamed rock 'n' roller with whom Nicks had a fling. "She just said, 'I just love this song. I'd like to do it just to commemorate that time in my life and that person,'" Parton told *The Hollywood Reporter.*

Stevie photographed in 1978.

23. STEVIE NICKS

"After the Glitter Fades" 1981

A prophetic Stevie crafts a timeless tale of resilience.

"AFTER THE GLITTER FADES" APPEARED WELL AFTER NICKS BECAME famous, so it's tempting to consider it a true story about how being in Fleetwood Mac wore her down. In reality, however, she wrote the song in 1972, when Buckingham Nicks was floundering after moving to Los Angeles and stardom felt very, very far away. "We were going nowhere fast," she told the radio station WLIR. "And I seemed to have some idea what was going to happen, that I was really gonna face some really serious glitter and see some serious glitter fade."

Buoyed by gentle pedal steel and twang-kissed Nicks vocals, "After the Glitter Fades" describes someone who maintains a love of music despite the tough reality of stardom: unfulfilling one-night stands, feeling emotionally numb and heartbroken, and dealing with the occasional lies. "That was a real premonition," Nicks told *High Times*. "I just had some idea about Fleetwood Mac. I wasn't talking about one-night stands with a man. I was talking about your one-night stands in a concert where you run in, played, and left."

Nicks actually wanted Dolly Parton to cut "After the Glitter Fades" because she was convinced the song "would be perfect for her," and even sent along a copy, but a cover never happened. Instead, country legend Glen Campbell did a lovely version of the tune, tapping into the country influences with a warm, solemn performance.

Stevie and Christine McVie live it up in 1976 while traveling with Fleetwood Mac.

24. STEVIE NICKS

"Think About It" 1981

A pep talk for Stevie and Christine McVie.

GIVEN FLEETWOOD MAC'S TANGLED INTERPERSONAL LIVES, it wasn't easy being—or staying—in the band. That certainly explains some of the impetus behind *Bella Donna's* ringing pop-rock gem "Think About It," which Nicks wrote in the mid-1970s as a pick-me-up for herself and Christine McVie; the latter was going through a divorce with Fleetwood Mac bassist John McVie at the time.

"In those days, there were no wardrobe mistresses or speech therapists or anything," Nicks told WLIR. "There was just me and Chris. All she had, really, was me. And so I really had to be her friend and be strong beside her at that point."

Shockingly, Nicks also confessed that she and McVie were ready to leave Fleetwood Mac over their issues with their respective exes/bandmates. "Think About It," however, was a reminder "that we were giving up a lot if we left," Nicks adds, "and that it was really something that should be taken to the heart and thought about heavily before we walked out."

Fittingly, the comforting narrator of "Think About It" encourages keeping a clear head and maintaining perspective during a turbulent time. Among other things, she reassures that heartbreak is temporary and it's important not to let negative feelings cloud your judgment. The narrator also points out that the other person's talent will help a person go far.

Throughout, Nicks's vocal delivery brims with conviction, a tonal match for the music, which she cowrote with E Street Band pianist Roy Bittan. Contributions from instrumental all-stars—piano from Little Feat's Billy Payne, organ from Heartbreaker Benmont Tench, and guitar from Elton John collaborator Davey Johnstone—only add to the confidence, making "Think About It" a low-key standout.

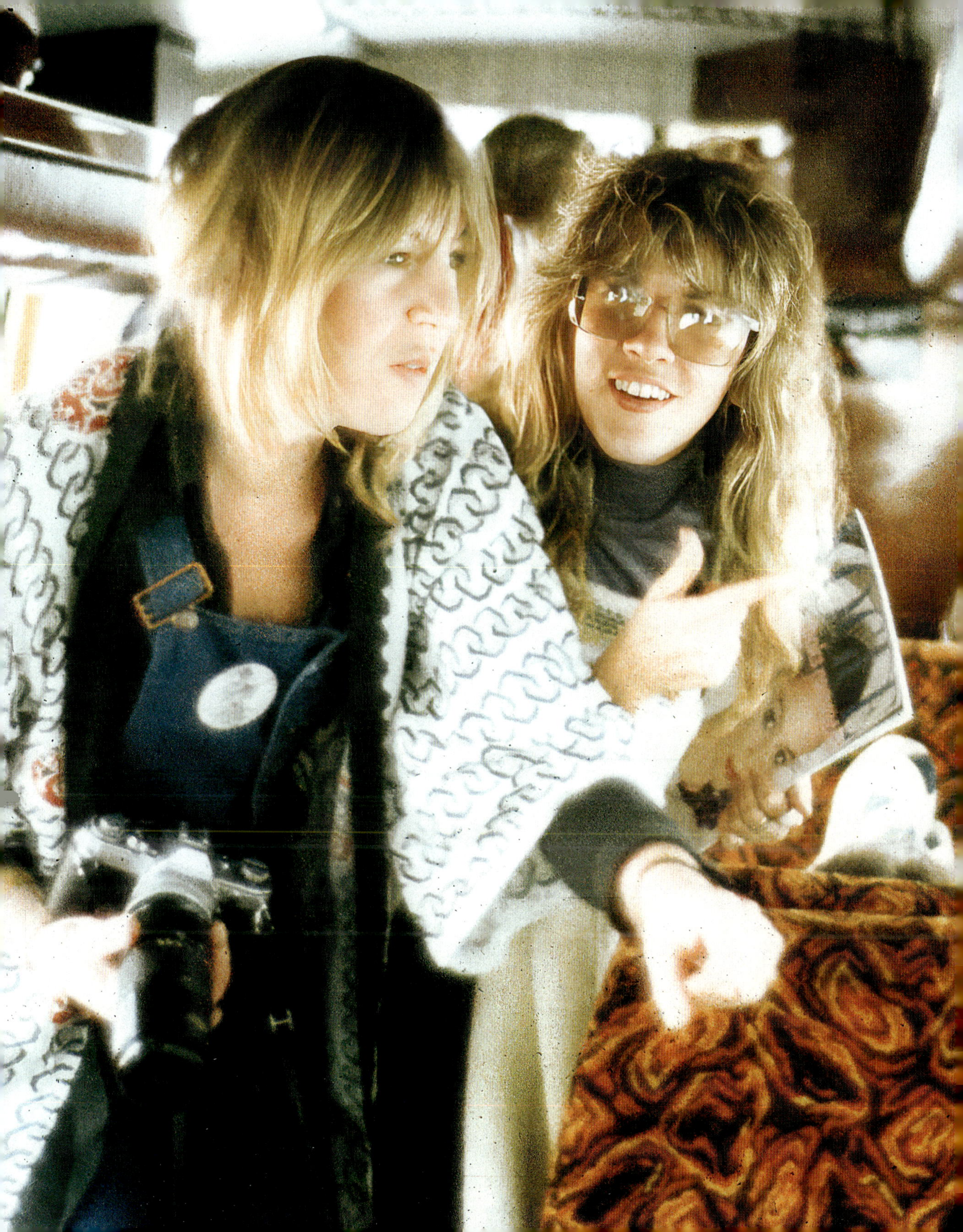

THE ENDURING FRIENDSHIP OF Stevie & Christine

When Mick Fleetwood first told Christine McVie that Stevie Nicks might be joining Fleetwood Mac, he reportedly told her, "They have a girl involved here. You're gonna have to meet her and see if you like her." As it turns out, he had nothing to worry about. "We met and I instantly liked her," McVie told *Rolling Stone*. "She and I are not competitive in any way at all. We're totally different, but totally sympathetic with each other . . . . We don't have any competition on stage. She is who she is. I am who I am."

By 1975, McVie had been a full-time member of Fleetwood Mac for several years, and was an integral part of the band's ever-evolving sound. Luckily, her songwriting complemented Nicks's approach perfectly. "Christine was the pop star," Nicks told *Vulture*. "She wrote all those really super pop hits. None of the rest of us could write those songs."

Over the years, the women were inseparable. "She was like my soulmate, my musical soulmate, and my best friend that I spent more time with than any of my other best friends outside of Fleetwood Mac," Nicks said in the same interview. "Christine was my best friend." Their musical chemistry was also singular. On the final Fleetwood Mac tour, the show ended with Nicks and McVie performing a lovely duet of "All Over Again," a lesser-known McVie song from Fleetwood Mac's 1995 album *Time*; the song's references to ending a long-term love while things were in a good place felt pointed and poignant.

Shockingly, McVie died unexpectedly of a stroke in November 2022 at the age of seventy-nine. Nicks was devastated that she was unable to say goodbye, telling *CBS News Sunday Morning* she had wanted to go "sit on her bed and hold her hand and sing 'Touched by an Angel' to her, until I was sure she heard it."

In March 2023, on the first night of a stadium tour with Billy Joel, Nicks honored McVie with a crushingly sad version of "Landslide," performing the song while a montage of photos of the two women flashed behind her. By the end of the song, Nicks was overcome with emotion and choking back tears, as the audience comforted her with applause and encouragement. "There's really not much to say," she said through her tears. "We just pretend that she's still here, that's how I'm trying to deal with it."

But in the *CBS News Sunday Morning* interview, Nicks talked about how she's keeping McVie's memory alive. "I feel her presence all the time," she says. "I especially feel her presence onstage. She's here." At that, Nicks touched a necklace she was wearing, revealing its charm contained some of McVie's ashes. "But as important as that, is that she's in my heart."

"She was like my soulmate, my musical soulmate, and my best friend . . ."

—STEVIE NICKS TO *VULTURE*

ENCHANTED FACTS ABOUT STEVIE

1 Born Stephanie Lynn Nicks, she earned the nickname Stevie because, as a child, she could not say her own name. Instead, she said "TeeDee," which eventually evolved into Stevie.

2 Nicks loves dogs and, over the years, has owned an Afghan Hound named Branwen and a Chinese Crested–Yorkshire Terrier mix named Sulamith. Her current dog is a white Chinese Crested named Lily.

3 When Stevie was in Fritz, the band once opened for Jimi Hendrix. "He actually dedicated a song to me," Nicks recalled during a radio show. "He looked over at me and said, 'This is for you, babe.'" What was the song? Stevie cannot remember.

4 Two of her favorite poets are Oscar Wilde and Edgar Allan Poe.

5 Nicks's snack weakness is animal crackers. "I know they're back there. I can smell them," she told a *Vulture* journalist. "I could trash this whole place finding those animal crackers."

6 Max, the cockatoo on the cover of *Bella Donna,* belonged to Stevie's brother, Christopher.

7 *Rolling Stone* named Nicks one of the 100 Greatest Songwriters of All Time and one of the 100 Greatest Singers of All Time.

8 Fleetwood Mac's *Rumours* won the Grammy Award for Album of the Year, but Stevie herself has never won a Grammy for her solo work, despite being nominated eight times.

9 When she and Lindsey Buckingham first joined Fleetwood Mac, some people debated whether she was a man or a woman because of her name.

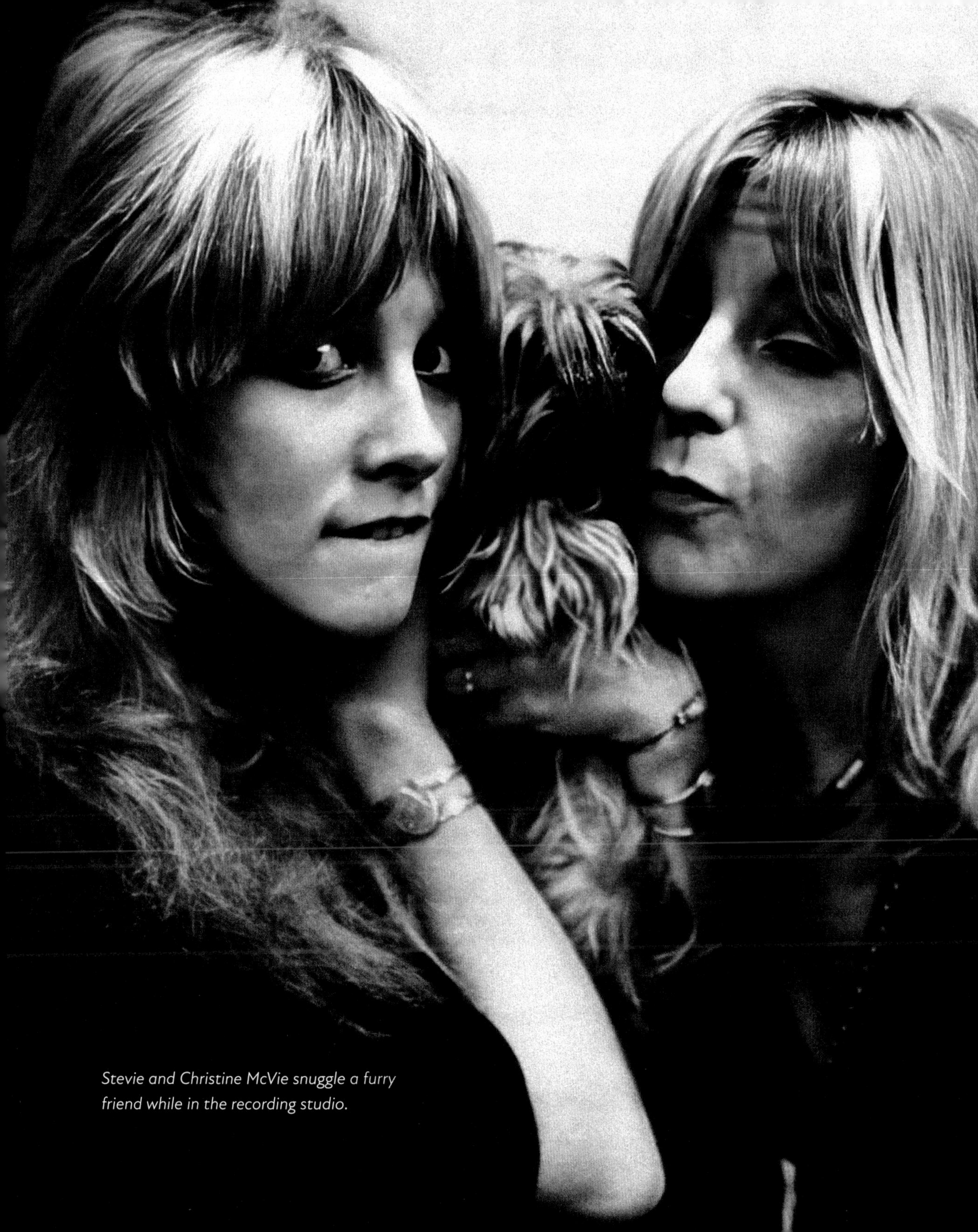

Stevie and Christine McVie snuggle a furry friend while in the recording studio.

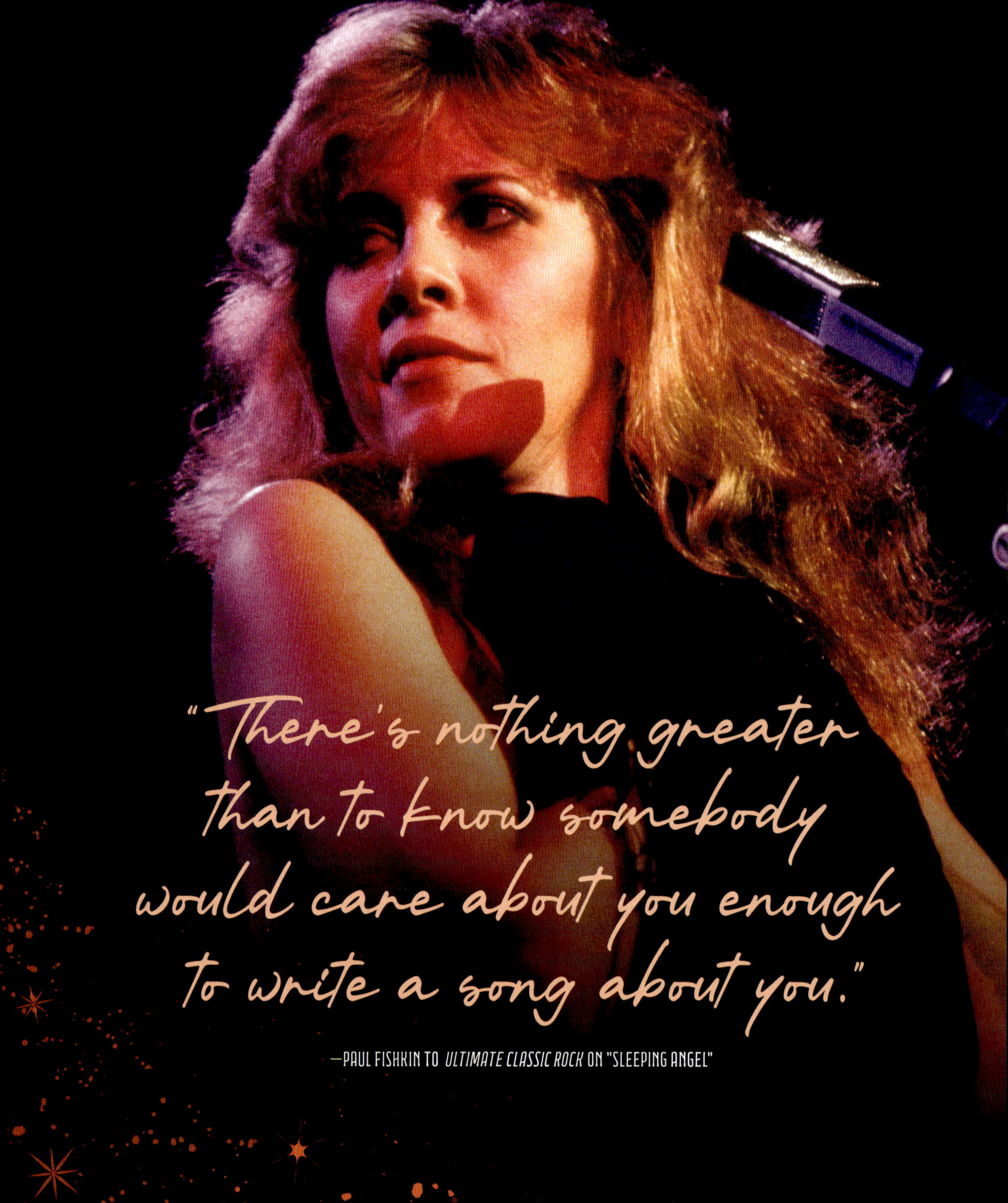

"There's nothing greater than to know somebody would care about you enough to write a song about you."

—PAUL FISHKIN TO *ULTIMATE CLASSIC ROCK* ON "SLEEPING ANGEL"

Stevie supported her debut solo album, Bella Donna, *with a well-received run of tour dates.*

25. STEVIE NICKS

"Sleeping Angel" 1982

A ballad about one of Stevie's love affairs.

IN THE 1982 MOVIE *FAST TIMES AT RIDGEMONT HIGH*, SWEET fifteen-year-old Stacy (Jennifer Jason Leigh) gets an abortion after she becomes pregnant by smooth-talking ticket scalper Mike Damone (Robert Romanus). The teens agree that Damone will pay half of the procedure's price (seventy-five dollars) and give Stacy a ride to the free clinic. Unfortunately, he fails to raise the money and ghosts Stacy; instead, she asks her brother Brad (Judge Reinhold) to give her a ride, pretending she has a bowling party to attend.

As this scene unfolds, Nicks's "Sleeping Angel," plays in the background. A tender ballad dominated by rich acoustic guitars and gentle organ swirls from Benmont Tench, the song was recorded for *Bella Donna*, but didn't make the final tracklisting. Instead, it surfaced on the *Fast Times at Ridgemont High* soundtrack. "What was driving the project [*Bella Donna*] was absolutely doing the right thing for the project," Paul Fishkin told *Ultimate Classic Rock*, theorizing why the song wasn't on *Bella Donna*. "Whatever anybody's personal desires were, they were secondary to getting the best record out."

Fishkin was particularly close to the song; Nicks wrote it about their short-lived romance, penning lyrics that reference a lack of trust, but yearn for freedom, space, and softness. He later complimented her vocal performance and told *Ultimate Classic Rock* he didn't mind being the subject of "Sleeping Angel," noting, "There's nothing greater than to know somebody would care about you enough to write a song about you."

Solo Tours

Today, Stevie Nicks is a twirling dervish who headlines stadiums and arenas as a solo act. But decades ago, in an interview with *Playboy*, she confessed she was nervous about going on the road by herself. "I hadn't been onstage alone before," she said. "It's a whole different can of beans to realize that if you're not out there—if you have to run to the wings for some powder or to get your hair brushed or because you're dripping wet—there is no one onstage who'll talk to the audience."

Ever resilient, Nicks adjusted rather quickly to solo stardom. In 1981, she booked the brief White Winged Dove Tour that culminated in four sold-out shows at the Fox Wilshire Theatre in Los Angeles. With many musicians who played on *Bella Donna* in tow—including organist/music director Benmont Tench, pianist Roy Bittan, and drummer Russ Kunkel—the show was a rousing success. A reviewer for the *Los Angeles Times* even called the December 8 concert "arguably the best pop-rock show I've seen this year." Incredibly enough, two other touring members from this time, guitarist Waddy Wachtel and vocalist Sharon Celani, are still part of Nicks's tours today.

Things picked up quickly from there. In 1983, she performed in front of a hundred thousand people at the US Festival and followed that up with the monthslong The Wild Heart Tour in North America. Three years later, she supported *Rock a Little* with extensive dates in Australia and North America and then finally did solo shows in Europe as well as the US and Canada after issuing 1989's *The Other Side of the Mirror*.

Unlike other artists, Nicks is rarely off the road; over the years, she's teamed up for tours with Don Henley, Rod Stewart, Billy Joel, and Tom Petty and the Heartbreakers. Remarkably, she has maintained this packed touring schedule alongside Fleetwood Mac's own busy concert calendar. And although Nicks certainly plays the band's songs in her solo sets—there's no way she could get away with skipping "Dreams" or "Gold Dust Woman"—the solo format is a "little looser," she told *The Creative Independent*.

"Fleetwood Mac rehearses for eight weeks solid, every day. It's a big rehearsal thing, and with my solo band we don't rehearse that long, because we're a smaller thing. We just go." That's evident from her epic banter: Going to a solo Nicks show is a lot like Storytime with Stevie, as it's not out of the ordinary for her to preface songs with lengthy remembrances or memories. "You know, when I walk out on the stage it's like that's when I'm really me," she said in a 1983 radio interview. "People say to me, 'There's never a look on your face like there is the look that is on your face when you're on that stage.' 'Cause that's where I belong."

"People say to me, 'There's never a look on your face like there is the look that is on your face when you're on that stage.' 'Cause that's where I belong."

—STEVIE NICKS

26. FLEETWOOD MAC

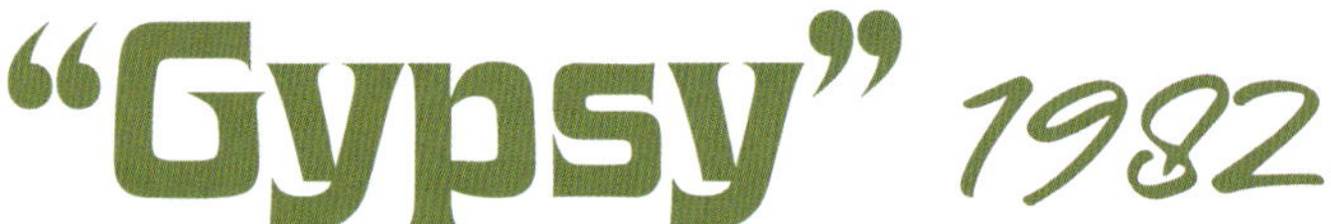

"Gypsy" 1982

An ode to younger, carefree days.

WHEN FLEETWOOD MAC RELEASED 1982'S *MIRAGE*, NICKS WAS IN a much different place in her career than she was when the group released their previous studio effort, 1979's *Tusk*. Thanks to *Bella Donna*, she had become a solo star who could headline tours and land hit singles on her own.

Still, Nicks stressed that she had no intention of parting ways with Fleetwood Mac. "I really believe that the spirit world guides that whole thing, and if it's not meant for me to be in Fleetwood Mac anymore, then something will happen," she said in 1982. "It would never be anything I would ever plan. It's gone on for so long that it's kind of like, Would you ever not go home to visit your family on Christmas? It's that big a part of your life."

"Gypsy," which was known in early press references as "Back to the Gypsy," was the second single released from *Mirage*. Written by Nicks in the late 1970s, "Gypsy" is *Rumours*-esque, thanks to twinkling piano and percussion, frothy harmonies, and a rumbling bassline, although Nicks possesses a country lilt in her voice that feels indebted to *Bella Donna*.

Lyrically, the song is a nostalgic, rose-colored look back at her earliest musical experiences, when she and Buckingham played together in the band Fritz. Nicks reminisces about her younger self: a carefree spirit in love with her simple life. "We had a king-size mattress, but we just had it on the floor," she told *Entertainment Weekly*. "I had old vintage coverlets on it, and even though we had no money it was still really pretty. . . . Just that and a lamp on the floor, and that was it—there was a certain calmness about it."

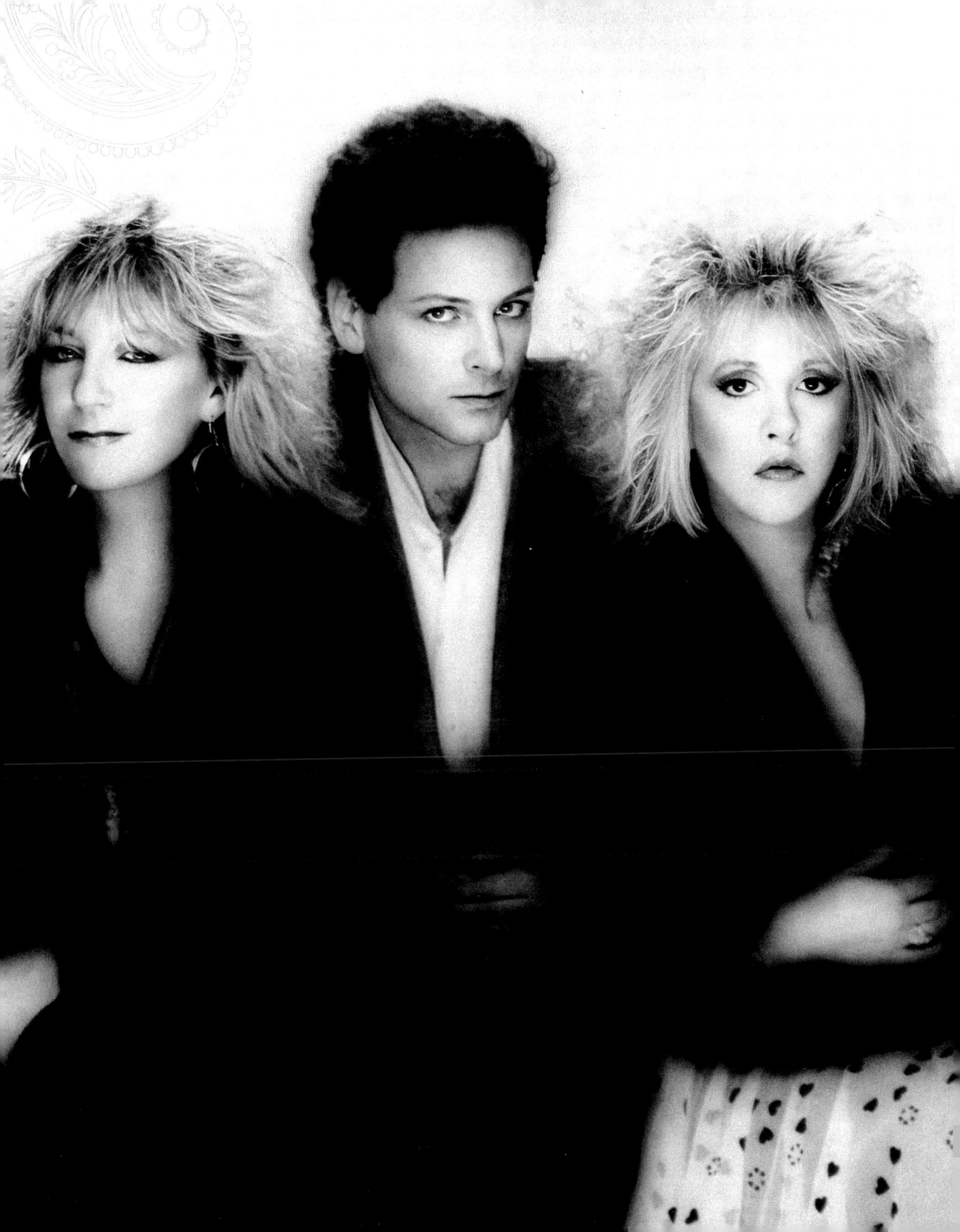

"Gypsy" also references the Velvet Underground, a store frequented by one of Nicks's style icons, Janis Joplin. "It was a tiny little store, but it had the most beautiful things," she told the *Los Angeles Times*. "Tunic tops that came down to your mid-thigh, and evening gown, old-lady nightgown material bell-bottoms that weren't really wide, but instead fell straight over a really high boot. It was in that room where I thought 'Wow! These are the kind of clothes I'm going to wear forever.'"

Despite all these fond remembrances, "Gypsy" possesses an air of melancholy. That's partly because Nicks added in references to her late best friend Robin Anderson [see page 112] and partly because she knows that she can't quite recapture the freedom of those halcyon days. Ultimately, however, "Gypsy" is sweet, as present-day Stevie describes the qualities of Fritz-era Stevie that she still keeps in her heart. "['Gypsy'] was written as an ode to who you were—and who you are," she said during a 2024 concert.

"Gypsy" was a major pop hit, reaching No. 12 on the Billboard Hot 100. And while it's an emotionally raw song for Nicks because of its associations with Robin, it became a live staple with signature moves: As the song nears its end, Nicks twirls around and around like a music box figurine, just like she does in the music video.

"... It was in that room where I thought 'Wow! These are the kind of clothes I'm going to wear forever.'"

—STEVIE NICKS TO THE *LOS ANGELES TIMES* ON CLOTHING STORE THE VELVET UNDERGROUND

MTV

Unlike many of their 1970s peers, both Nicks and Fleetwood Mac had a smooth transition into the music video era. During MTV's first day on the air, the channel aired the clip for "Stop Draggin' My Heart Around" four times and Fleetwood Mac's "Tusk" once. Around the release of *Mirage*, MTV launched a "One Night Stand with Fleetwood Mac" contest: The lucky winner (and three friends!) would fly on a private Learjet to have dinner with the band and catch them in concert. (Out of two hundred thousand entries, the eventual winner was a Toledo, Ohio, resident named Randy Lane, who ended up chatting with John McVie about sailing.)

The music video for "Gypsy" was also quite popular in the channel's early days. Premiered on the same day *Mirage* hit stores—the first time that ever happened on MTV—the video was directed by Russell Mulcahy, who was known for cinematic clips for Duran Duran, Elton John, and Ultravox. The noirish "Gypsy" clip featured Nicks daydreaming about romantic historical moments, and then flashing back to the present day, where she fancifully spins around.

It was an intense video shoot physically—and, as it turns out, emotionally. "There's a scene in 'Gypsy' where Lindsey and I are dancing," Nicks said in the 2011 book *I Want My MTV: The Uncensored Story of the Music Video Revolution*. "And we weren't getting along very well then. I didn't want to be anywhere near Lindsey; I certainly didn't want to be in his arms. If you watch the video, you'll see I wasn't happy. And he wasn't a very good dancer."

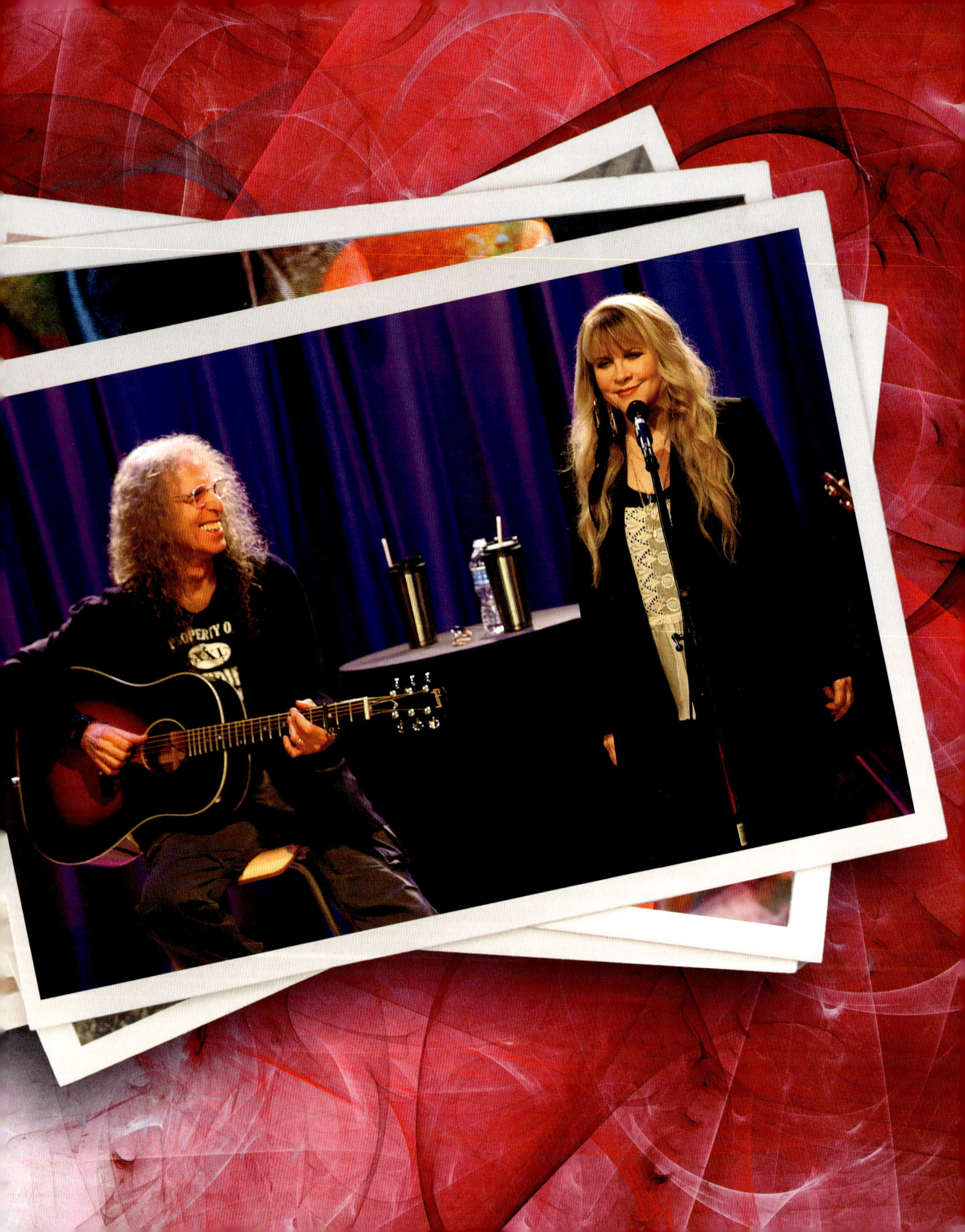

Stevie (pictured with guitarist Waddy Wachtel) performs at the GRAMMY Museum in 2011.

27. STEVIE NICKS

"If Anyone Falls" 1983

A new songwriting collaboration.

AS NICKS BEGAN RECORDING *THE WILD HEART*, A STUDIO OWNER named Gordon Perry (the first husband of Nicks's longtime backing vocalist Lori Perry) slipped her an instrumental called "The Last American" by a Houston-based musician named Sandy Stewart. Inspired, Nicks wrote lyrics to that song—rechristening it "If Anyone Falls"—and another tune called "Nothing Ever Changes" that very night. The timing seemed perfect for Stewart, as she had been searching for lyrics for the song. But then she received even better news. "The next thing I know, I'm on the phone and Gordon's saying, 'You can't have it back. They want to use it on Stevie's next album,'" Stewart told *Record* magazine.

It was the start of a beautiful songwriting partnership. "From that day onward, Sandy and I considered ourselves . . . kind of the Rodgers and Hammerstein of rock," Nicks told MTV. "If someone can write a track that I really love, I'll be glad to write a song to it, because I've got about 800,000 pages of words."

With its sharp-edged electric guitars and Stewart's buoyant keyboards, "If Anyone Falls" felt fresh and contemporary. The lyrics were also infused with the intense romantic feelings of a new relationship—no surprise, as in the liner notes to her 1991 *Timespace* compilation, Nicks reveals that she wrote "If Anyone Falls" when she was falling in love with someone. "He was everything I wanted to be; a real rock and roller . . . and a lover of the Stones . . . small and frail sometimes, but in many ways the strongest person I had ever known." Given that she noted the song was inspired by her guitarist, Waddy Wachtel, chances are good she was talking about him.

"It was good to have somebody that knew the real you besides just your mom and dad," Nicks said on VH1's Behind the Music *of her friend Robin.*

28. STEVIE NICKS

"Nightbird" 1983

A heartbreaking song about one of Stevie's dearest friends.

"NIGHTBIRD" WAS INSPIRED IN PART BY ROBIN ANDERSON, who supported her music career, listening to early songs and later touring with her as a speech therapist. In fact, Nicks later credited her friend with rescuing her voice, "with a lot of patience and love," when it faltered while on tour with Fleetwood Mac. "She was the one person that knew me for what I really was and not for the famous Stevie," Nicks said on VH1's *Behind the Music*. "And it was good to have somebody that knew the real you besides just your mom and dad."

Tragically, the very day *Bella Donna* reached No. 1 on the *Billboard* album charts in September 1981, Robin was diagnosed with terminal leukemia and given mere months to live. She died in October 1982. "Without a doubt, it was the absolute high and low of success," Nicks admitted on VH1's *Behind the Music*. "I didn't really ever get to enjoy *Bella Donna* at all because my friend was dying. Something went out that day; something left that day."

A devastated Nicks poured her grief into music, settling into her living room with Sandy Stewart to develop "Nightbird." Although this was a different way of working—Nicks usually wrote lyrics to full musical tracks Stewart sent from afar—the pair's in-person songwriting chemistry was strong. "I started singing and pacing and wondering if I was doing the right thing, because this was a very important song to me," Nicks said in a 1983 radio interview. "[Sandy] was very compassionate to me, especially at that time, just rode with me until I was able to just start singing something, and she just started playing the right thing."

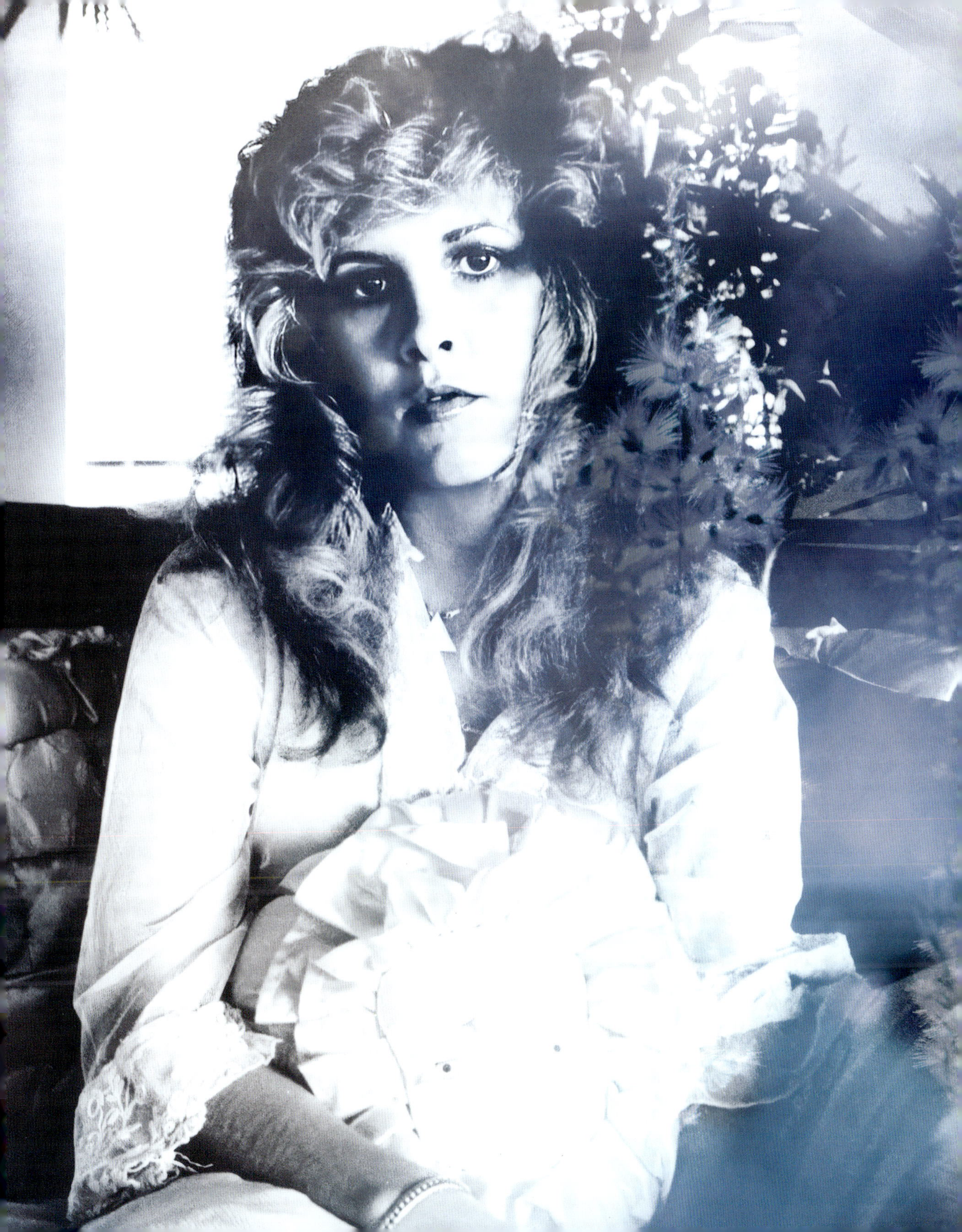

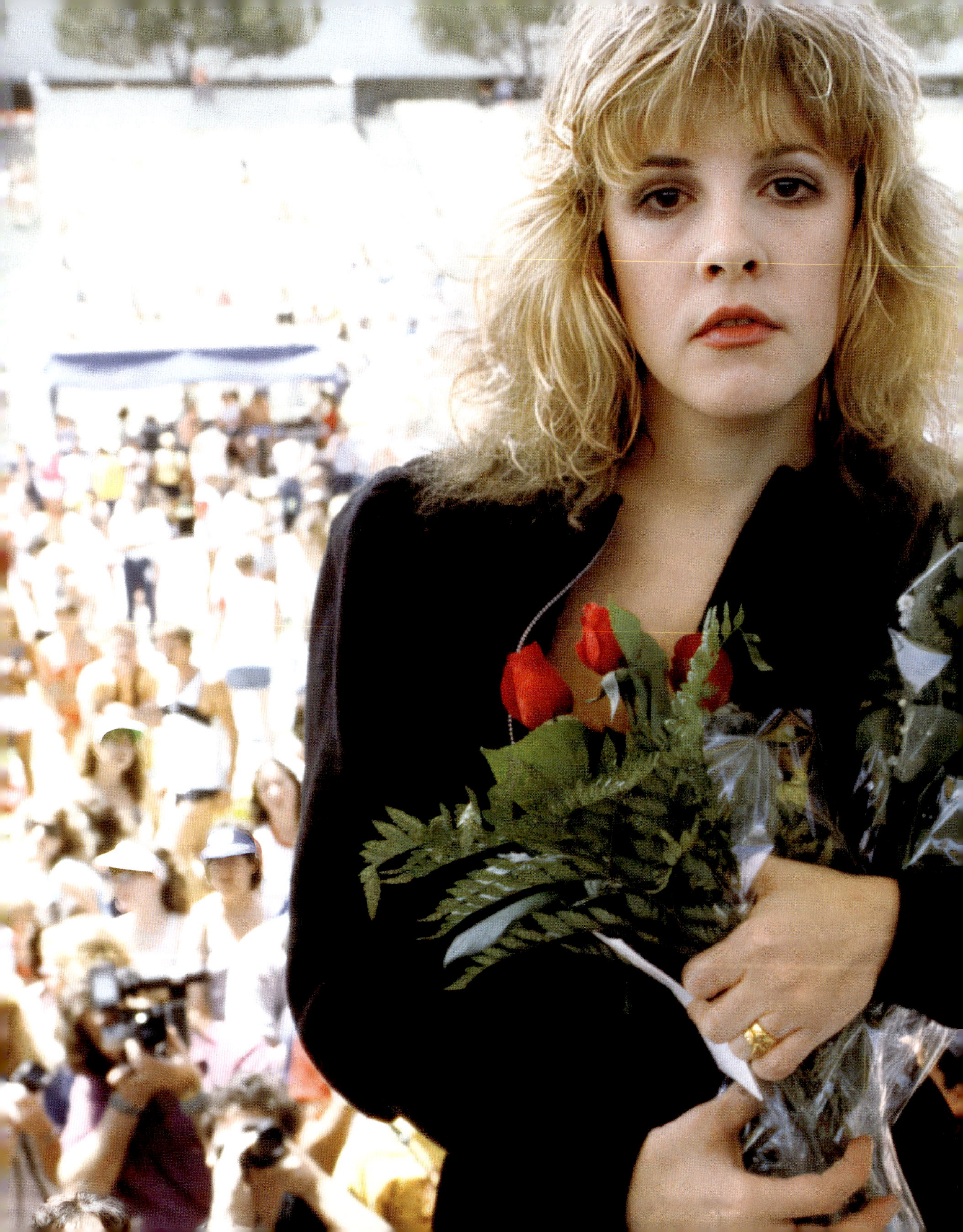

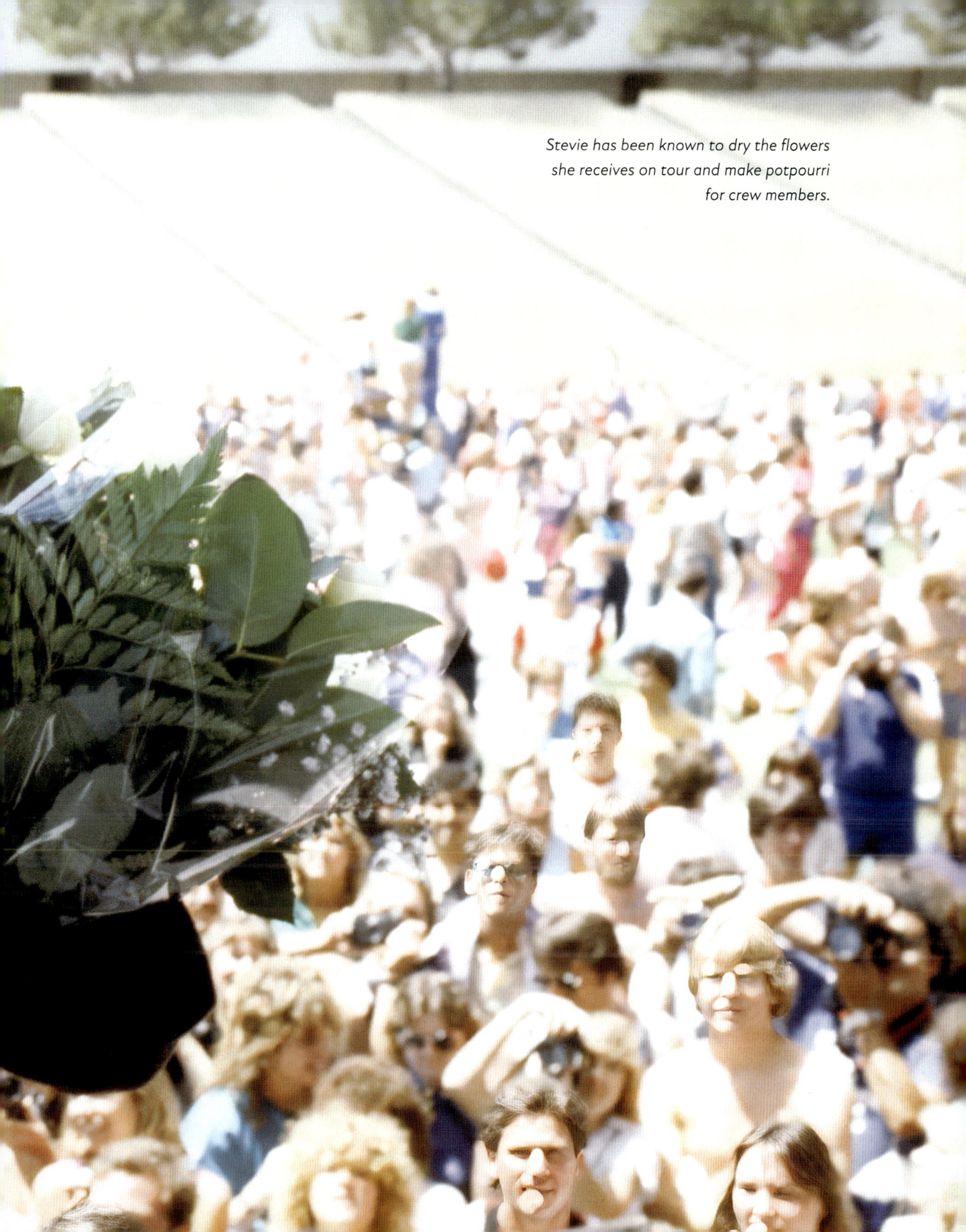

Stevie has been known to dry the flowers she receives on tour and make potpourri for crew members.

The duo ended up writing the song "from scratch" very quickly, Nicks shared. "Me pacing and her playing her little synthesizer on the floor in the living room. It's the first time I've ever done that." With fragile, gentle vocals from both Nicks and Stewart, the song aches with sadness. Nicks references how she wasn't prepared for winter—a clear allusion to how stunned she is over Robin's illness—and uses the ghostly image of beckoning someone to walk through her shadow.

But like many Nicks songs, "Nightbird" contains several layers of meaning. "Robin had the worst leukemia that UCLA Medical Center had ever seen," Nicks said in a 1983 radio interview. "And Robin didn't have any time. So, it's like, the song is really about the fact that it's very difficult to be a rock 'n' roll singer." This fits the chorus, which mentions crying singers wrapped in capes, calling out for both the night and the titular nightbird.

Appropriately, the song resembles a lullaby, with swaying grooves, oceanic synthesizer licks, and sparkling piano from David Foster. "Nightbird" was a top 40 hit in America. However, Nicks has only played the song live twice, during 1983 TV appearances on *Saturday Night Live* and *Solid Gold*.

"It was not planned for me to sing with Stevie until two days before [Saturday Night Live], and it was an unbelievable experience, one I will carry with me always."

—LORI NICKS TO ROCKALITTLE.COM

Stevie's SINGERS

The lyrics of "Nightbird" reference people who sing at night, which Nicks meant as an allusion to her stalwart backing vocalists, Sharon Celani and Lori Perry. She first met Perry—who later married Stevie's brother, Christopher, and changed her last name to Nicks—after moving to Los Angeles in the early 1970s. Lori became an integral part of Nicks's solo work, both live and on record, with the *Saturday Night Live* performance of "Nightbird" particularly standing out. "That performance is probably the highlight of my live singing career with Stevie," she told the Nicks Fix website. "It was not planned for me to sing with Stevie until two days before the show, and was an unbelievable experience, one I will carry with me always."

Nicks's first encounter with Celani was also quite memorable: In 1977, she saw her in Hawaii at a legendary club called the Blue Max, singing Warren Zevon's "Poor Poor Pitiful Me." The performance was so good that Nicks introduced herself and asked, right then and there, if Celani would ever consider working with her. "I didn't know this girl," Nicks said in a 1983 radio interview. "This could have been an unpleasant person, you know, that I had just nailed myself into a relationship with." However, Nicks's instincts were right on: To this day, Celani is still one of her backing singers, having accompanied Nicks both on solo work and with Fleetwood Mac.

Stevie and then-husband Kim Anderson attend the 1983 American Music Awards.

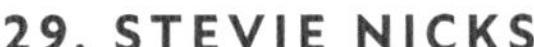

29. STEVIE NICKS

"Stand Back" *1983*

How a Prince song inspired Stevie.

ON JANUARY 29, 1983, STEVIE NICKS MARRIED KIM ANDERSON, the widower of her best friend Robin Anderson. The wedding came just three months after Robin died of leukemia; tragically, she had also just given birth to a premature baby boy.

"I was determined to take care of that baby, so I said to Kim, 'I don't know, I guess we should just get married,'" Nicks told *US Magazine*. "...It was a terrible, terrible mistake. We didn't get married because we were in love, we got married because we were grieving and it was the only way that we could feel like we were doing anything."

Unsurprisingly, the marriage—Nicks's only one—was short-lived, lasting just three months. But the nuptials did end up producing one of her biggest and most enduring solo hits: 1983's "Stand Back."

On their wedding day, the couple were heading to their honeymoon in Santa Barbara and Prince's sleek "Little Red Corvette" came on the car radio. Nicks was floored—and inspired. "I start singing all these words, and I'm like, 'Pull over, we have to get a cassette player! And we have to record this!'" she told MTV News. "I'm writing in the car—here we are, newlyweds, and we get to our hotel and we're setting up the tape recorder and I've made up my whole new melody to [the song]."

Feeling emboldened, Nicks decided to call up Prince himself and ask him to play on the song when she finally recorded the tune. ("I track down Prince's phone number—and because I'm Stevie Nicks, I can get it," she quipped to MTV News.) She confessed to writing her own song to the foundation of "Little Red Corvette" and offered him 50

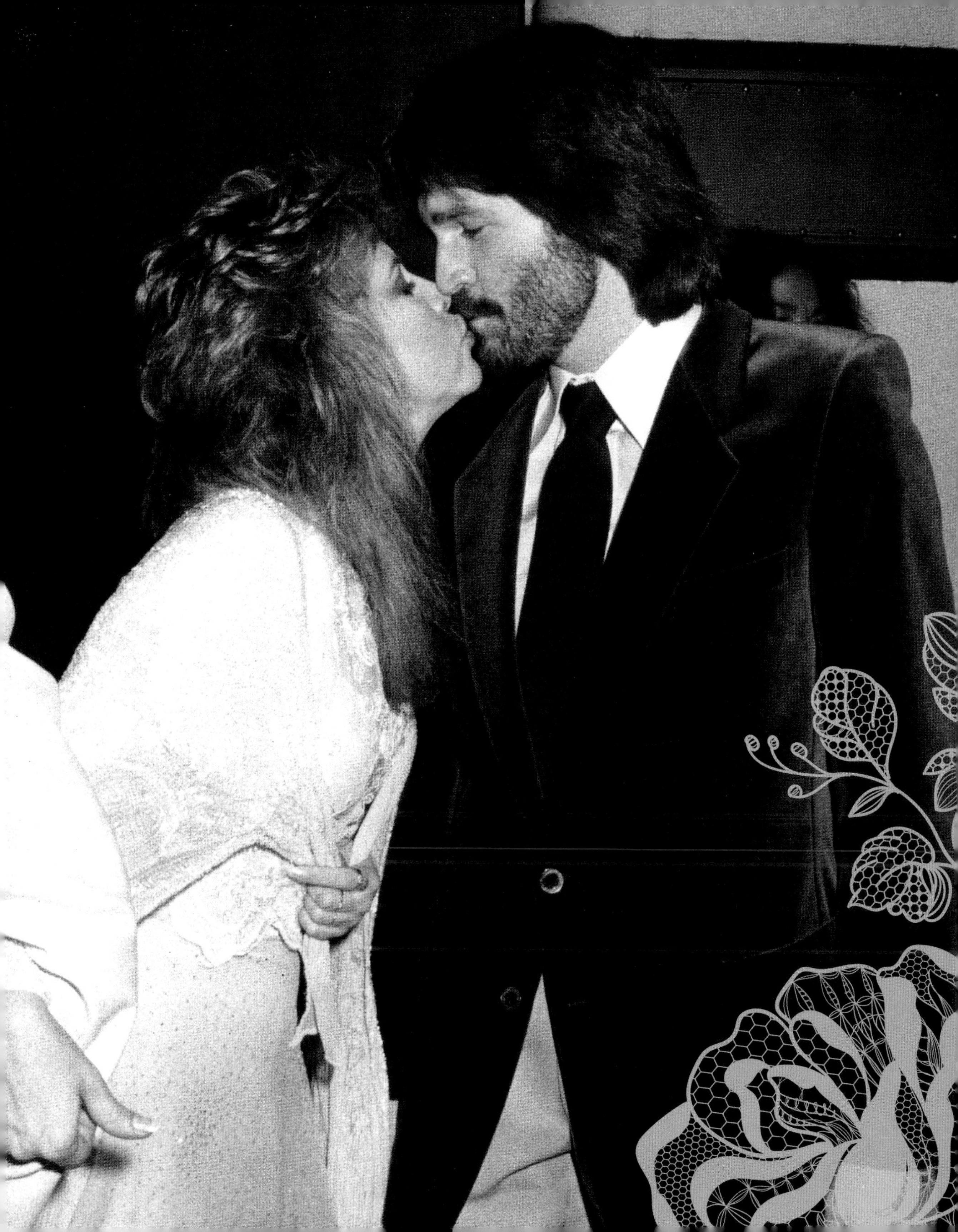

percent of royalties. (He never took her up on the generous proposal.) Nicks also wondered if he was free to come to the studio.

Incredibly enough, Prince was. Within the hour, he was there listening to the song, while Nicks "turned extremely white and started to shake" from nerves, as she put it to *Details*. Things moved quickly from there, she added. "He walked over to the piano and put on a really incredible keyboard track. And not only did Prince make it up right on the spot, he played it with only two fingers. Then he left."

In a 2010 radio interview published years later in Duane Tudahl's *Prince and the Purple Rain Era Studio Sessions: 1983 and 1984* book, Prince himself also noted the session was quick. But he also recalled having to program the drum machine, "because people were using live drums at that point . . . so I went down there and programmed it for them and pretty much played most of the song there in about twenty or thirty minutes."

The end result of the collaboration was one of the best pop singles of the 1980s—a galvanizing song that starts with strutting drums and vibrant synthesizers and levels up with guitar from Toto's Steve Lukather and a positively tenacious Nicks vocal lead. "When it starts, it has an energy that comes from somewhere unknown . . . and it seems to have no timespace," she wrote in the liner notes for *Timespace: The Best of Stevie Nicks*. "I've never quite understood this sound . . . but I have never questioned it."

Accordingly, Nicks has never been very specific about what "Stand Back" is based on, though she's alluded to it being about a fight or anger. But it's clear the narrator is smarting from being treated poorly and is working out their pain while trying to stay optimistic. As a result, the song bursts with both determination and indignation—an unstoppable combination when you need a jolt of self-confidence.

"Stand Back" was a huge hit that reached No. 5 on the Billboard Hot 100 and has remained a staple of Nicks's live shows, both solo and with Fleetwood Mac. After Prince died in 2016, she honored him during her solo tours with rather entertaining retellings of how the pair made "Stand Back." In the end, however, "It never belonged to me," she said in a 1991 tour book. "It has always belonged to the world—and to Prince, who inspired the entire song."

STEVIE *Speaks*

Stevie and Prince had met years before at a record label party; hilariously, she told him, "You're going to have to learn how to talk more," because he was so quiet.

"I track down Prince's phone number—and because I'm Stevie Nicks, I can get it."

—STEVIE NICKS TO MTV NEWS

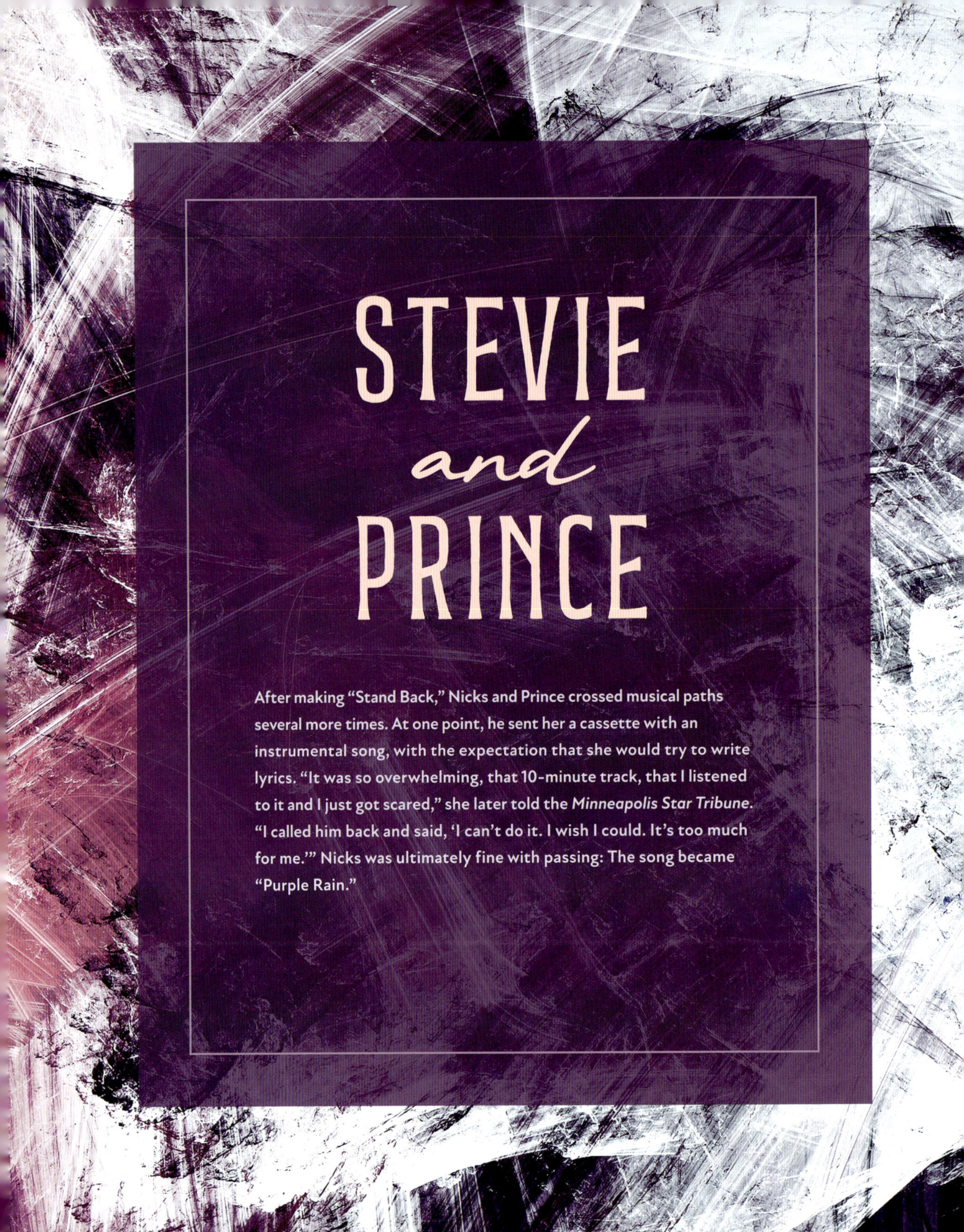

STEVIE *and* PRINCE

After making "Stand Back," Nicks and Prince crossed musical paths several more times. At one point, he sent her a cassette with an instrumental song, with the expectation that she would try to write lyrics. "It was so overwhelming, that 10-minute track, that I listened to it and I just got scared," she later told the *Minneapolis Star Tribune*. "I called him back and said, 'I can't do it. I wish I could. It's too much for me.'" Nicks was ultimately fine with passing: The song became "Purple Rain."

> "It was so overwhelming, that 10-minute track, that I listened to it and I just got scared . . ."

—STEVIE NICKS TO THE *MINNEAPOLIS STAR TRIBUNE* ON A SONG PRINCE SHARED WITH HER

In July 1983, Nicks played the Met Center in Minneapolis on The Wild Heart Tour. After the show, Prince swooped in and picked her up in his purple Camaro; the pair raced back to his house—it was purple, naturally—at a breakneck speed of 100 mph. A writing session commenced but was then abandoned for the night. "I've just done a show and I'm tired, so I go upstairs and sleep on the floor of his purple kitchen," Nicks recalled to *Mojo*. "In the morning he wakes me up and I have some coffee and I sing a little part on the song." She had to split for the airport soon after and the song, which was apparently called "I Know What to Say to You," remains unreleased.

Unfortunately, Nicks said she and Prince eventually stopped talking after the *Purple Rain* movie premiere in 1984 because she had a viscerally negative reaction to a scene where he hit Apollonia. "I freaked and had to go sit in the bathroom," she recalled in 1994. "Afterward I went back to see him, and when he asked why I'd left, I had to tell him, 'When you popped Apollonia, it kinda popped my brain.' He looked at me like it just killed him."

Not long after, she wrote "Thousand Days" about her "non-relationship with Prince," as she put it to *Billboard*. First demoed during the *Rock a Little* era as a song with stormy guitars, urgent saxophone, and anguished vocals, the tune alludes to a relationship in which clashing personalities cause friction. But despite this tumult, the narrator still cares about the other person; as a result, the lyrics also contain hints of wistfulness and pangs of longing.

Nicks happened to base "Thousand Days" on that fateful night in the purple house. She was "smoking my pot" but Prince "didn't agree with my lifestyle," she told *Billboard*. "I like him, but we were just so different there was no possible meeting ground." A completed version of "Thousand Days" later surfaced on the B-side of "Street Angel" singles and then on several compilations in a slightly more polished form that amplified the melancholy at the song's core.

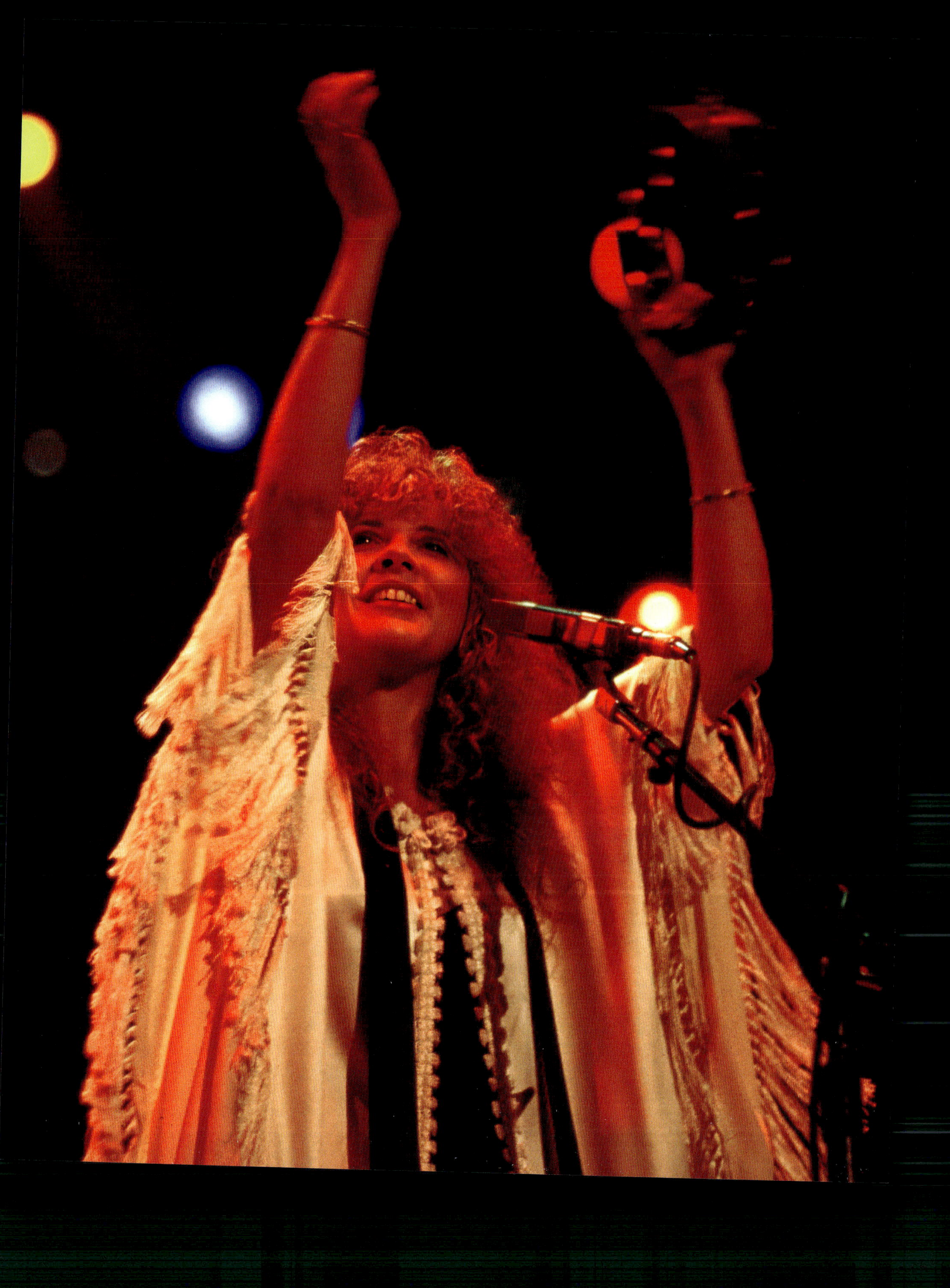

Stevie shows off her tambourine skills during the Detroit date of the Tusk Tour.

30. STEVIE NICKS

"Enchanted" 1983

A classic rocker written during a car ride.

AS ANNIE LEIBOVITZ PHOTOGRAPHED STEVIE NICKS FOR A 1981 *Rolling Stone* cover, Nicks posed and twirled for the camera while cheerfully singing along to a playlist of tunes. These included tunes by other people (Todd Rundgren's "I Saw the Light"), as well as familiar gems from Fleetwood Mac and her solo career. Interestingly enough, however, one of the tunes she belted out was a then-unreleased "Enchanted," a rollicking song in the vein of a barnstorming 1950s rock 'n' roll tune. But the upbeat tone was deceptive: The narrator of "Enchanted" despairs over yet another broken relationship and points out that the ex didn't put any effort into her.

Nicks composed the song around the time she wrote the title track of *The Wild Heart*, while riding in a limousine from New York City to Long Island. "We heard the instrumental part out of the speakers, and we hooked up our TCD-5, which is the saviour of our singing lives," she said in the press kit for the album. "So we sang and recorded and by the time we got there the song was written. Constructive traveling, I call it." Although "Enchanted" wasn't released as a single, Nicks clearly adored the song's title and what it represented, using its name for both a 1998 boxed set (*Enchanted: The Works of Stevie Nicks*) and a tour. It also became a live favorite for her, making the setlist of many Nicks solo tours in the twenty-first century.

The Wild Heart is Stevie's second solo album.

31. STEVIE NICKS

"Wild Heart" 1983

A mission statement for Stevie's growing musical boldness.

NICKS OFTEN TOOK INSPIRATION FROM MANY DIFFERENT places while writing songs. Take "Wild Heart," which she wrote about the movie *Wuthering Heights,* likely the classic 1939 film version starring Laurence Olivier. "I wrote it about Heathcliff and Cathy, and the fact that they were one person, that they couldn't be together and they couldn't be separate, and about the power and the drama of the closing deathbed scene," she said in the liner notes to the 2016 reissue of *The Wild Heart*. "All those amazing things he says to her."

From a musical standpoint, "Wild Heart" embodied the bold, unfettered vibe of the album. Nicks recorded the song live alongside musicians such as Sandy Stewart on keyboards and Brad Smith on drums, underscoring the song's dramatic nature by belting out her lyrics with bristling urgency. The result was a panoramic anthem that also set the tone for *The Wild Heart* era.

The empowered chorus "was becoming my anthem after *Mirage* and *Bella Donna*," Nicks says in the liner notes. "Basically I was saying, 'Don't accuse me of anything, don't tell me what I can and cannot do, and don't blame it on me, blame it on my wild heart.'" That's certainly not a bad thing, however. "I played it for Tom Petty and he said, 'This is an epic,'" she told *Video Rock Stars* magazine. "And that's just what it is, the real story of what we all go through, everybody . . . of how wild our hearts really are and we can't help it, because this is just the way it is."

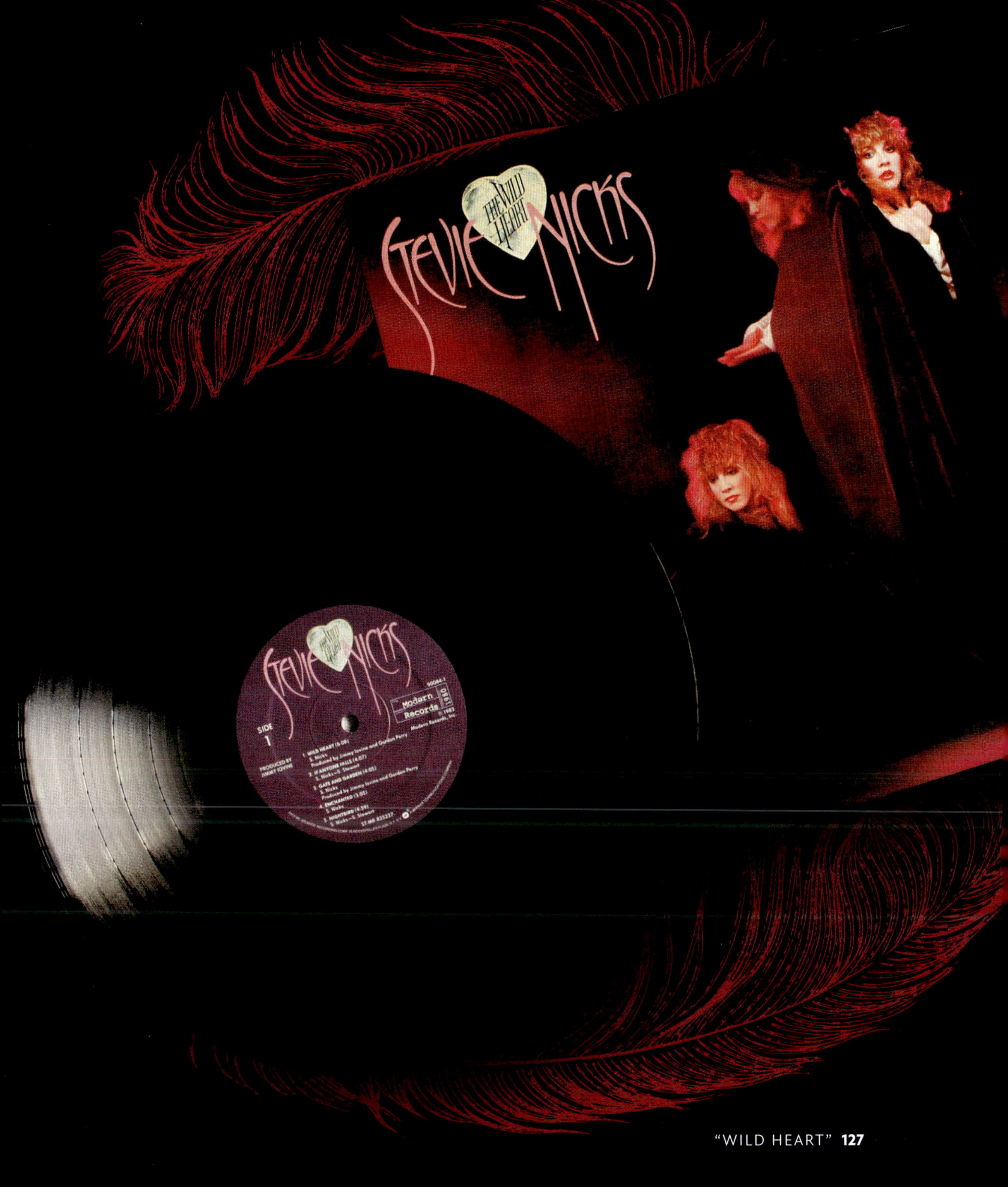
STEVIE NICKS
THE WILD HEART
STEVIE NICKS
SIDE 1
PRODUCED BY JIMMY IOVINE
1. WILD HEART (6:08)
S. Nicks
Produced by Jimmy Iovine and Gordon Perry
2. IF ANYONE FALLS (4:07)
S. Nicks—S. Stewart
3. GATE AND GARDEN (4:05)
S. Nicks
Produced by Jimmy Iovine and Gordon Perry
4. ENCHANTED (3:05)
S. Nicks
5. NIGHTBIRD (4:59)
S. Nicks—S. Stewart
ST-MR-835237
90084-1
Modern Records
1980
℗ 1983 Modern Records, Inc.

Mick Fleetwood and Stevie perform live onstage in 1983.

32. STEVIE NICKS

"Beauty and the Beast" *1983*

A modern fairy tale modeled after Stevie's complicated life.

NICKS ONCE CALLED *BEAUTY AND THE BEAST* HER FAVORITE FAIRY tale, noting she was particularly fond of the 1946 Jean Cocteau–directed movie adaptation of the story, which she saw while having an affair with bandmate Mick Fleetwood. That movie—along with Fleetwood, who certainly resembled the hirsute, dapper gentle giant—inspired the majestic 1983 song about an ill-fated romance.

"It matched our story because Mick and I could never be," Nicks told *Entertainment Weekly*, cognizant of the fact that Fleetwood's then-marriage was turbulent and that this affair could hurt Fleetwood Mac. "Lindsey had barely survived the breakup of Lindsey and Stevie . . . [and would not] survive the relationship of Stevie and Mick." In fact, after Fleetwood told Buckingham he and Stevie were dating ("Even though I thought it was totally the wrong thing to do," Nicks says), they promptly split up. "But of course Lindsey never forgave me for years, if ever," she says. "All the great love stories are the love that cannot be."

Nicks originally recorded a piano demo of "Beauty and the Beast" after a show in Dallas at Gordon Perry's "magical" studio, with backing vocals from Lori Perry and her best friend Carolyn Brooks. Later, in New York City, Nicks hired an orchestra, which added bittersweet glamour to the music in a three-hour session.

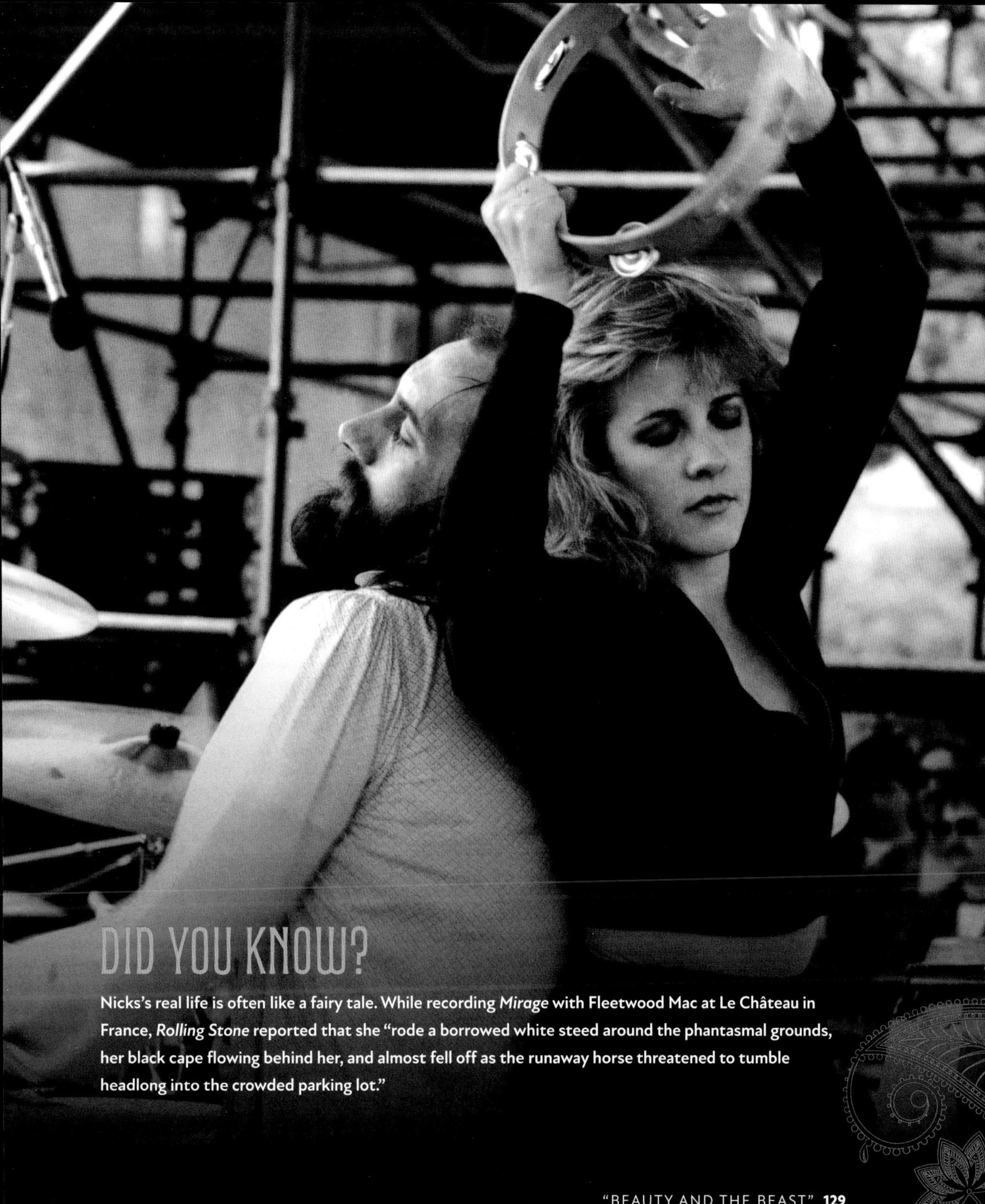

DID YOU KNOW?

Nicks's real life is often like a fairy tale. While recording *Mirage* with Fleetwood Mac at Le Château in France, *Rolling Stone* reported that she "rode a borrowed white steed around the phantasmal grounds, her black cape flowing behind her, and almost fell off as the runaway horse threatened to tumble headlong into the crowded parking lot."

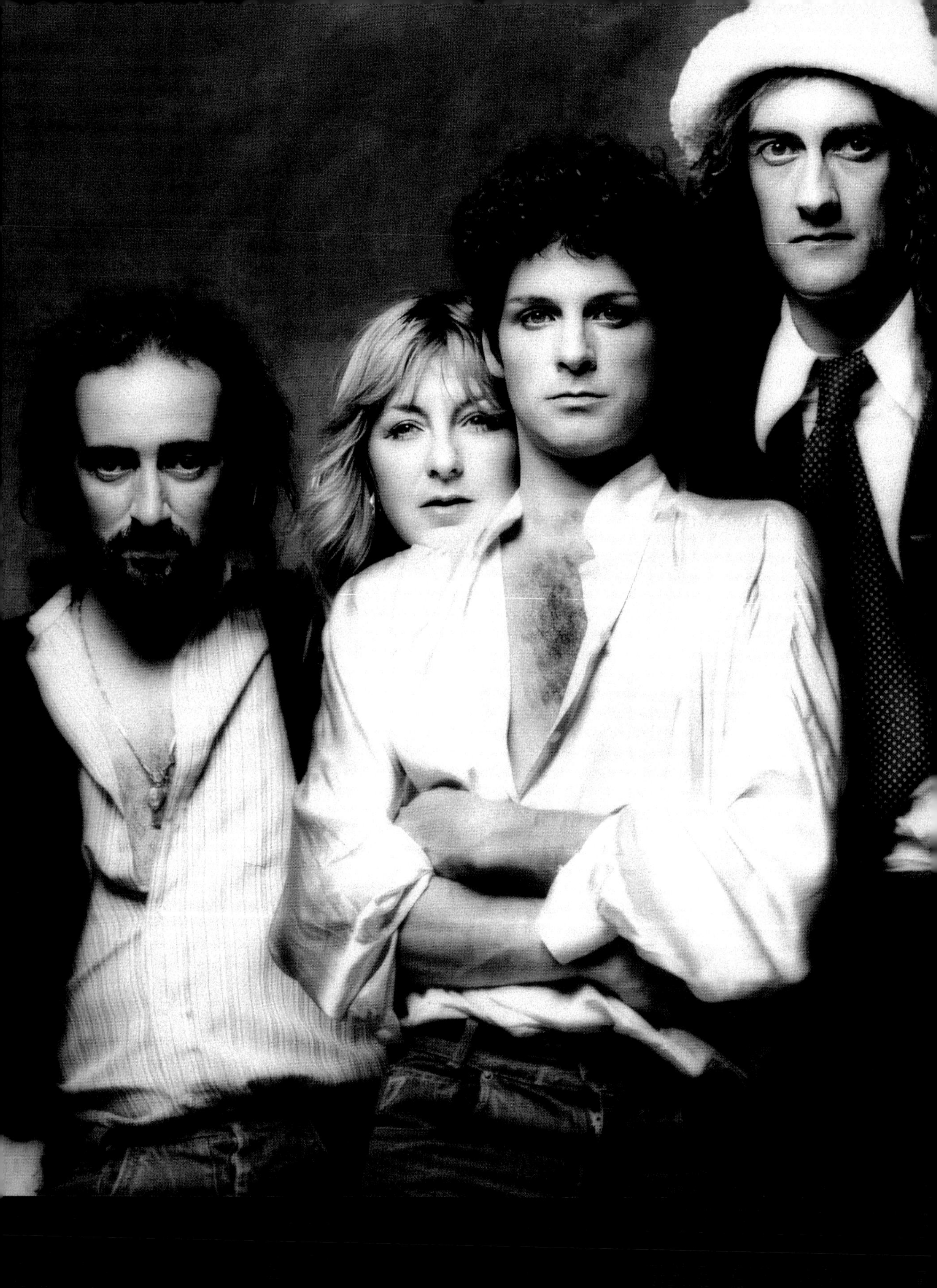

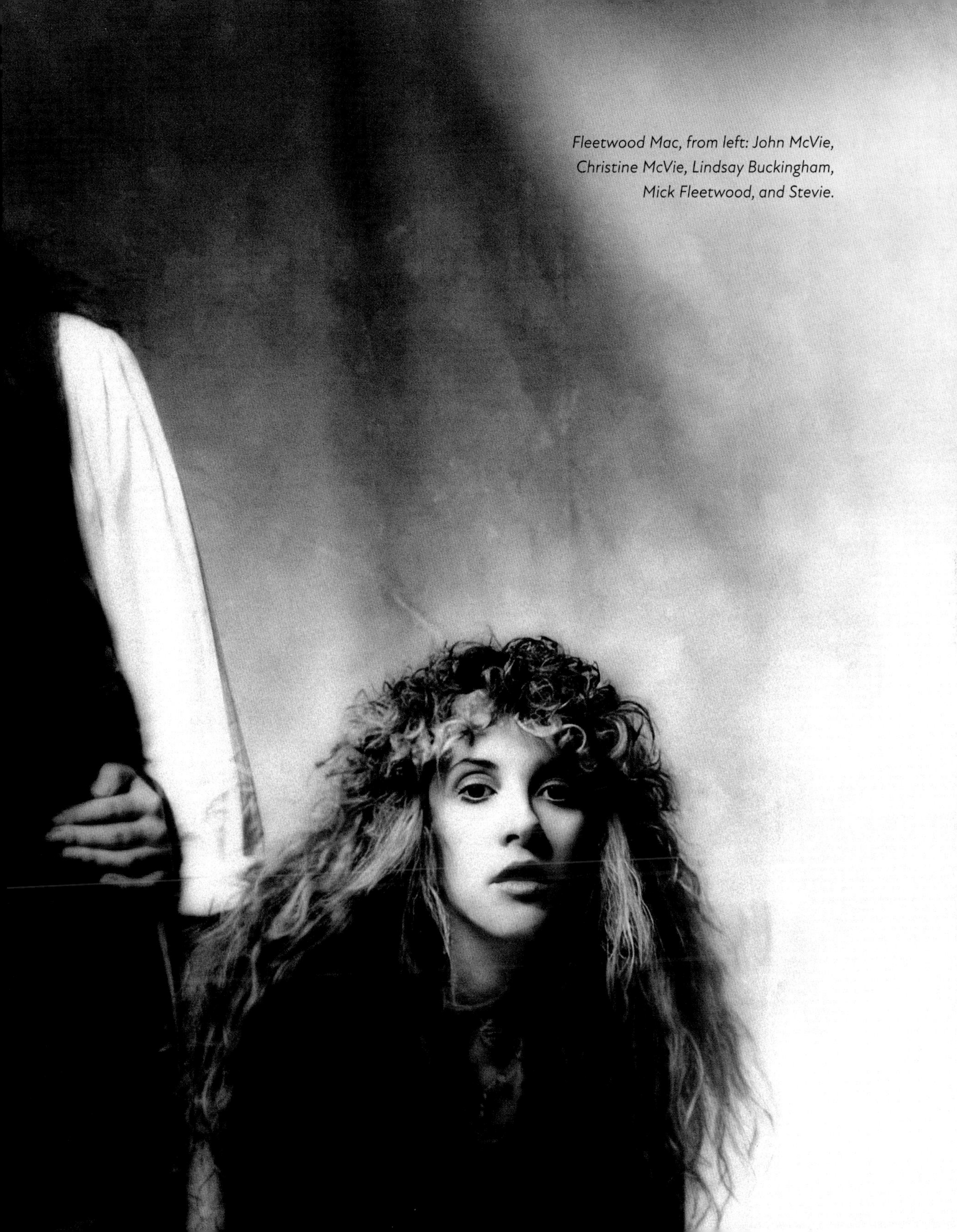

Fleetwood Mac, from left: John McVie, Christine McVie, Lindsay Buckingham, Mick Fleetwood, and Stevie.

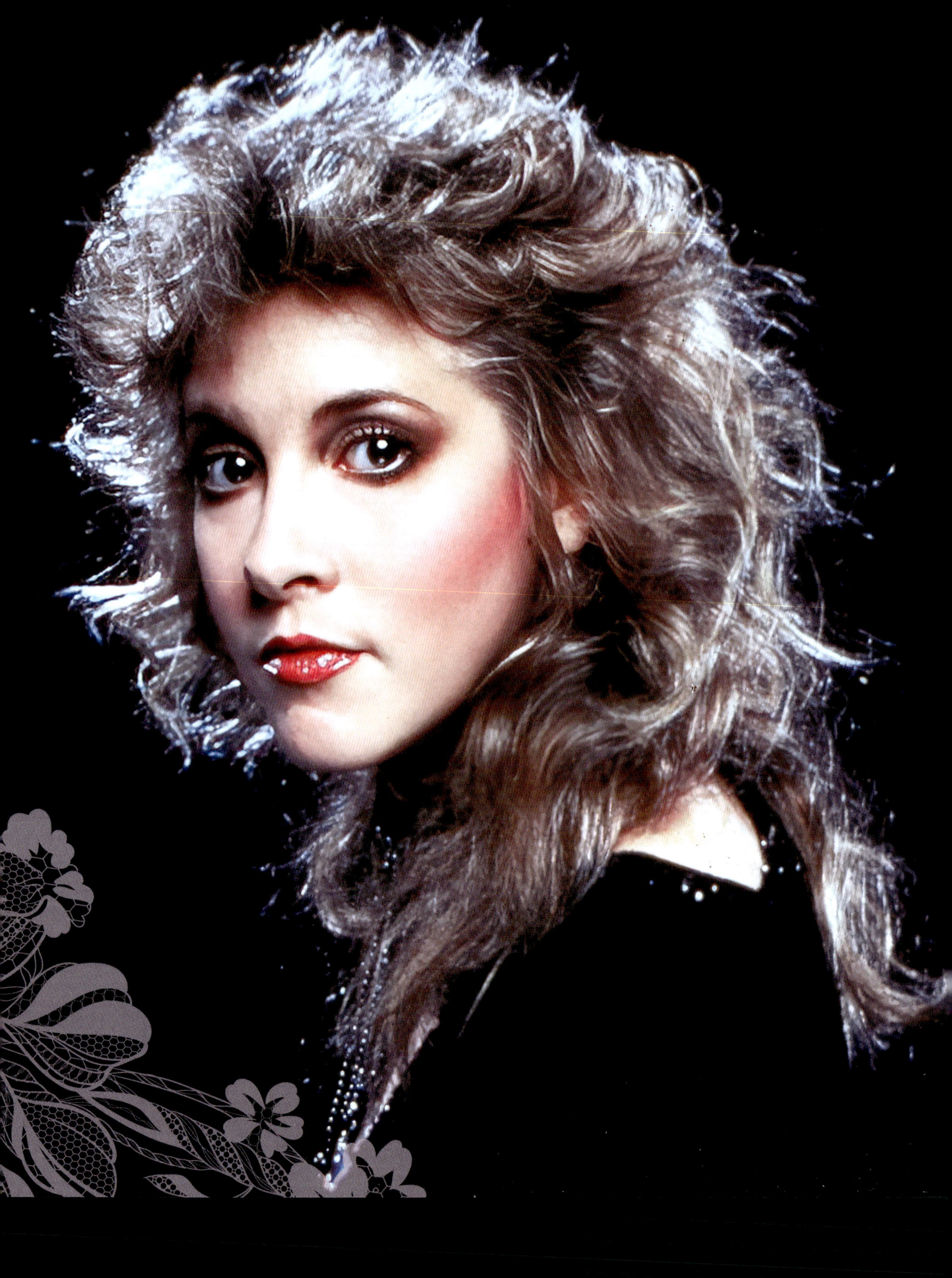

Stevie promoted her 1980s solo albums with increasingly lengthy tours.

33. STEVIE NICKS

"Talk to Me" *1985*

An epic 1980s power ballad.

NICKS SPENT MORE THAN A YEAR WORKING ON *ROCK A LITTLE*, the follow-up to *The Wild Heart*. It was a bumpy process: She and producer Jimmy Iovine parted ways before the album was done, and she excised a few songs, notably a duet of Warren Zevon's "Reconsider Me" with Don Henley. In a 1985 interview, Nicks tried to verbalize the issue with the album and came up short. "For many reasons—all different kind of strange reasons wound up into one—it wasn't right," she said, comparing it to having "the wrong pair of shoes or something. It was wrong."

Still, *Rock a Little* spawned several hits, including "Talk to Me," which topped *Billboard*'s rock radio charts, reached No. 4 on the Hot 100, and earned Nicks a Grammy nomination for Best Female Rock Vocal Performance. Written by Chas Sandford, who also cowrote John Waite's "Missing You," the smoldering power ballad encourages open lines of communication. "This was a hard song to sing, but I had loved 'Missing You' and I loved the words to 'Talk to Me,'" Nicks said in the 1991 *Timespace* compilation. "It took a long time to finish it though, because I couldn't quite get the right feeling on it."

What ended up making the song work? Legendary session drummer Jim Keltner, who contributed overdubs and then "stayed to be an audience to push me a little, to make me get a great vocal," Nicks added. "So I had someone to sing to, and I got the vocal. I put some tambourine on it, and it was finished forevermore."

Stevie's TOP HAT

Once you find a look that works for you, stick with it. That's certainly the mantra of Stevie Nicks, who settled on a style in the late 1970s and has stuck with it ever since.

One of her most recognizable accessories is a black top hat—"the little top hat that could," as she described it to *V Magazine* in 2009—which she was frequently photographed wearing onstage while touring with Fleetwood Mac during the band's heyday.

During a 2023 show, Nicks recalled how she came to acquire the hat. While on tour in the late 1970s, she went antique shopping on a snowy day in Buffalo, New York, with John and Christine McVie. In a nondescript shop, "we found my first top hat," Nicks told the crowd, and then mimicked bowing and tipping her hat, as the crowd roared its approval.

As with her shawls, the top hat holds a special place in her collection. "I still have it," she told *V*. "It's at home in a box. I keep everything. There were a few classic pieces that got lost or stolen along the way, but everything else I saved."

Over the years, Nicks has worn other top hats during pivotal moments. For example, she wore a black felt top hat with a jaunty turquoise peacock feather during a photo shoot when she appeared on *Saturday Night Live* in 2024. At a MusiCares charity auction weeks later, this hat—which Nicks autographed with her signature and "additional celestial doodles" like stars—fetched an incredible $58,500.

Stevie shows off one of her dapper top hats during the Tusk *Tour.*

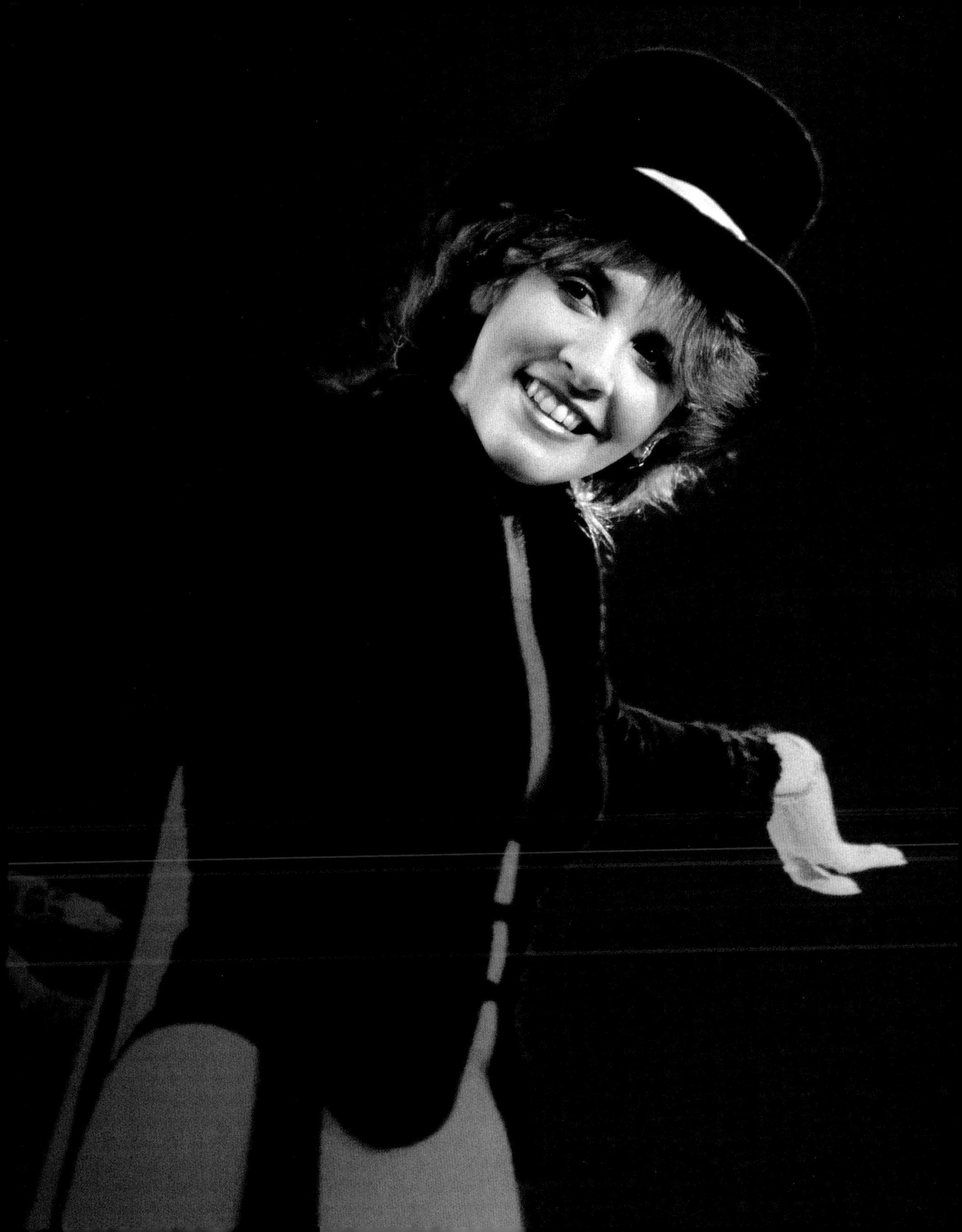

Stevie had a major hit in the mid-1980s with "I Can't Wait."

34. STEVIE NICKS

"I Can't Wait" 1985

The rock 'n' roll goddess claims her crown.

BY THE MID-1980S, NICKS HAD FIRMLY ESTABLISHED HERSELF AS A rock 'n' roll queen outside of Fleetwood Mac. Look no further than "I Can't Wait," a blazing rocker with hollering vocals, lacquered synthesizers, and electric guitars that flash like jagged lightning bolts. It's a sonic match for the lyrics: The narrator burns with passion for an ex–romantic partner whose ambivalence is maddening and alluring. "To understand this song, you sort of have to let yourself go a little crazy," she wrote in the *Timespace* liner notes. "Love is blind, it never works out, but you just have to have it."

"I Can't Wait" started with a musical track with "this incredible percussion thing" given to Nicks by her old pal Rick Nowels. (It turns out Nowels, who later found commercial fame with Belinda Carlisle and Lana Del Rey, had known Nicks since they were teenagers.) She was bowled over. "I listened to the song once, and pretended not to be that knocked out, but the second Rick left, I ran in my little recording studio and wrote 'I Can't Wait,'" she said in the *Timespace* liner notes. "It took all night, and I think it is all about how electric I felt about this music."

Nicks and Nowels then recorded the song while the inspiration was still fresh. "I sang it only once, and have never sung it since in the studio," she revealed. "Some vocals are magic and simply not able to beat. So I let go of it, as new to me as it was. But you know, now when I hear it on the radio, this incredible feeling comes over me, like something really incredible is about to happen."

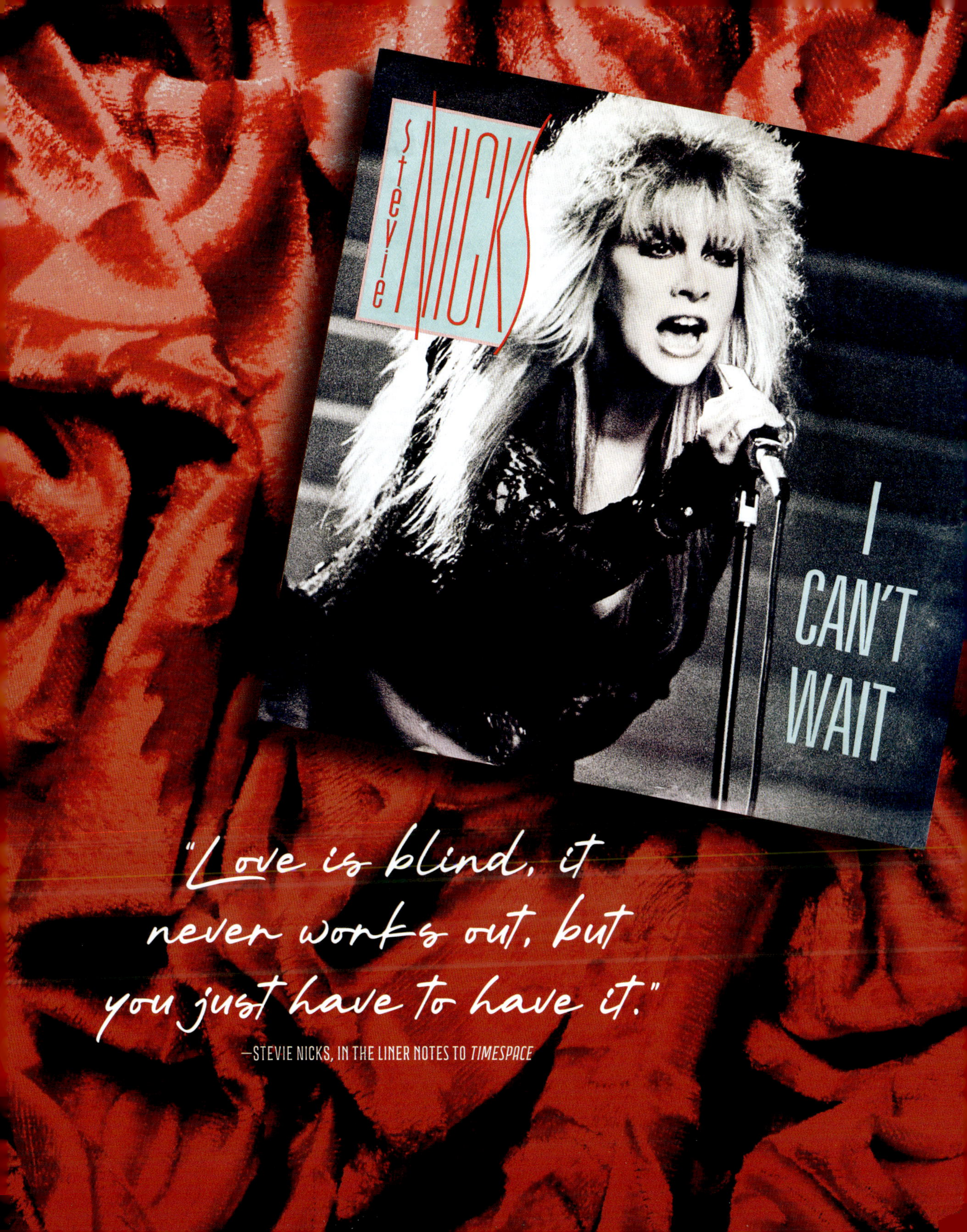

"Love is blind, it never works out, but you just have to have it."

—STEVIE NICKS, IN THE LINER NOTES TO *TIMESPACE*

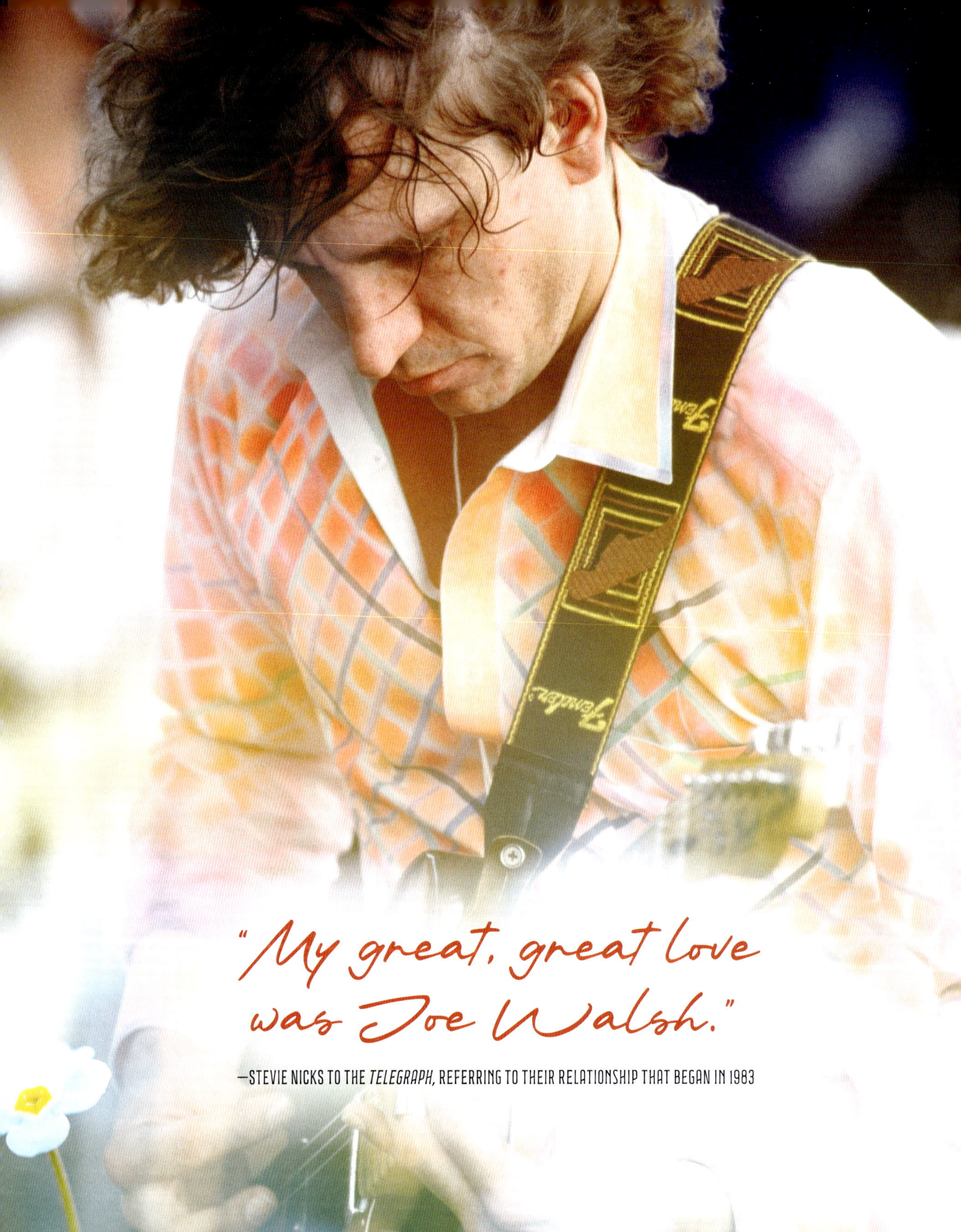

"My great, great love was Joe Walsh."

—STEVIE NICKS TO THE *TELEGRAPH*, REFERRING TO THEIR RELATIONSHIP THAT BEGAN IN 1983

Joe Walsh performs at the second Farm Aid concert in 1986.

35. STEVIE NICKS

"Has Anyone Ever Written Anything for You" 1985

A heartbreaking song offering solace amidst grief.

THE SOMBER PIANO BALLAD "HAS ANYONE EVER WRITTEN ANYTHING for You" closes *Rock a Little* on a serious note. Amidst sweeping orchestral swells, Nicks frames this song as a gift to someone who's going through a tough time. She encourages this person to keep going, because they matter and make a difference in her life.

Nicks wrote the song for rocker Joe Walsh. "In my own way, this is probably my most intense song," she said on *VH1 Storytellers*, before recounting the time she toured with Walsh after releasing *The Wild Heart*. "I was very uptight about something that was going on," Nicks explained. "I don't even remember what was going on. But Joe felt it was important in the scheme of our lives to tell me a story that would make me rise above all of it."

Walsh shared that his four-year-old daughter was killed in a car accident while going to nursery school and then took Nicks to a park in Boulder, Colorado, with a small drinking fountain dedicated to his child. Nicks was incredibly moved by the story—and when she got home to Phoenix, she poured this emotion into songwriting. "I got out of the car, I walked into the front entryway, where my Bösendorfer piano is, I sat down at the piano and I wrote this song," she said. "And I wrote it in about five minutes, the whole thing."

On Tambourine

At a 1991 show at the Whisky a Go Go in Los Angeles, Roger McGuinn brought Stevie Nicks to the stage for a cover of the Bob Dylan–penned "Mr. Tambourine Man." The pair's voices sounded heavenly together, particularly on the song's gorgeous harmonies.

McGuinn recorded "Mr. Tambourine Man" while with the Byrds, of course. But this collaboration was fitting for another very good reason: Nicks is also synonymous with the percussive musical instrument. When she's not singing one of her iconic tunes onstage, she is often seen doing elaborate dance moves while shaking a tambourine adorned with flowing ribbons. These movements are often unselfconscious, as if she's infused with the spirit of the music happening around her.

Nicks picked up the tambourine while still playing in Fritz. "The reason I started playing was so when I wasn't singing I had something to do," she said in a fan Q&A. "It became more important in Fleetwood Mac, because I only sing a third of the time, so I had more time to perfect my tambourine playing."

In the studio, her tambourine playing wasn't always welcome. In the book *Stevie Nicks: Visions, Dreams & Rumours*, author Zoë Howe notes that circa *Rumours*, Mick Fleetwood's parts were used on the recording and Nicks's tambourine was "always dampened with gaffer tape" on and offstage to diminish its impact.

Nicks was clearly undeterred. Fans have compiled YouTube playlists with footage of her tambourine shimmies from across the years (sample video title: "Queen of the Tambourine"). The evolution is fascinating: In the late 1970s, her playing added a mystical edge to Fleetwood Mac's sprawling live jams. In later concerts with the band, her tambourine added percussive force to songs like "Go Your Own Way." And during her solo shows up until the present day, her tambourine is like a comforting talisman and an extension of her fantastical stage presence.

Playing the tambourine with such vigor isn't always easy, as she revealed in a 2013 interview in which she mentions Fleetwood Mac concerts stretching beyond the two-and-a-half-hour mark. "I've got pains in my fingers from playing tambourine, so I don't know how Mick [Fleetwood] does it."

Neil Finn, who played with Fleetwood Mac on their final tour to date, noticed the endurance needed as well: "Sometimes Mike [Campbell]'s solos would go on and Stevie would get exhausted playing tambourine. She'd be, 'Fucking hell, Lindsey only did 12 bars!'"

Naturally, Nicks ensured that her Barbie doll comes with a miniature version of her ribbon-laced tambourine. And over the years she's switched up the instrument's accoutrements; for example, a tambourine used on 1997's The Dance Tour boasted black and cream lace ribbons with faux pearl accents.

DID YOU KNOW?

In a 2020 MusiCares benefit auction, an autographed Nicks tambourine sold for $10,240.

"I only sing a third of the time [in Fleetwood Mac], so I had more time to perfect my tambourine playing," Stevie once said in a fan Q&A.

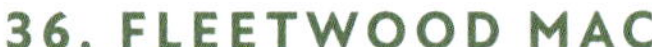

Fleetwood Mac had multiple hits in 1987 from Tango In The Night.

36. FLEETWOOD MAC

"Seven Wonders" 1987

A fanciful song that earned a second life as a witchy anthem.

IN 1987, FLEETWOOD MAC RELEASED THEIR FIRST ALBUM IN five years, *Tango in the Night*. In a change from previous efforts, Nicks didn't write the major hits from the album. Instead, Lindsey Buckingham ("Big Love") and Christine McVie ("Little Lies," "Everywhere") picked up much of the slack. This division of labor came partly because Nicks was absent from most of the proceedings; among other things, she was promoting *Rock a Little* and also went to rehab for her cocaine addiction.

When Nicks did join the recording sessions, the scenario was less than ideal, starting with the fact that the band was recording at Buckingham's house. "I didn't find that to be a great situation for me," she said in 2016. "Especially coming out of rehab." In fact, the group was tracking vocals in the master bedroom, which she describes as being "extremely strange. In all fairness, it was like the only empty room and they had a beautiful master bedroom all set up like a vocal booth but I found it very uncomfortable, personally."

Despite these circumstances, Nicks did sing lead and earned a writing credit on the sparkling "Seven Wonders," which was otherwise composed by her solo collaborator Sandy Stewart. (The solitary lyric Nicks wrote in the song references someone named Emmeline; she misheard Stewart's preferred lyrics but insisted on keeping her version because she liked the name.) "Seven Wonders" embodies Fleetwood Mac's sound on

Tango in the Night: plush digital production dominated by layers of evocative synthesizers and modern sonic flourishes.

Fittingly, Stewart's lyrics were fanciful, featuring a narrator who's determined to find their own beauty in the world (i.e., by seeing all seven wonders) so they'll be sated even if a potential romance doesn't work out. Nicks sounds more muted than usual, giving her voice a wistful tone and suiting the song's vibe to a T.

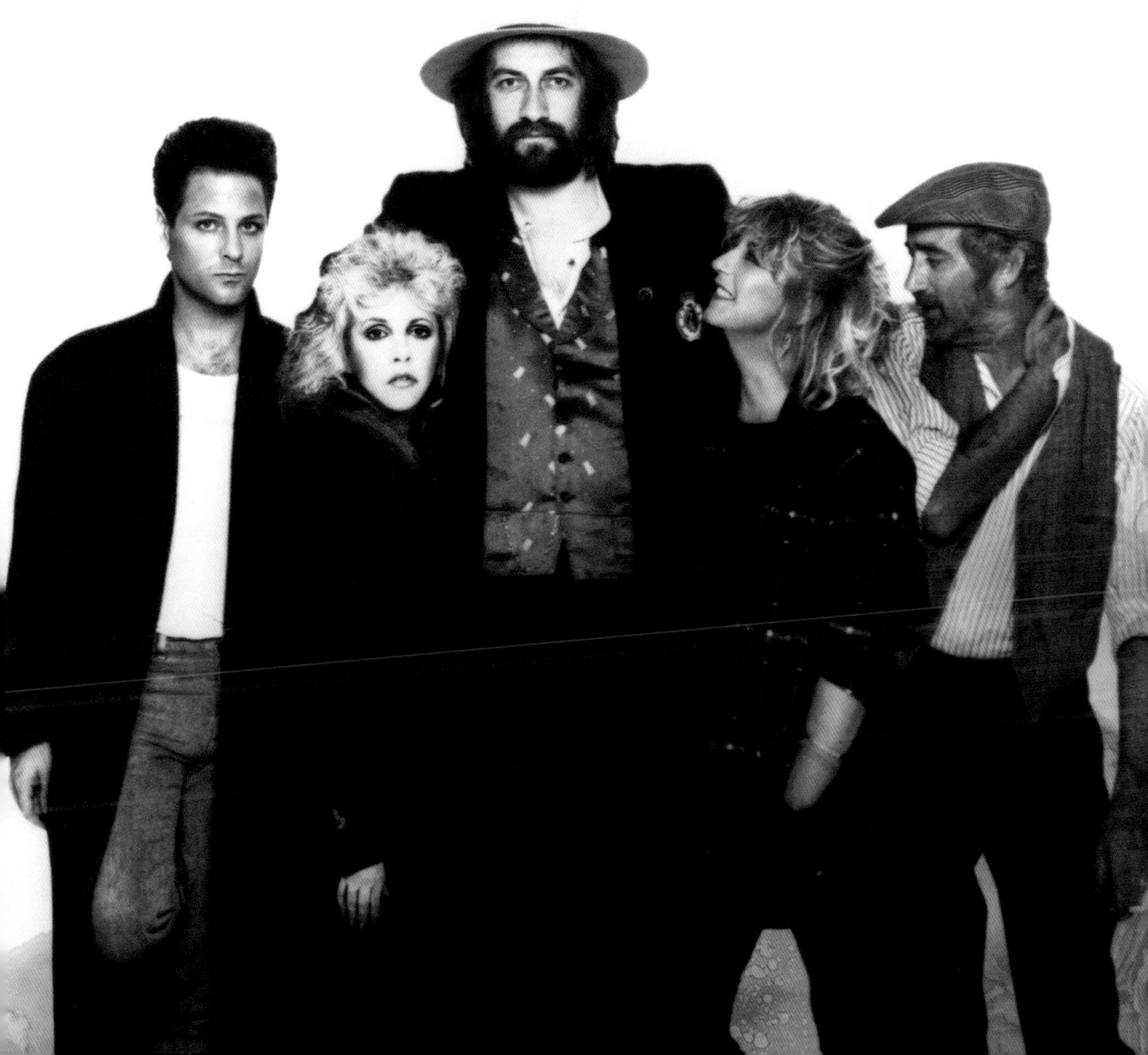

American HORROR Story

In the 2010s, "Seven Wonders" had an unexpected pop culture resurgence as a result of its inclusion on *American Horror Story: Coven*. In response, Fleetwood Mac even added it into their setlists in 2014 and 2015 for the first time since the late 1980s. The song's presence on the show was no accident: Nicks loomed large over that season's storyline, providing inspiration for characters and (fittingly) serving as the namesake of an episode called "The Magical Delights of Stevie Nicks."

Nicks had previously crossed paths with *American Horror Story's* co-creators, Ryan Murphy and Brad Falchuk, through her involvement in a Fleetwood Mac–inspired episode of another show they created, *Glee*. And she was intrigued when Murphy told her about *American Horror Story: Coven* and the oddball character Misty Day (Lily Rabe), a friendless loner who lives in a forest and only "has an eight-track and a couple of [my] albums," she told the *Los Angeles Times*. Nicks was thrilled at being described as Misty's "friend and her mom and her conscience," she added. "That's what I've always ever wanted to be to anybody with my songs. So, yes, I was like, 'Absolutely, Ryan, you can use my music.'"

"[Being described as Misty's] friend and her mom and her conscience . . . That's what I've always ever wanted to be to anybody with my songs . . ."

—STEVIE NICKS TO THE *LOS ANGELES TIMES*

Nicks also acted in several episodes, performing "Rhiannon" and "Has Anyone Ever Written Anything for You." That Nicks appeared on camera like this was surprising, as she insisted that she wasn't an actress, recalling a traumatic fourth grade experience involving "an incredibly bad play" in which she "played one of the last two surviving girls in the Alamo," she shared with the *Los Angeles Times*. "It was so bad that I came home—in the fourth grade!—and said to my mother, 'Never put me in a drama class again! Ever! Because I suck! I'm a terrible actress, mom!'"

But the ways her life and music intertwined with the show were uncanny. For example, when she viewed the script for one episode, she realized the witches test was called The Seven Wonders. "I called Ryan late at night and said, 'You know, Fleetwood Mac has a song called 'Seven Wonders,'" Nicks said during a Facebook Q&A. "And he hung up and said, 'OK! I have to go write it in!' So the whole end was written as part of the Seven Wonders test." For a cherry on top, Nicks appeared in this episode and performed the song—blessing the witches with her presence to bring them all good luck.

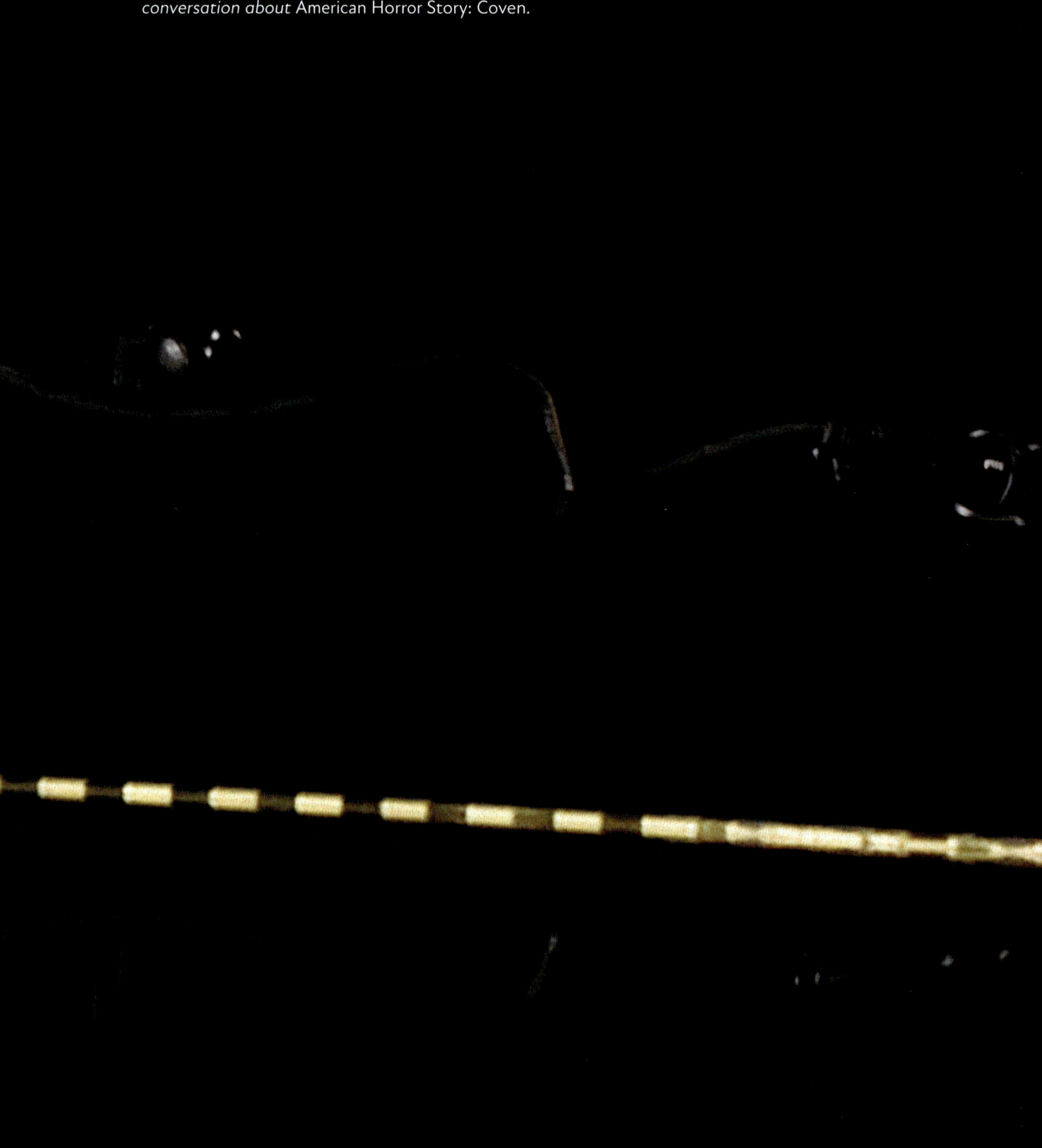

conversation about American Horror Story: Coven.

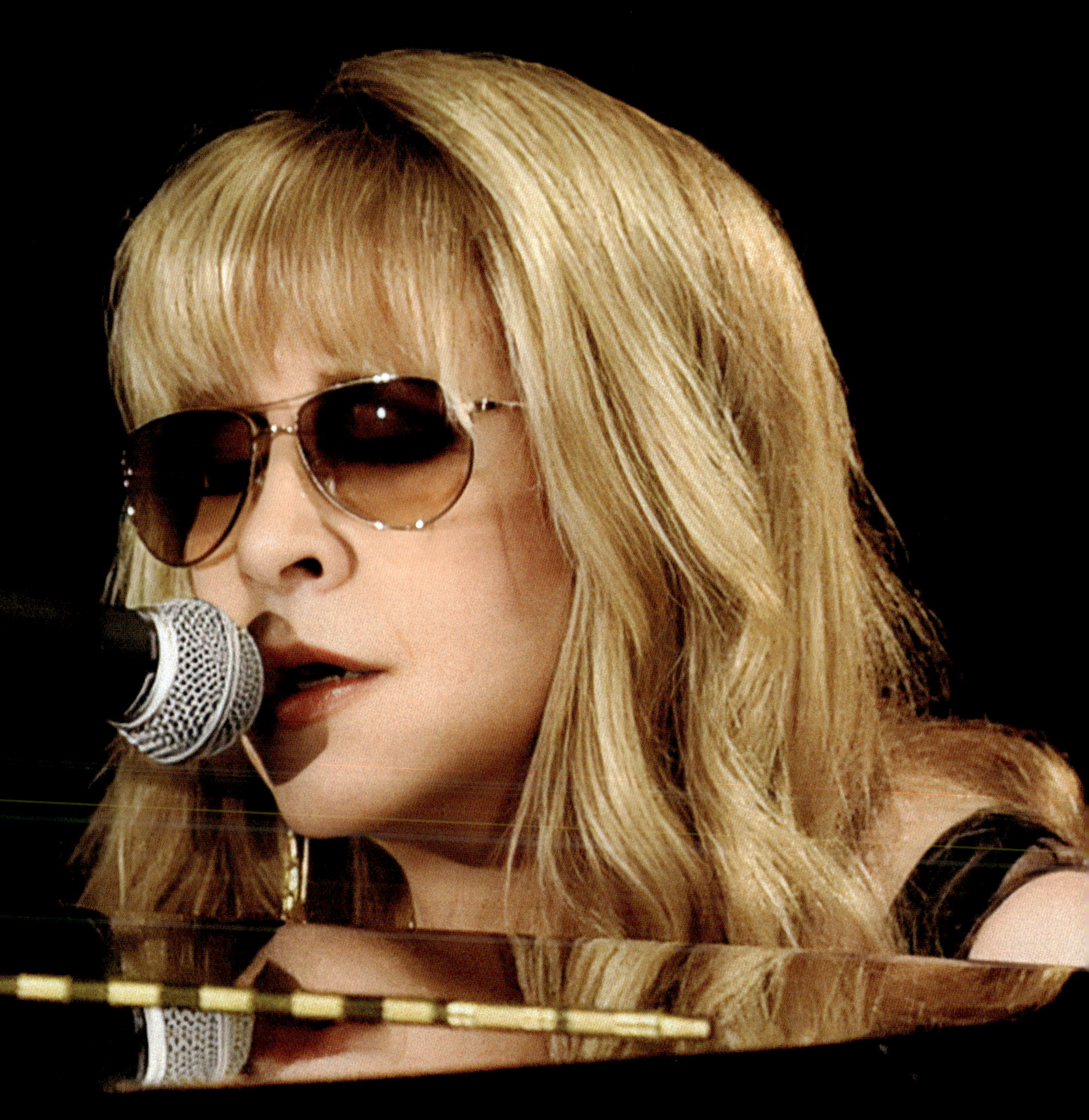

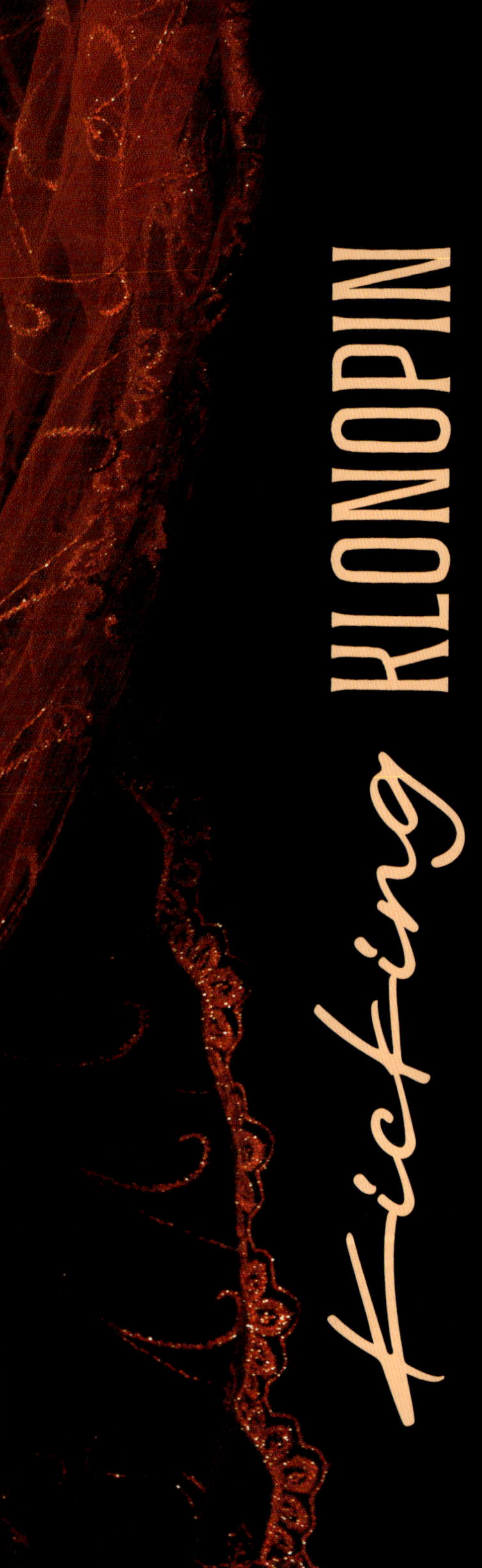

Kicking KLONOPIN

During the recording of Fleetwood Mac's "Seven Wonders," Nicks's voice was affected because she started drinking brandy before singing—a habit complicated by the fact that she had also been prescribed Klonopin after going to rehab in late 1986 for her cocaine addiction. The new prescription had an immediate negative impact on her health.

"[I was] not quite understanding why I was feeling so weird and this doctor kept saying, 'This is what you need,'" she said in 2017. "It's the typical scenario of a groupie doctor. Discuss rock and roll with you, so in order to do that he would keep upping your dose so you'd come in once a week." Nicks soon developed an addiction to Klonopin, which loomed large over her life well into the 1990s, affecting everything from her weight to her songwriting. "He stole eight years of my life," she told *Rolling Stone*, describing the prescribing doctor.

Unfortunately, this altered state had a negative impact on 1994's *Street Angel*, which Nicks recorded just before going to rehab again for more than six weeks, this time to detox from Klonopin. "I was totally clear when the record went out. So I really saw how not good it was," she said in a 2001 radio interview. "I tried to fix it in a couple of months' time, but it was just not possible, and I was so depressed about it." Thankfully, Nicks redeemed herself with the late-1990s Fleetwood Mac reunion and then her subsequent solo work—and now speaks about her experiences to deter others from going down the same path.

Stevie photographed in 1991.

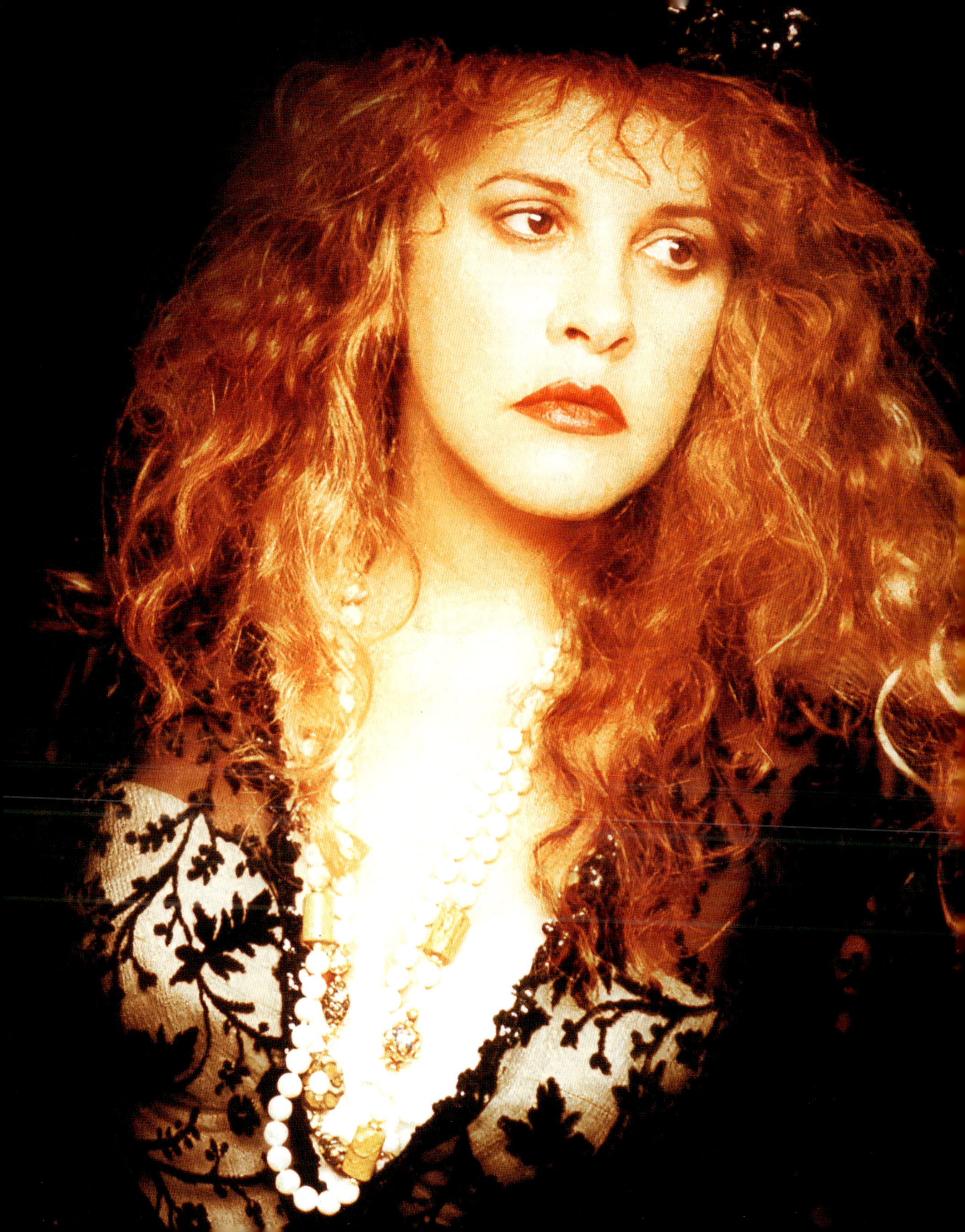

Stevie embraced 1980s musical trends and sounds within her solo work.

37. STEVIE NICKS

"Rooms on Fire" *1989*

A true story about a star-crossed love affair.

NICKS CLOSED OUT THE 1980S ON A HIGH NOTE WITH HER fourth solo album, *The Other Side of the Mirror*, which spawned the hit single "Rooms on Fire." Her last top 40 hit to date, the dizzying Gothic-pop swirl—which featured plaintive acoustic guitar from Rick Nowels, who cowrote the song, and bewitching synth flourishes—also reached No. 1 on *Billboard*'s rock radio chart.

In a 1989 BBC interview, Nicks called "Rooms on Fire" a deeply personal song about "a girl who is a rock 'n' roll star who has pretty much accepted the fact that she will never ever be able to be married or have those children that she wanted or the husband that she wanted or that deep, deep love that she wanted and she's accepted it." However, this perpetually lovelorn figure still experiences passion, Nicks stressed to *Record Mirror*. "The single is about when you're in a crowded room and you see a kind of person and your heart goes, 'Wow!' The whole world seems to be ablaze at that particular moment."

As it turns out, Nicks based these insights on real life: In the liner notes to *Timespace*, she all but revealed the subject of the song was Rupert Hine, with whom she had an intense (but short-lived) fling while he produced *The Other Side of the Mirror*. "It always seemed to me that whenever Rupert walked into one of these old, dark castle rooms, that the rooms were on fire," she wrote. "There was a connection between us that everyone around us instantly picked up on, and everyone was very careful to respect our space."

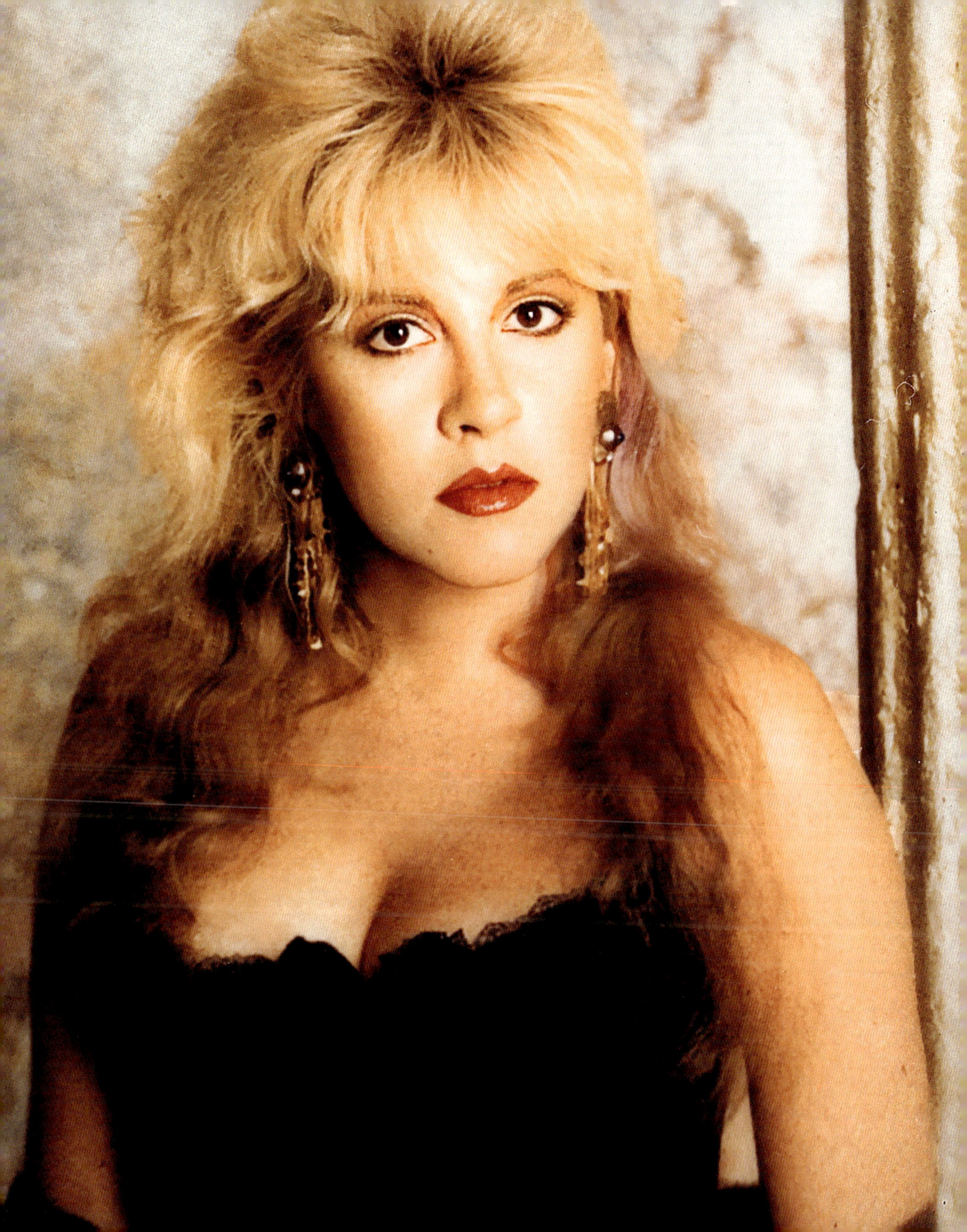

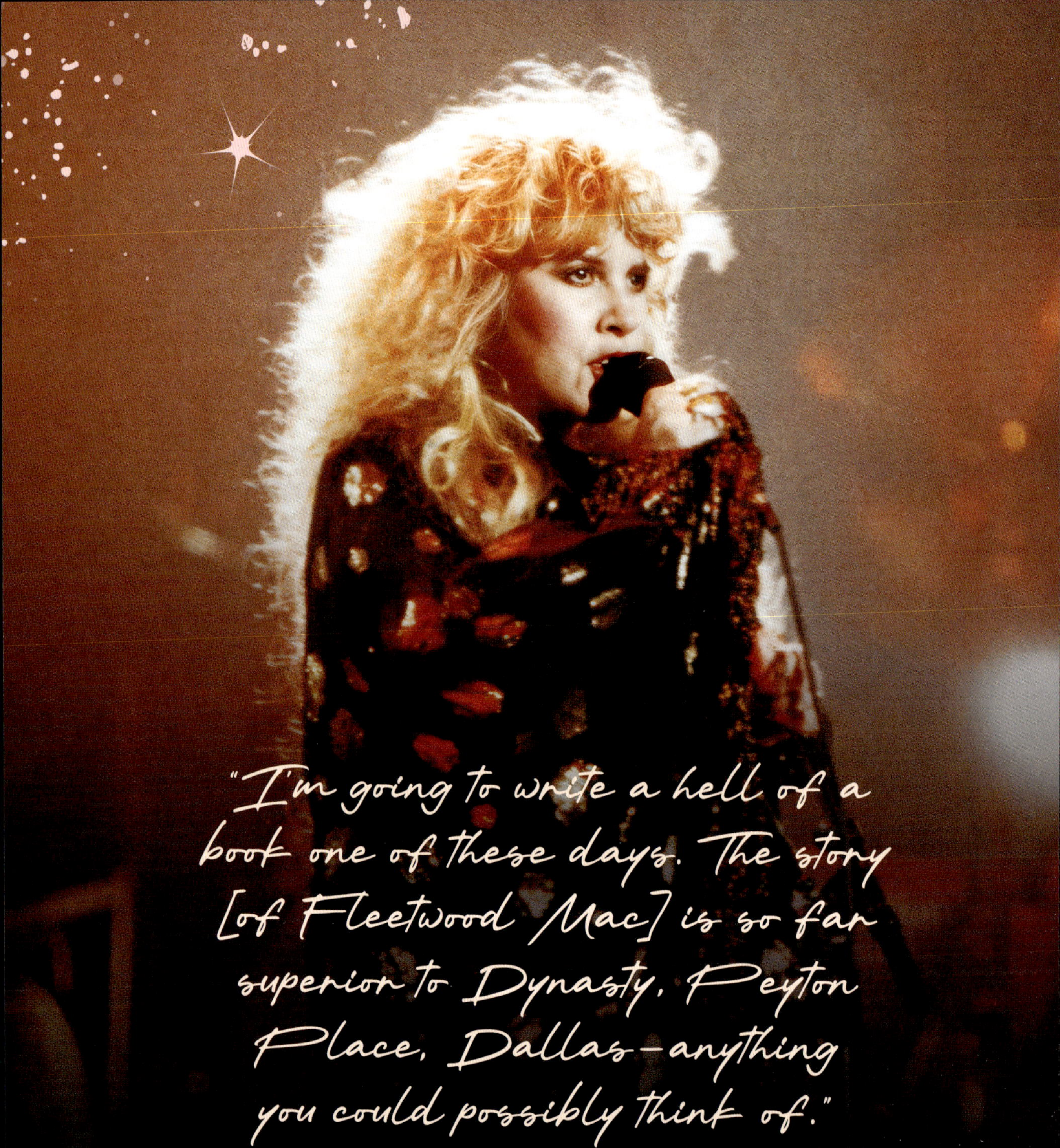

"I'm going to write a hell of a book one of these days. The story [of Fleetwood Mac] is so far superior to Dynasty, Peyton Place, Dallas—anything you could possibly think of."

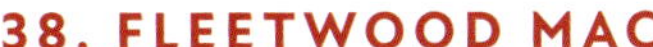
Stevie performs live on August 25, 1990, in Manchester, England.

38. FLEETWOOD MAC

"Affairs of the Heart" 1990

A bright spot during a turbulent time for the Mac.

IN A 1989 INTERVIEW WITH *JUKE NATIONAL ROCK WEEKLY*, NICKS assured that she was "absolutely in love with being in Fleetwood Mac. Everything about it thrills me." That includes the band's ups and downs, she added. "Truly, you cannot find a crazier soap opera television than Fleetwood Mac's story. We've loved each other, we've hated each other, and we've bled on each other. At the end of the day, I can't find a better bunch of people that I love and respect."

Fleetwood Mac's 1990 album *Behind the Mask* emerged during an especially tumultuous time for the band. Lindsey Buckingham had departed from the group several years before, replaced by two guitarist-vocalists, Billy Burnette and Rick Vito. Nicks and Christine McVie, meanwhile, had vowed to stop touring with Fleetwood Mac at the end of dates supporting *Behind the Mask*; among other things, Nicks was irate over being unable to include "Silver Springs" on her *Timespace* compilation. [See page 50.]

But before all this came "Affairs of the Heart," a classic, easygoing Fleetwood Mac pop-rocker in which Nicks muses about romantic choices—and the unexplainable emotional lure of short-lived (and ill-suited) relationships. To underline her point, she quotes lines from poet Alfred, Lord Tennyson, giving the song an elegant air.

Timeline of the Fleetwood Mac Lineup

1967–1974

British vocalist-guitarist Peter Green formed Fleetwood Mac in 1967, naming the group after two of his bandmates: drummer Mick Fleetwood and bassist John McVie. In the subsequent years, the band went through multiple lineup changes, most notably by adding vocalist-keyboardist Christine McVie in 1970.

NEW YEAR'S EVE 1974

In late 1974, guitarist Bob Welch decided to go solo and leave Fleetwood Mac. In response, Mick Fleetwood hired two musicians: guitarist-vocalist Lindsey Buckingham and vocalist Stevie Nicks. With their addition, the classic Fleetwood Mac lineup of Fleetwood, Nicks, Buckingham, John McVie, and Christine McVie was born. They went on to great success in the 1970s and into the 1980s.

1987

After the release of *Tango in the Night*, Lindsey Buckingham quit Fleetwood Mac before the band's tour. He was replaced by two guitarist-vocalists: Billy Burnette and Rick Vito.

1990

Angry that she could not include her beloved song "Silver Springs" on her *Timespace* compilation, Nicks left Fleetwood Mac after touring for *Behind the Mask* wrapped in December 1990. Christine McVie also said she would stop touring with the group but would still record and be a member

1991 Vito departed Fleetwood Mac to go solo, leaving Mick Fleetwood and John McVie the sole remaining touring members.

1993 The classic lineup—Fleetwood, Nicks, Buckingham, and both McVies—reunited and played "Don't Stop" for newly inducted President Bill Clinton.

1994–1995 A new-look Fleetwood Mac featuring Fleetwood, John McVie, Billy Burnette, Dave Mason, and Bekka Bramlett launched a tour and released the album *Time*; Christine McVie appeared on the latter.

1997 With Mason, Burnette, and Bramlett having departed Fleetwood Mac in the preceding years, the classic lineup reunited for a TV special and live album, *The Dance*, and a subsequent tour.

1998 In 1998, after being inducted into the Rock & Roll Hall of Fame and performing at the Grammys, Christine McVie left Fleetwood Mac again.

2003–2014 The *Rumours*-era lineup—sans Christine McVie—toured extensively in support of 2003's *Say You Will* and also launched tours tied to a 2009 UK reissue of *The Very Best of Fleetwood Mac* and 2013's *Extended Play*. In 2013, Christine McVie rejoined the band to play "Don't Stop" at two shows in London.

2014 To the delight of fans, Christine McVie rejoined the band full-time for the On with the Show Tour.

2018 Buckingham parted ways with Fleetwood Mac and was replaced by Tom Petty and the Heartbreakers guitarist Mike Campbell and Crowded House's Neil Finn. This lineup embarked on the An Evening with Fleetwood Mac tour through 2019.

2022 Christine McVie died on November 30, 2022, effectively ending Fleetwood Mac.

Stevie spread her creative wings in the early 2000s.

39. STEVIE NICKS

"Every Day" 2001

A fresh chapter for the sober Stevie.

NICKS TECHNICALLY STARTED WORKING ON HER FIRST SOLO STUDIO album in seven years, *Trouble in Shangri-La*, in late 1994, right after the release of *Street Angel* and her stint in rehab for Klonopin addiction. The Fleetwood Mac reunion and 1998's *Enchanted* boxed set pulled her away from new solo work—but once she finished the album, she explained how much it meant to her, especially given *Street Angel*'s lukewarm reception.

"*Trouble in Shangri-La* is saying a lot more than just, 'Here's some really nice songs for you to listen to,'" Nicks said in a 2001 interview. "It's saying, 'My life was almost gone and what saved me is my music.'" Given this, it's easy to interpret the album's first single, "Every Day," as a love letter to music; Nicks sings of an all-encompassing passion for something (or someone) that inspires her and keeps her alive.

"Every Day" was cowritten by Damon Johnson of the rock band Brother Cane and John Shanks; the latter, who also produced the song, is also known for his work with Kelly Clarkson, Melissa Etheridge, and Michelle Branch. Fittingly, the sweet song feels like it could appear in a rom-com film; its lush harmonies, majestic piano and strings, and folksy acoustic guitars cushion Nicks's vocals like a warm blanket.

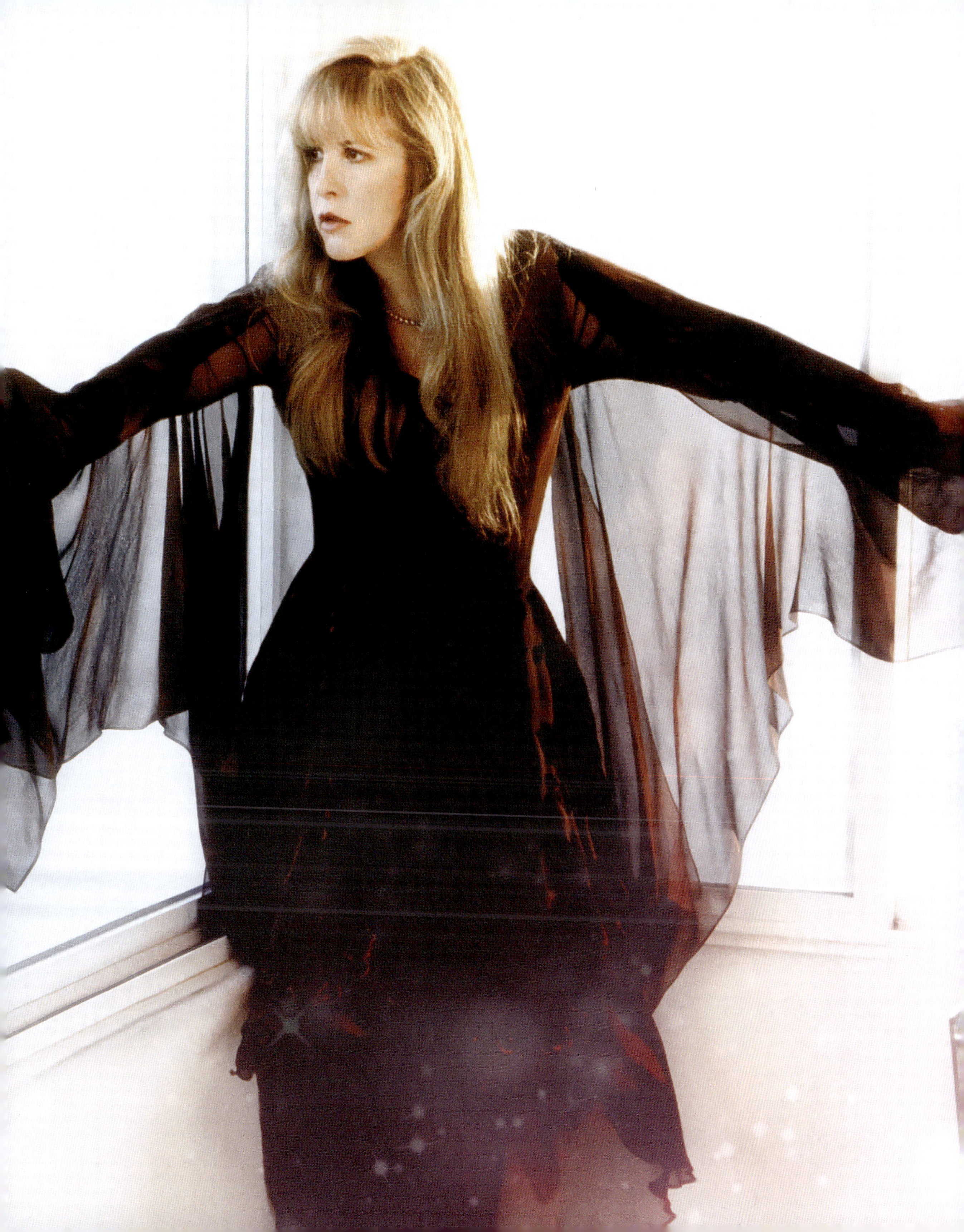

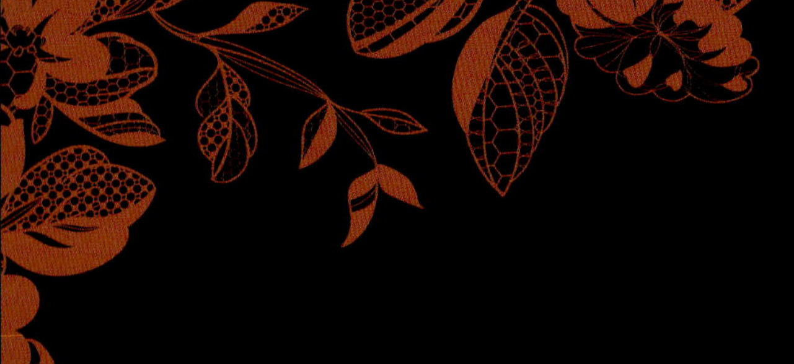

Stevie lends her talents to Stormy Weather 2002, which benefits The Walden Woods Project.

40. STEVIE NICKS

"Fall from Grace" 2001

A complex song about conflict.

TUCKED AWAY NEAR THE END OF *TROUBLE IN SHANGRI-LA*, "FALL from Grace" is a ferocious, Tom Petty-esque rocker describing a tumultuous partnership. The narrator notes the sacrifices she's made to protect the peace—being a sounding board, acquiescing to someone else's wants and needs, minimizing herself—before realizing that the relationship is irreparably damaged, just like the doomed nursery rhyme character Humpty Dumpty. By the end of the song, however, the storm clouds have cleared and the narrator wonders, like a phoenix rising from the ashes, whether a second chance is possible.

"Fall from Grace" can be interpreted as being about a romance, but its lyrics could also chronicle any kind of bumpy relationship. And in a 2001 interview with Wall of Sound, Nicks confirmed that "Fall from Grace" was "really about Fleetwood Mac onstage," as she put it. "That's always mostly going to be about me and Lindsey, just about our energy and what a trip it is to be in Fleetwood Mac."

To deepen the mystery, Nicks prefaced a 2024 live performance of the song by noting "Fall from Grace" was "written about an argument," before adding, "And I did it for a year probably on the road and then I decided I didn't want to be involved in that argument anymore so I stopped doing it for a long time." But she missed the song, she remarked, which is why she re-added it to her setlist.

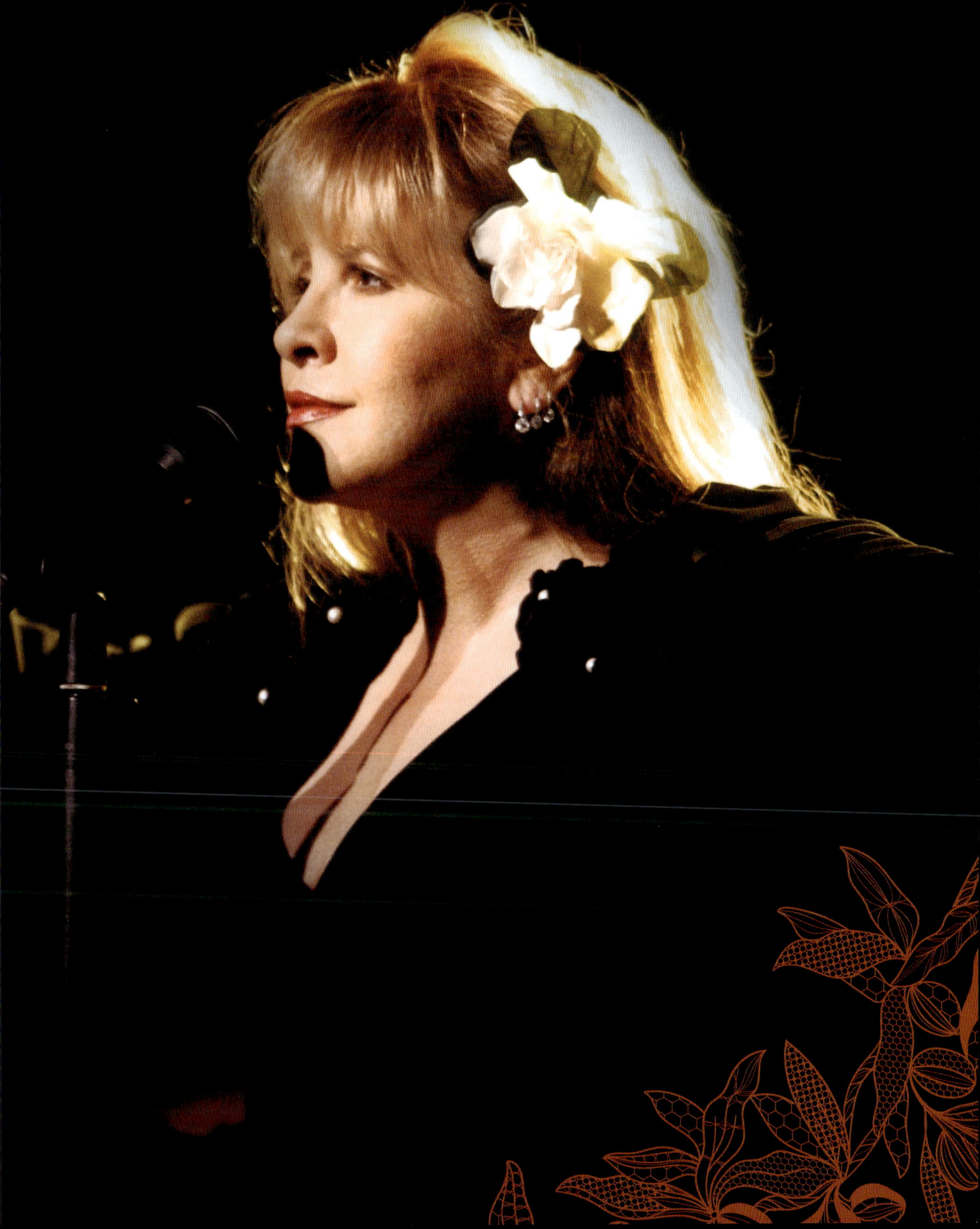

The Night of 1000 STEVIES

The 2001 movie *Gypsy 83* follows Gypsy Vale (Sara Rue) and Clive Webb (Kett Turton) as they travel from Ohio to New York City with the goal of reaching the Night of 1000 Stevies event in New York City. This was no fictional event: Held since 1991 in New York City, the night is billed by organizers as "the ultimate Stevie Nicks celebration—a riot of shawls, lace, baby's breath, twirling, tambourines and great performance" that's "neither a contest nor a karaoke show." In short, that means vocalists, drag performers, and dancers all dressed to the nines like Stevie—all eras, of course. "Everybody can dress up like me, because there's so many different mes," Nicks once told *Rolling Stone*. "You can be any me you want."

Cofounded by Chi Chi Valenti and Johnny Dynell, the night has drawn luminaries such as Boy George, Debbie Harry, and Cyndi Lauper and expanded to New Orleans as well due to its popularity. Nicks has also blessed the event and even sent a video for the twenty-first edition (theme: "The Wild Heart") in which she lightly threatened to one day show up to the event in disguise. In 2025, the Night of 1000 Stevies theme was "Dances of Rhiannon." Fittingly, the event featured the New York Studio of Irish Step Dance doing a routine to "Fire Burning"; the Welsh Nicks tribute singer Rhiannon UK covering "Gold Dust Woman"; as well as dancers, tap burlesque performers, and singers.

"Everybody can dress up like me, because there's so many different mes . . . You can be any me you want."

—STEVIE NICKS TO *ROLLING STONE*

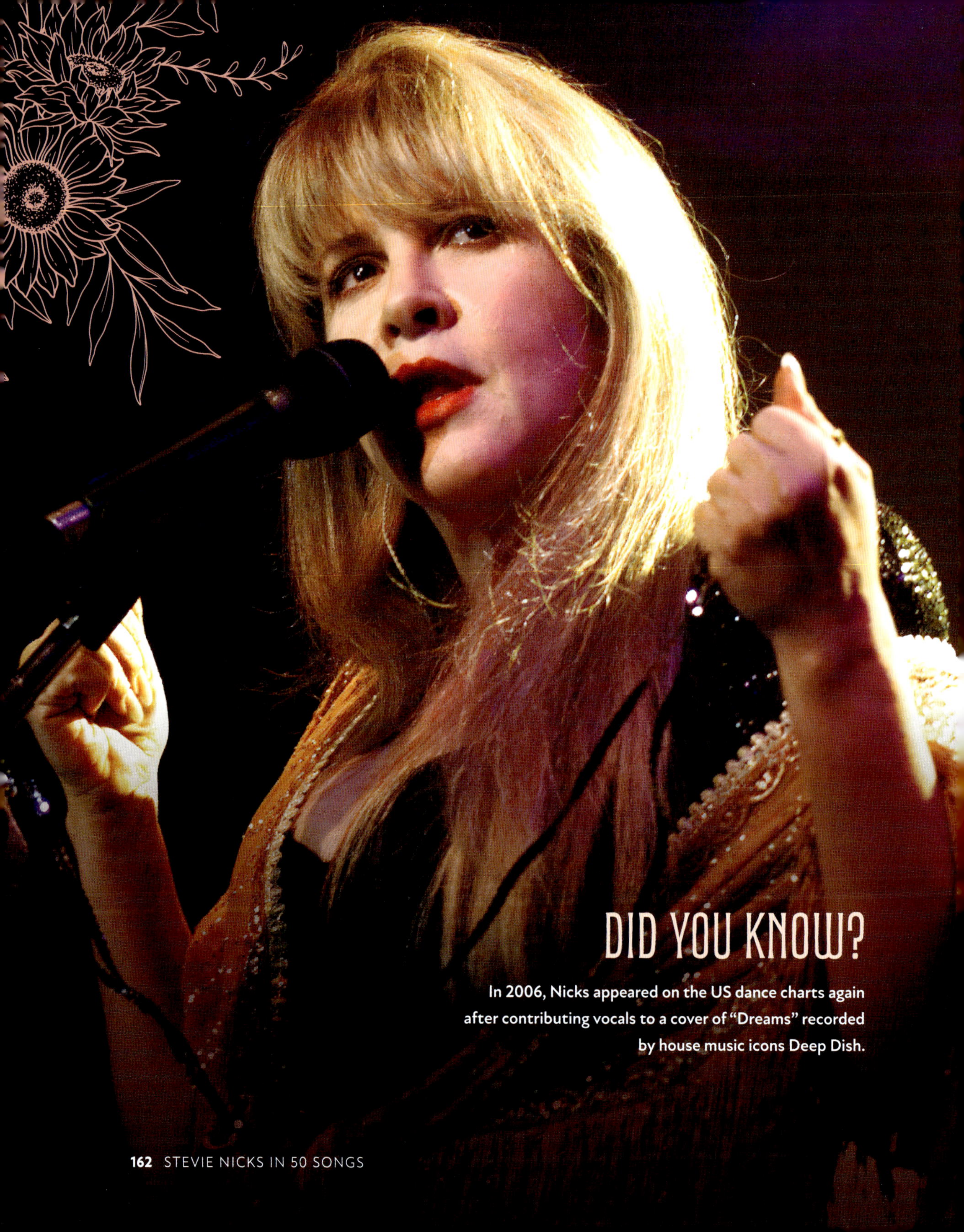

DID YOU KNOW?

In 2006, Nicks appeared on the US dance charts again after contributing vocals to a cover of "Dreams" recorded by house music icons Deep Dish.

Stevie made a big commercial comeback with 2001's Trouble in Shangri-La, which spawned the Grammy-nominated "Planets of the Universe."

41. STEVIE NICKS

"Planets of the Universe" 2001

This heavy breakup song earned Stevie a Grammy nomination.

WHEN NICKS SPLIT UP WITH BUCKINGHAM IN 1976, SHE COPED by pouring her heart into music. Out came the biting (if cathartic) breakup song "Planets of the Universe," which was demoed for *Rumours* but held back until *Trouble in Shangri-La*. The lyrics observe that the world (and galaxy) keeps turning despite a crumbling relationship that's losing its luster.

The extended single version amplifies her anger: After expressing regret for putting in so much romantic effort, she coldly tells the ex to go away, and then, as electric guitar rages in the background, she practically snarls that he'll never forget their relationship. "It's one of the heaviest songs I've ever written and I wrote it in anger in all my drama—as dramatic as I was and probably still am," Nicks said in 2001. "I went back and wrote the first part of the song a couple months ago because I wanted to soften it a little bit."

Interestingly, the delicate acoustic guitar at the start sounds like "Rhiannon," which is no accident: In a 2001 radio interview, Nicks explained that "Planets of the Universe" is one of her eleven songs that she has in mind if she's ever able to do the long-awaited "Rhiannon" film. [See page 28.] Dance remixes of "Planets of the Universe" propelled the song to No. 1 on *Billboard*'s club play chart; the original song, meanwhile, earned Nicks a Grammy nomination for Best Female Rock Vocal Performance.

42. STEVIE NICKS

"Sorcerer" 2001

A sweet song decades in the making.

THE MYSTICAL FOLK SONG "SORCERER" IS ANOTHER NICKS composition with a convoluted history. She wrote it during the Buckingham Nicks era; in fact, the duo demoed the song in 1974 and actually played it live during early 1975 shows. "It was really about the city of Hollywood and how strange it was to us," Nicks told VH1 in 2001. "It was all about models and rock 'n' roll and drugs and scary people. I was a very, very prudish little girl from San Francisco who had strict parents, I had not had a lot of freedom, and coming into this town was freaky."

From there, Nicks demoed the song a few times before it surfaced in 1984: recorded by Marilyn Martin for the soundtrack to the movie *Streets of Fire*. Years later, Nicks reclaimed "Sorcerer" for *Trouble in Shangri-La*, recruiting Sheryl Crow to add guitar and backing vocals. This version is classic Nicks, with its lilting acoustic riffs, mesmerizing harmonies, and a vocal melody that flits around like a butterfly.

MARILYN MARTIN

Marilyn Martin first linked up with Nicks on The Wild Heart Tour when she was touring with opener Joe Walsh. "We were doing soundcheck one day when the tour began, and Stevie was watching," Martin told the Nicks Fix. This led to her singing with Nicks on the tour and providing backing vocals on *Rock a Little*. Martin's husband, Greg Droman, meanwhile, engineered *Tango in the Night*.

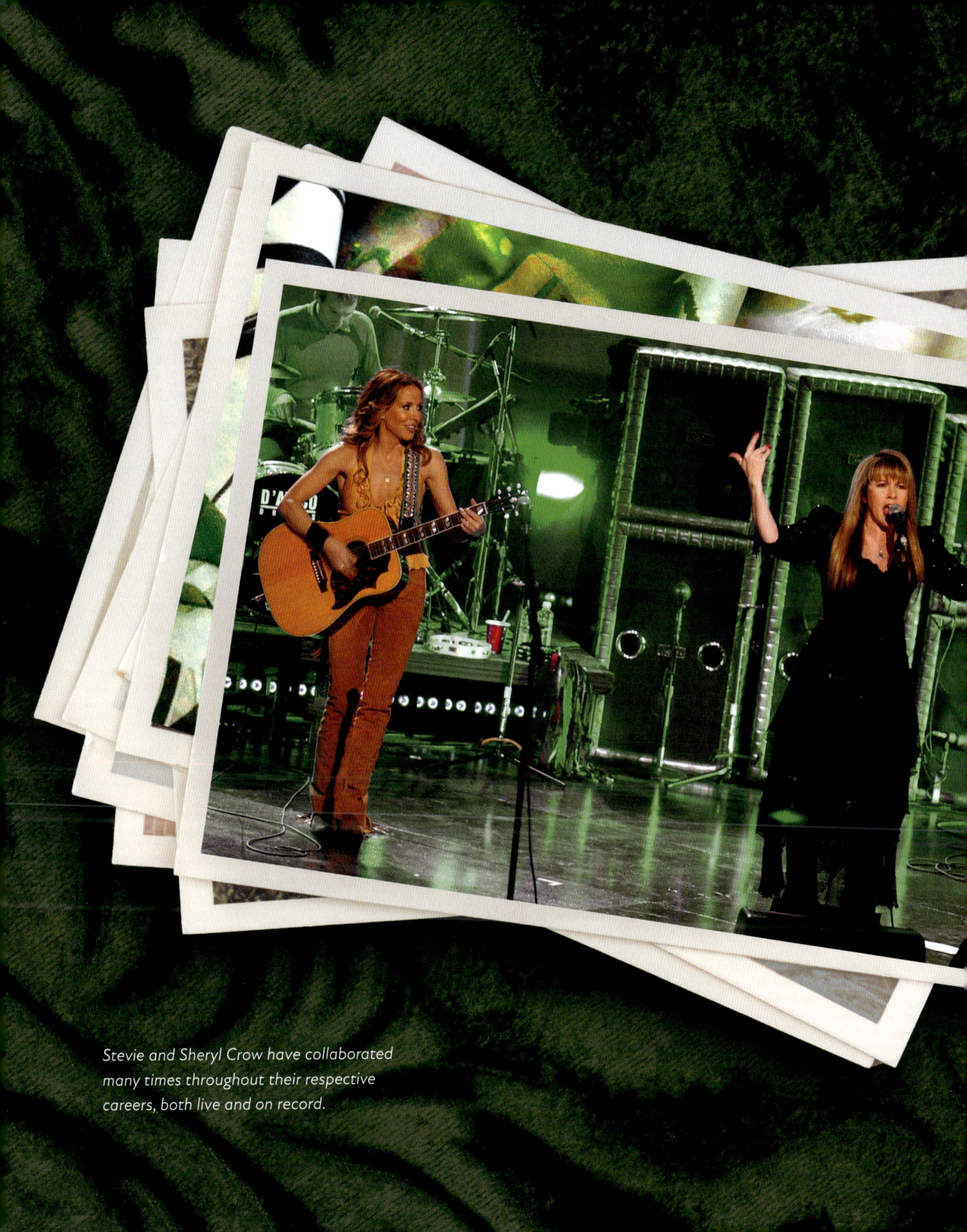

Stevie and Sheryl Crow have collaborated many times throughout their respective careers, both live and on record.

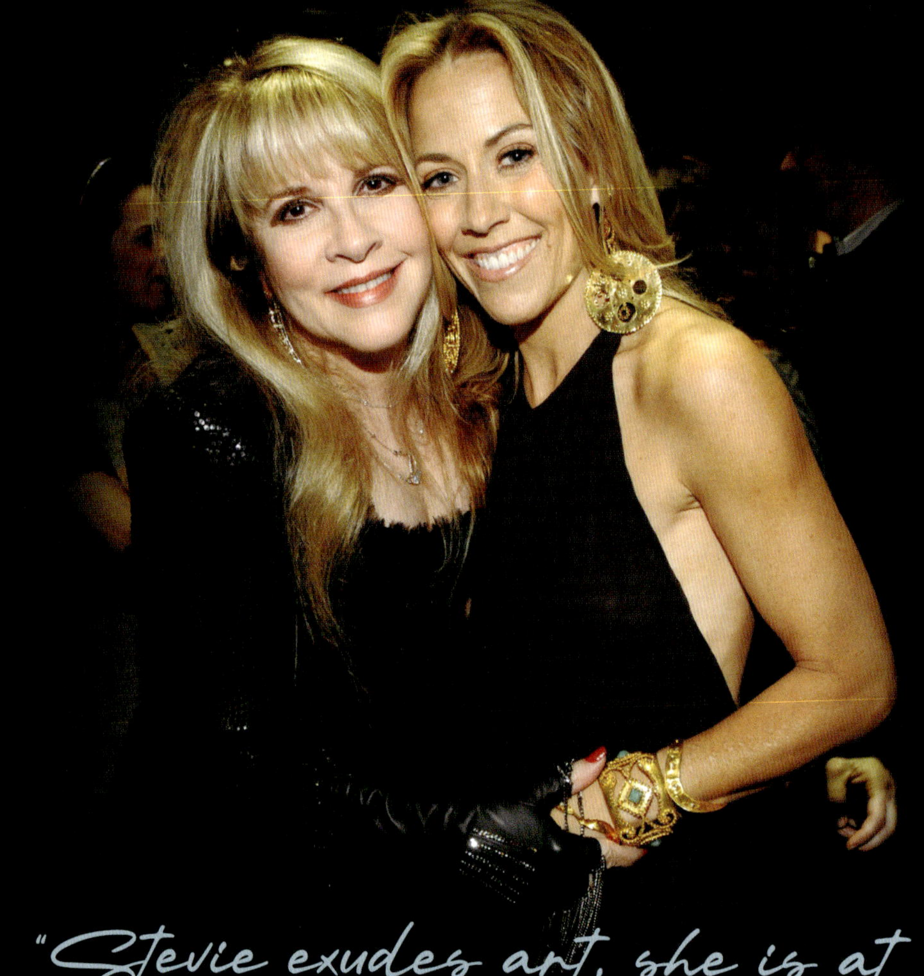

"Stevie exudes art, she is at all times authentic. She's the sister I don't see enough, but she never leaves my heart."

—SHERYL CROW

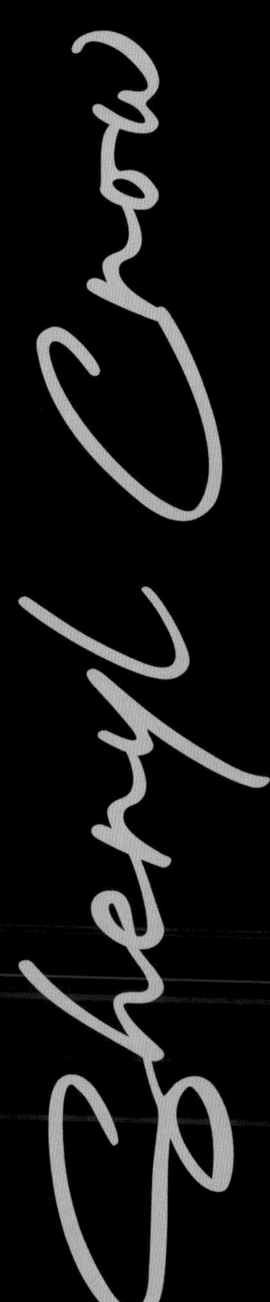

Sheryl Crow ended up coproducing five songs on *Trouble in Shangri-La*, a collaboration that was a long time coming. Growing up in small-town Missouri, she was a massive Nicks fan. "Even when I was at school, I had my hair cut like hers and I was wearing shawls and stuff and my friends thought I was a freak," she told *The Independent*. "Also her singing style. Somewhere in there, she came out of blues and country, and when I first heard it, it validated what I liked."

As it happens, Crow's bluesy rocker "All I Wanna Do" caught Nicks's ear in 1994—and the next year, the icon recorded Crow's "Somebody Stand by Me" for the soundtrack of 1995's *Boys on the Side*. The two women met for the first time at the movie's premiere and then crossed paths again at a benefit hosted by Don Henley. Along the way, Nicks floated the idea of Crow producing something for her. "We really planned it out," Nicks said in 2001. "We wanted to work together and we wanted to sing together. Sheryl's a harmony singer, and I'm a harmony singer."

Indeed, the *Trouble in Shangri-La* experience was so positive that Nicks and Crow have spent the subsequent decades supporting each other's endeavors, both live and in the studio. "I'm a rock star and I always wanted to be one," Nicks told *The Independent*. "Sheryl is a rock star too, and under that umbrella, each of us listens to what the other says. If Sheryl says, 'I don't think you should do that,' I'm probably not going to do it. Only a few people in my life have that authority."

Crow inducted Fleetwood Mac into the Rock & Roll Hall of Fame in 1998, giving a speech in which she called Nicks the "Dark Angel that I wanted to be." In turn, Nicks added vocals to multiple songs from Crow's 2002 full-length *C'mon, C'mon* (album tracks "C'mon, C'mon" and "Diamond Road" and the B-side "You're Not the One"). That same year, the pair joined forces on a TV special to raise awareness for breast cancer and performed a dynamic mini-set that included a moving take on Crow's "Strong Enough" and a cover of the Allman Brothers' "Midnight Rider."

Much later, Crow collaborated with Nicks and Maren Morris on the country-flecked 2019 single "Prove You Wrong." In a press release, Crow gushed about her friend: "Stevie exudes art, she is at all times authentic. She's the sister I don't see enough, but she never leaves my heart." And when Crow was inducted into the Rock & Roll Hall of Fame in 2023, there was Nicks onstage, adding golden harmonies on Crow's "Strong Enough" and "Everyday Is a Winding Road."

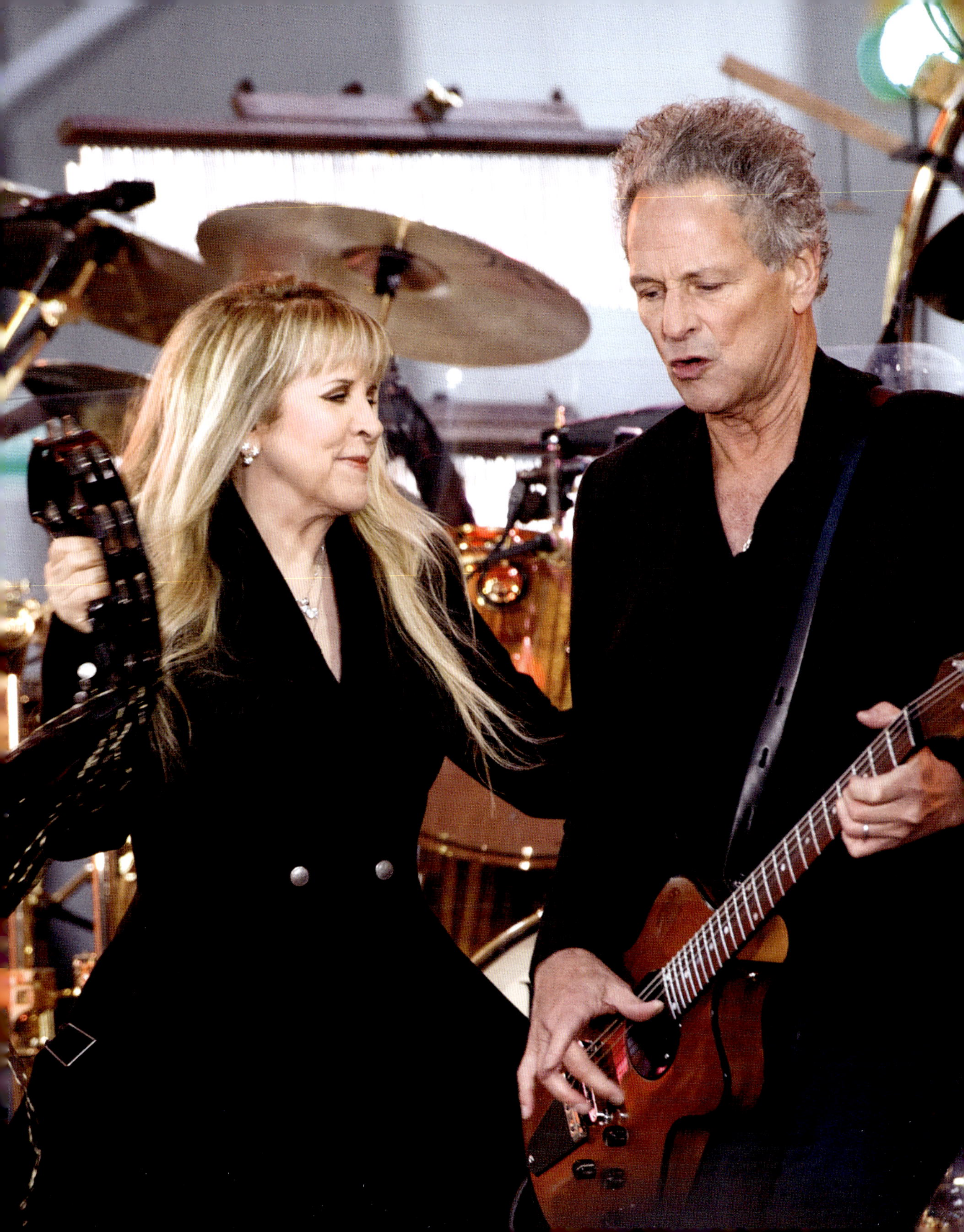

Stevie and Lindsey Buckingham perform with Fleetwood Mac in 2014 on NBC's TODAY show.

43. FLEETWOOD MAC

"Say You Will" 2003

Closing Fleetwood Mac's studio chapter with a Stevie highlight.

SAY YOU WILL WASN'T JUST NICKS'S FIRST STUDIO ALBUM with Fleetwood Mac since 1995; It also ended up being the band's final full-length. But as Nicks told *Performing Songwriter*, the musical ambition that's always coursed through the band was present. "This wasn't going to be just a dumb, stupid album. It's not going to be because we just felt like doing a record. This is because we needed to do this, and this musical entity needed to come through all of us, and we are serious as a heart attack about this."

Nicks wrote the title track, with lyrics describing a once-in-a-lifetime love that's intimate and transformative. In the chorus, the narrator asks for a second chance with this partner—but even if that doesn't happen, the second verse stresses that the beauty of this connection remains a fond memory. If you guessed the song is about Lindsey Buckingham, you'd be right—but Nicks revealed to *Performing Songwriter* she was also inspired to write the song after seeing a film about the jazz trumpeter Arturo Sandoval, likely 2000's *For Love or Country: The Arturo Sandoval Story*. She wrote the chorus first and then tackled the verses, where she took inspiration from other great romances: "I went back over all my relationships with people and think of different ways that I have felt when I wanted basically to burst into song and sing that chorus."

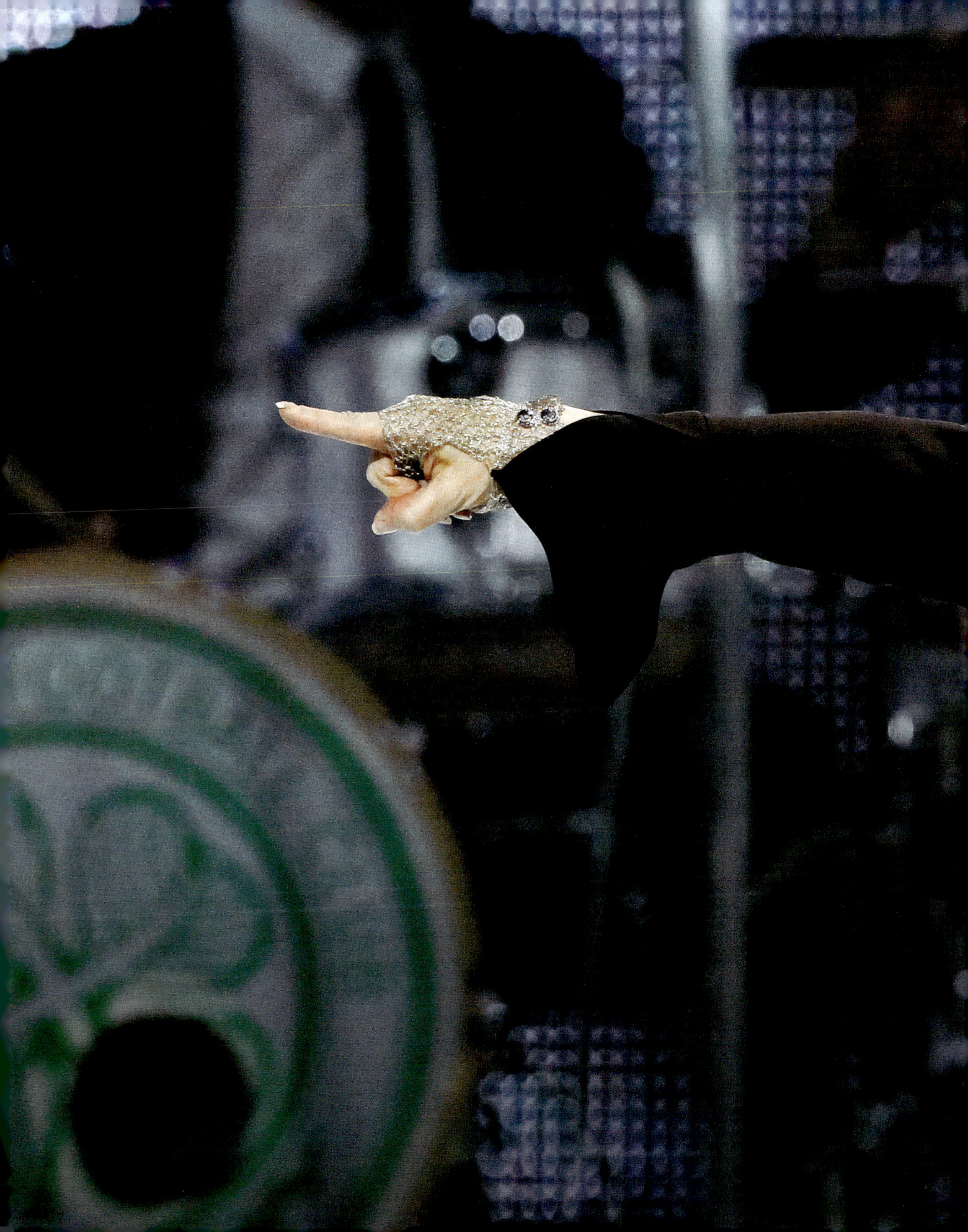

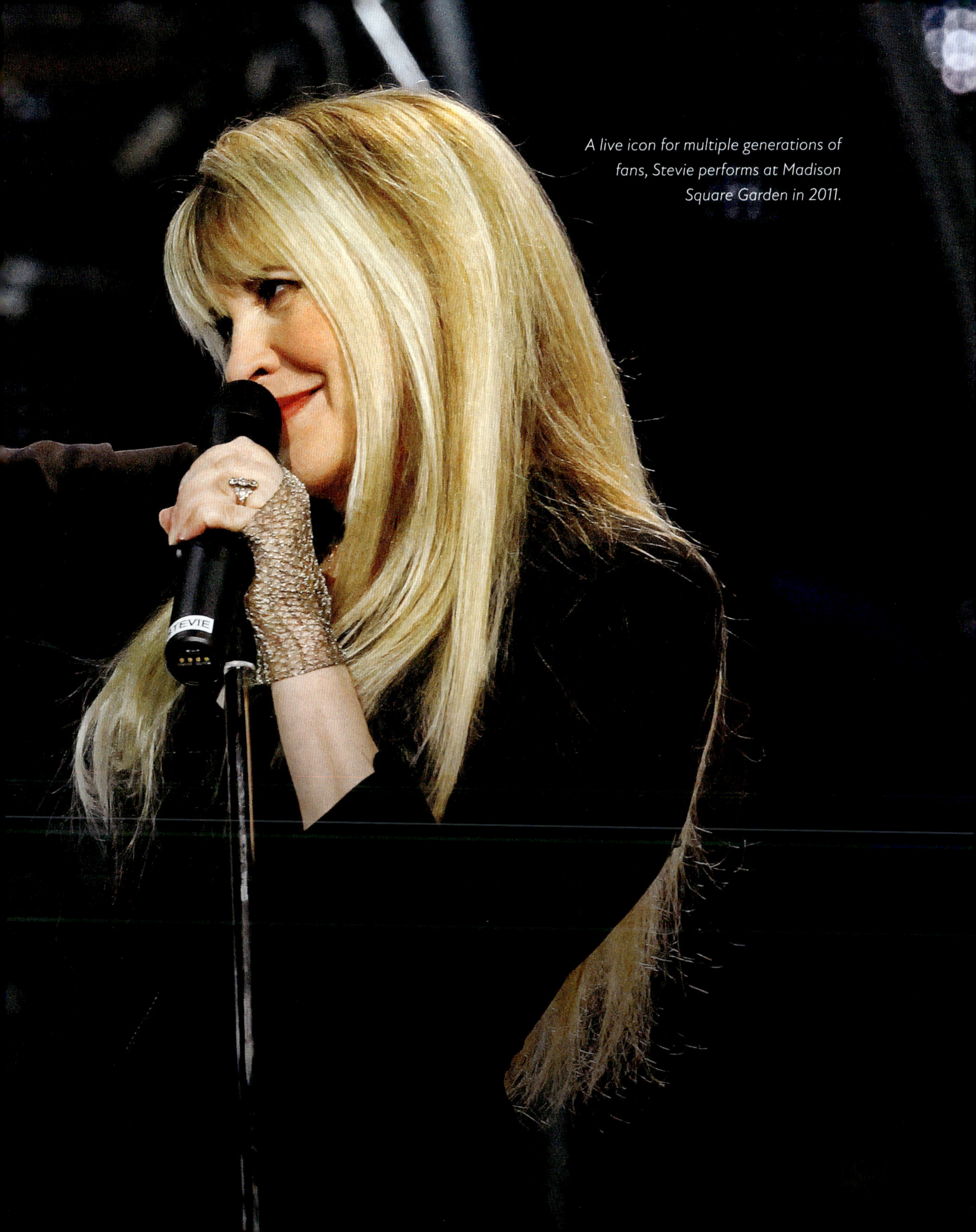

A live icon for multiple generations of fans, Stevie performs at Madison Square Garden in 2011.

An appropriately witchy Stevie arrives at 2012's The Twilight Saga: Breaking Dawn - Part 2 *Los Angeles premiere.*

44. STEVIE NICKS

"Secret Love" 2011

Her first album in a decade dug up old ghosts.

NICKS TOOK A DECADE TO FOLLOW UP *TROUBLE IN SHANGRI-LA* with a new solo record, *In Your Dreams*. As it turns out, the full-length came about after she wrote the song "Moonlight (A Vampire's Dream)" upon seeing the 2009 movie *The Twilight Saga: New Moon*. "I don't care if it sells any records or not, I can't just put out this one song," Nicks said she told her record company. "I said, 'I'm going to have to build a record around this song.'"

As with most of her solo albums, *In Your Dreams* features a mix of new songs (including a bunch written with Dave Stewart of the Eurythmics) and older material. For example, Nicks wrote the album's first single, the easygoing pop-rocker "Secret Love," in 1975, but never brought it to Fleetwood Mac. "Which is crazy because this is a very easy, simple, precise song that Lindsey Buckingham would've loved, and Fleetwood Mac would've loved," she told *TODAY*. "I put it away right after I joined the band, and for some reason, I never put it on any of my records either."

However, she kept her demo cassette and found it tucked away in a box at her parents' house in Phoenix. (Oddly enough, the demo did somehow leak, as her assistant discovered a higher-quality version of the song on YouTube.) Produced by Stewart, "Secret Love" is about two people in a rapidly disintegrating clandestine affair, even though the narrator assures they're simply looking for some temporary affection.

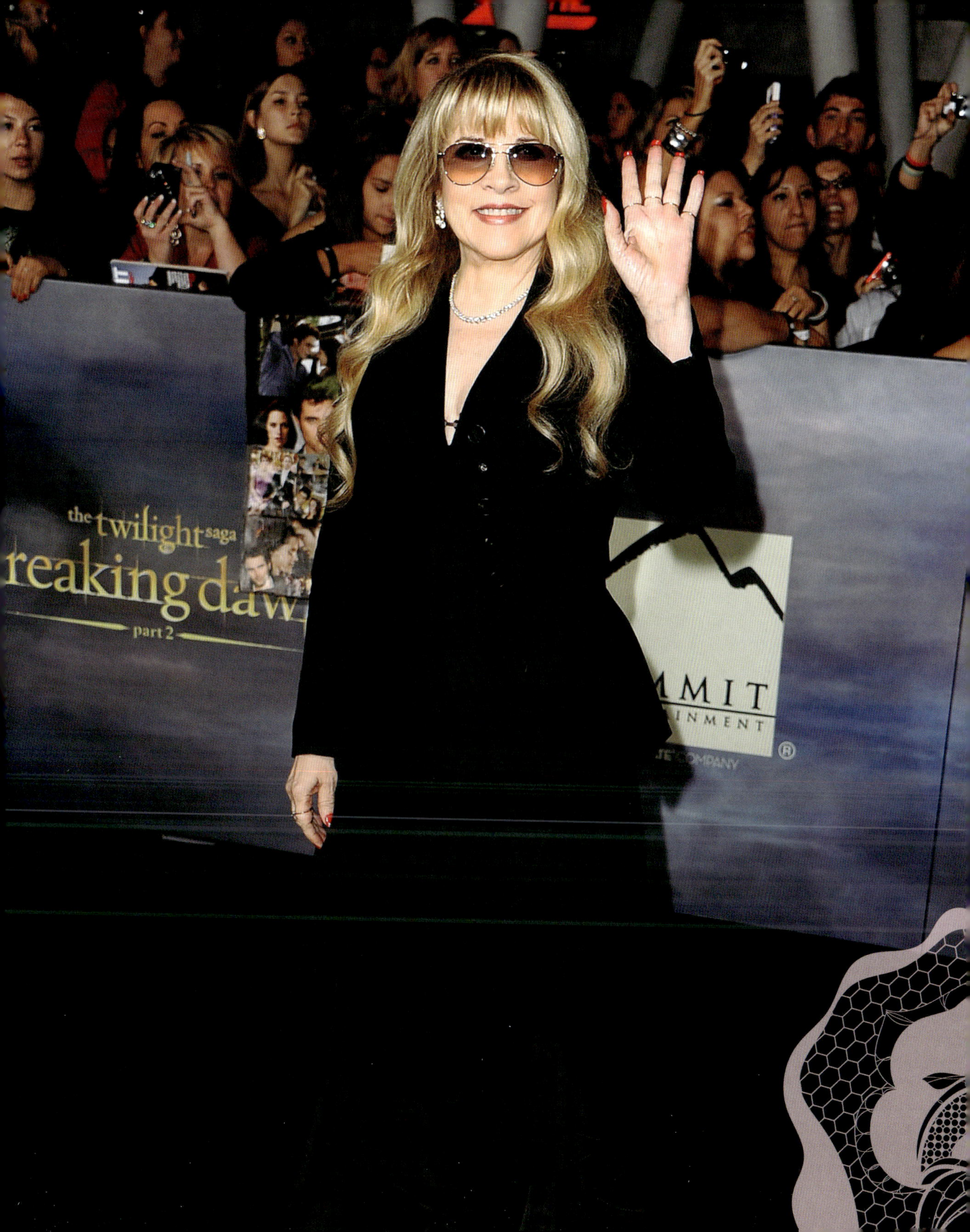
the twilight saga
reaking daw
part 2
MMIT

"Soldier's Angel" 2011

Stevie uses her songwriting gift to honor those who served.

IN 2005, NICKS STARTED VISITING SOLDIERS RECUPERATING at the Walter Reed National Military Medical Center in Bethesda, Maryland. She would spend nearly all day talking to them, often gifting them iPods full of music, which "would break the ice and they would open up to me and talk to me," she told the *Atlanta Journal-Constitution* in 2011. "I have many secrets that I carry. I probably know more about the war than most people, and their secrets are safe with me." Understandably, these visits affected her deeply. "It has been a life changer," she added. "I walked in there a rock star with very few problems and walked out of there a soldier's mother."

After one marathon visit, she wrote a poem that she gave to soldiers and their families, vowing to turn the comforting words into a song. However, she was stymied by writer's block until 2009, when she happened to be in London the day news broke that seven British soldiers had been killed in Iraq. Moved by the incident, she wrote a journal entry that ended up giving her the words of the chorus.

Musically, Nicks also had trouble finishing "Soldier's Angel." But she knew one person who could help her finish the song: Lindsey Buckingham, who gladly came in and added guitars and harmonies. "Not only did we create something that's probably as Buckingham Nicks as we have been since 1973, but . . . I think that song really brought Lindsey and I back together," she told *Billboard*. "He said to me as he was leaving on that second day, 'I feel like we're closer than we've been in 30 years.'" "Soldier's Angel" remains one of Nicks's most enduring songs. In 2022, she started playing the tune live once again to honor people in Ukraine, using the song also to ask for donations to the UN's crisis relief fund.

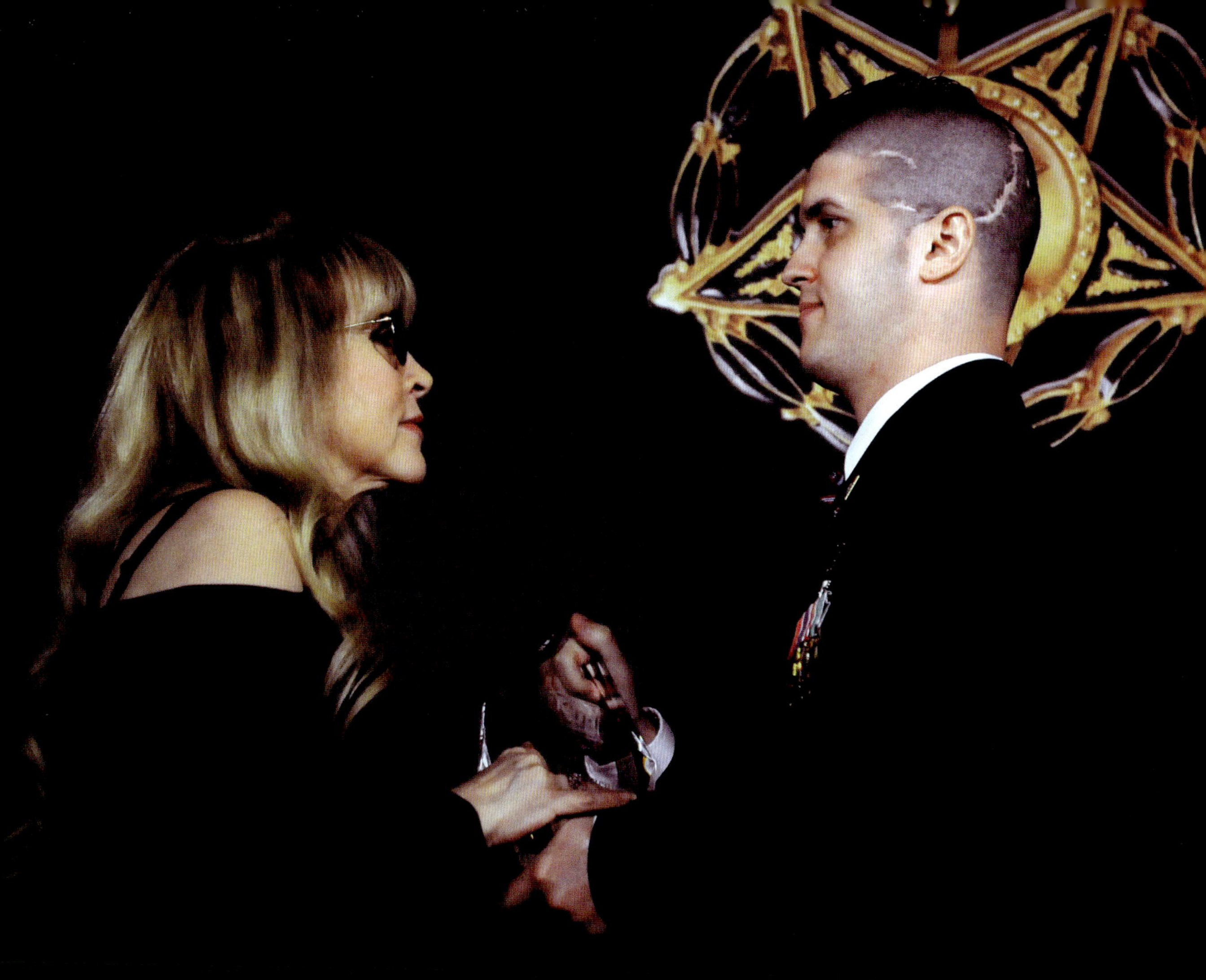

"I walked in there a rock star with very few problems and walked out of there a soldier's mother."

– STEVIE NICKS TO THE *ATLANTA JOURNAL-CONSTITUTION*

Supporting VETERANS

After discovering how much soldiers liked receiving iPods full of music, Nicks decided to form a nonprofit, Stevie Nicks's Band of Soldiers, to dole out the devices. According to a 2007 interview in *The Independent*, these iPods had close to one thousand songs, "a big mix of slow jazz, rap, R&B and music closer to her own style," as the article put it. "I realised I wanted to do something, but what can you do?" Nicks said. "A little tiny iPod is perfect. They are too ill to be downloading music. What better [gift] can I give them than music?" (The nonprofit is still in existence, but tax returns show it doesn't appear to be active at the moment.) To honor this work, Nicks received the prestigious USO Achievement Award in 2015.

However, even before this gesture, Nicks was a supporter of veterans. In the midst of 1991's Gulf War skirmish Operation Desert Storm, she was moved to write a letter to comfort deployed soldiers that was subsequently printed in the military newspaper *Stars and Stripes*. "I would tell them about Rhiannon, and about my treasured gold cross, and I would send them my feeling of sanctuary," she said in the *Timespace* liner notes. "I would do what I do when I sing. . . . I would try to make them forget, even if for a moment, and they could come into my world." On the heels of this letter, she wrote lyrics for the song "Desert Angel," pairing them with solemn music by Mike Campbell of Tom Petty and the Heartbreakers, as another way to send solace from the US.

"I realised I wanted to do something . . . They are too ill to be downloading music. What better [gift] can I give them than music?"

– STEVIE NICKS TO *THE INDEPENDENT*

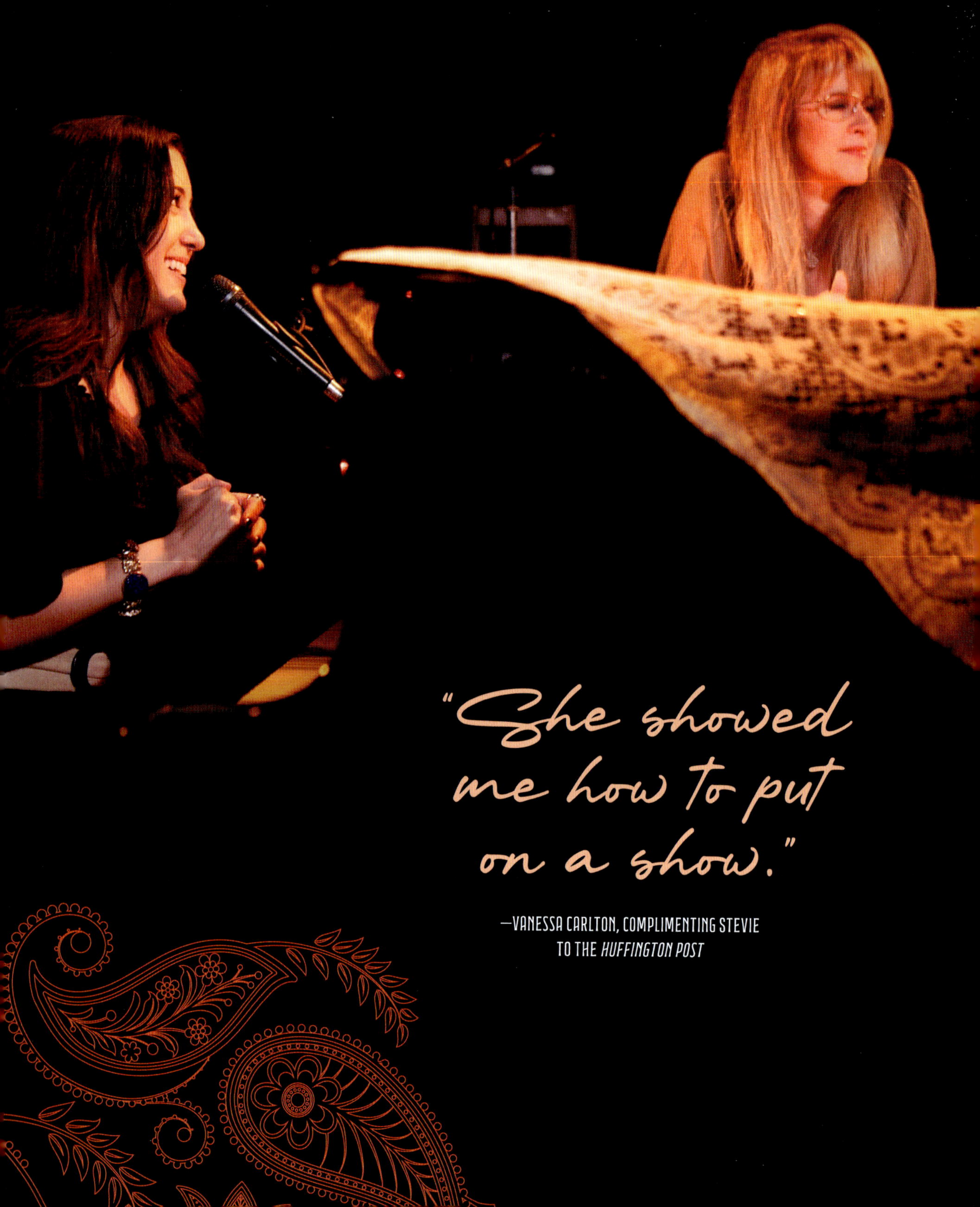

"She showed me how to put on a show."

—VANESSA CARLTON, COMPLIMENTING STEVIE TO THE *HUFFINGTON POST*

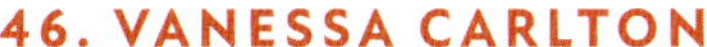
Vanessa Carlton performs with Stevie at the Roxy in 2007 and frequently opens the icon's shows.

46. VANESSA CARLTON

"Carousel" 2011

A song expressing gratitude for love—and mothers everywhere.

IN 2014, NICKS DUSTED OFF AND RECORDED A STASH OF HER OLD demos on the compilation *24 Karat Gold: Songs from the Vault*, including *Tusk* coulda-been "The Dealer" and a stunning song she wrote with Sharon Celani in Hawaii called "Blue Water." The collection also included a cover of Vanessa Carlton's 2011 song "Carousel," a piercing piano number about the comforting idea that love never really disappears and second chances are always possible.

It's "the only song I've ever written in a dream that sounded great in the morning," Carlton told Songfacts, noting the musical idea woke her up at 3:30 a.m. "I had the scale and I had the rhythm of the chorus, which is like you're resting on the one note." She played this part on her piano and headed back to sleep.

Carlton and Nicks are longtime friends. The two women first toured together in 2005. "She showed me how to put on a show," Carlton told the *Huffington Post*. "As much as she herself is crafting and creating all of this stuff on her own, it's really interesting to see how important the other element is to her, to serve and really entertain." Years later, Nicks officiated Carlton's wedding to Deer Tick's John McCauley.

As it turns out, Carlton returned these kindnesses during a very trying time: the death of Nicks's mom, Barbara. In late December 2011, Nicks received a phone call from her brother. "He said, 'Stevie, I know I'm not really what you'd call a really spiritual guy, but I think I just had a visitation from our dad,'" she later recalled, "and he said, 'Son, go get your mother from the hospital and bring her home.'" On the way to get her mom, it came up that

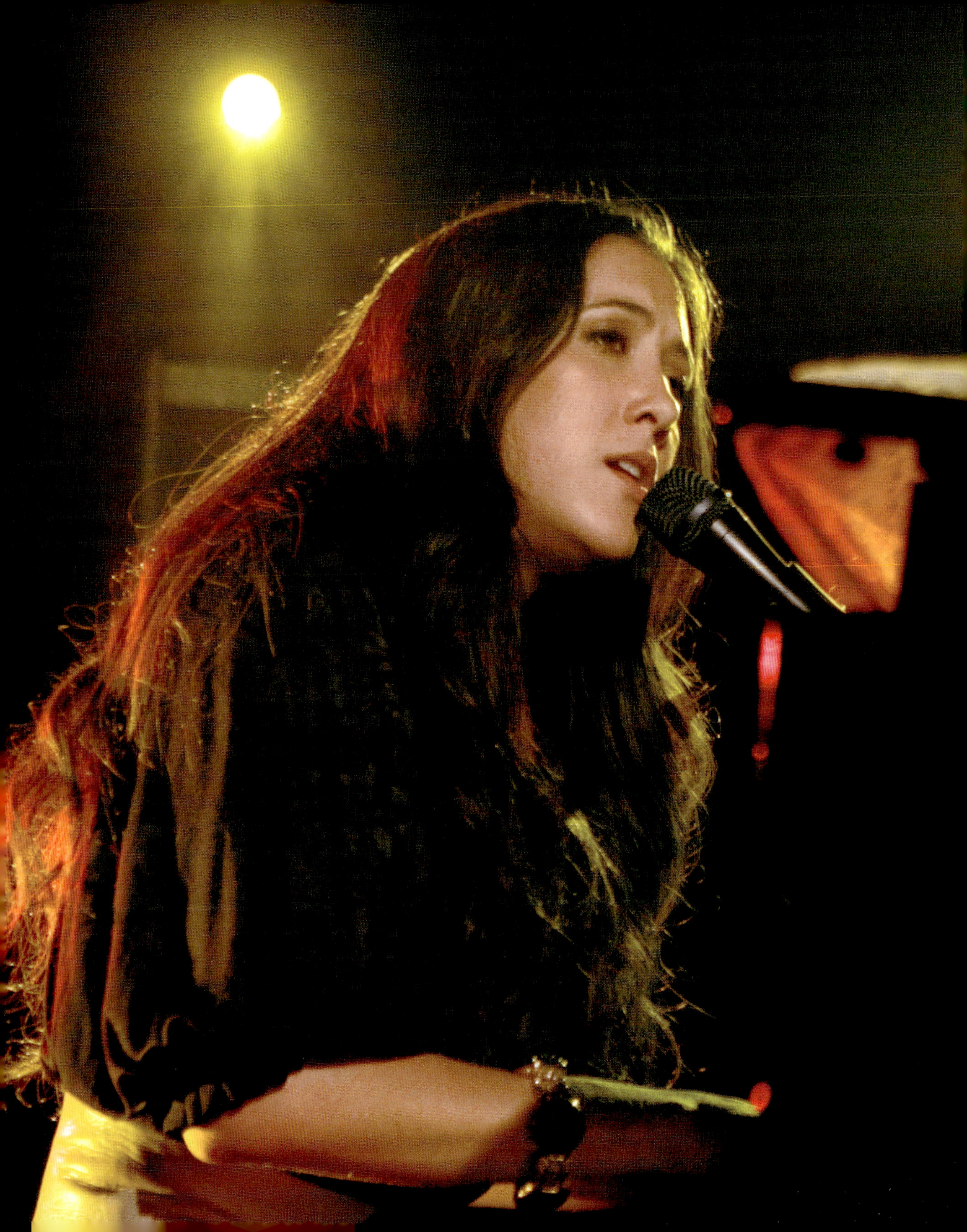

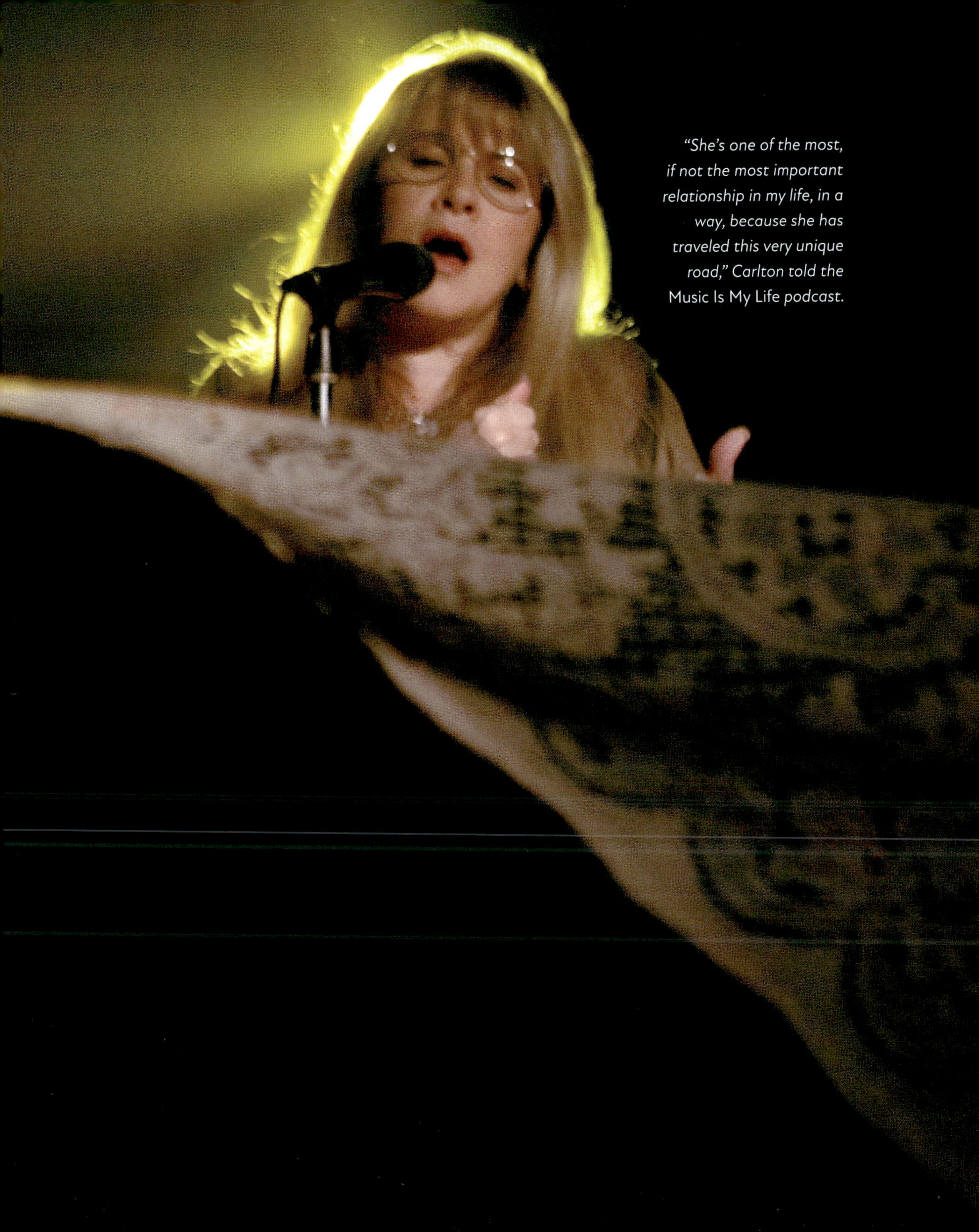

"She's one of the most, if not the most important relationship in my life, in a way, because she has traveled this very unique road," Carlton told the Music Is My Life *podcast.*

Nicks's mom loved "Carousel"; Carlton, who happened to be visiting the family for the holidays, "started to sing it in the backseat by herself in her beautiful, tiny little voice," Nicks said.

Barbara Nicks died the very next day; poignantly, Carlton was still by Stevie's side. Several years later, Nicks decided to record and release her own version of "Carousel" as a gesture of gratitude. Her take is dainty folk music with strings and light acoustic accents. "I thought it was important to record this song for her, for her relationship with her mom, for everybody in that room's relationship with their mother," Nicks said. "To understand that things are taken away from you very fast and there's nothing you can do, and you should really take advantage of people while they're here because so quickly they can be gone . . . and friendship and what friendship means, what real love and real friendship means."

When Nicks recorded her version, she asked her niece, Jessi, to sing alongside her and Carlton, "so that it would be Barbara's friend Vanessa, Barbara's daughter Stevie, and Barbara's granddaughter Jessi" contributing vocals together. Unsurprisingly, their voices dominate the version, winding over and around one another like gossamer braids. "I thought that Jessi did an amazing job singing on it," Nicks later said. "Waddy [Wachtel] helped her with an amazing part to sing, so it's really like a little Crosby, Stills, and Nash song, the way that we three girls did it."

"I thought it was important to record this song for [Vanessa], for her relationship with her mom, for everybody in that room's relationship with their mother."

–STEVIE NICKS

Stevie as INSPIRATION

"I always wanted to be inspirational to other singers," Nicks said in a 2001 interview. "And I wanted to be a success story for women where they can say, 'Well, she made it. I can make it, too.'" Mission very much accomplished. Dozens of artists have covered her songs—for example, Florence and the Machine, Tori Amos, and Courtney Love have all tackled "Silver Springs"—and her intergenerational admirers include Michelle Branch, Belinda Carlisle, Halsey, and Mary J. Blige.

Nicks has also inspired and mentored countless female singers, including Lorde ("If she had been my age, and our age, she probably would have been the third girl in Fleetwood Mac," Nicks once said); the rock band HAIM, whose members have collaborated with Nicks; and Natalie Maines of the Chicks.

Maines sang on *Trouble in Shangri-La's* "Too Far from Texas" and was impressed by Nicks's approach to music. "[She's] very supportive of other females in the industry," Maines told Howard Stern. "I think lots of women are competitive. She really wants you to succeed."

For Nicks, being that steady presence is deeply meaningful. "They know they can call me. I'm never far away," she said in 2014, referencing her status as a guiding force. "I like to say a fairy godmother as opposed to a mom because I don't become their moms. . . . They don't need another mom, but maybe they need a fairy godmother."

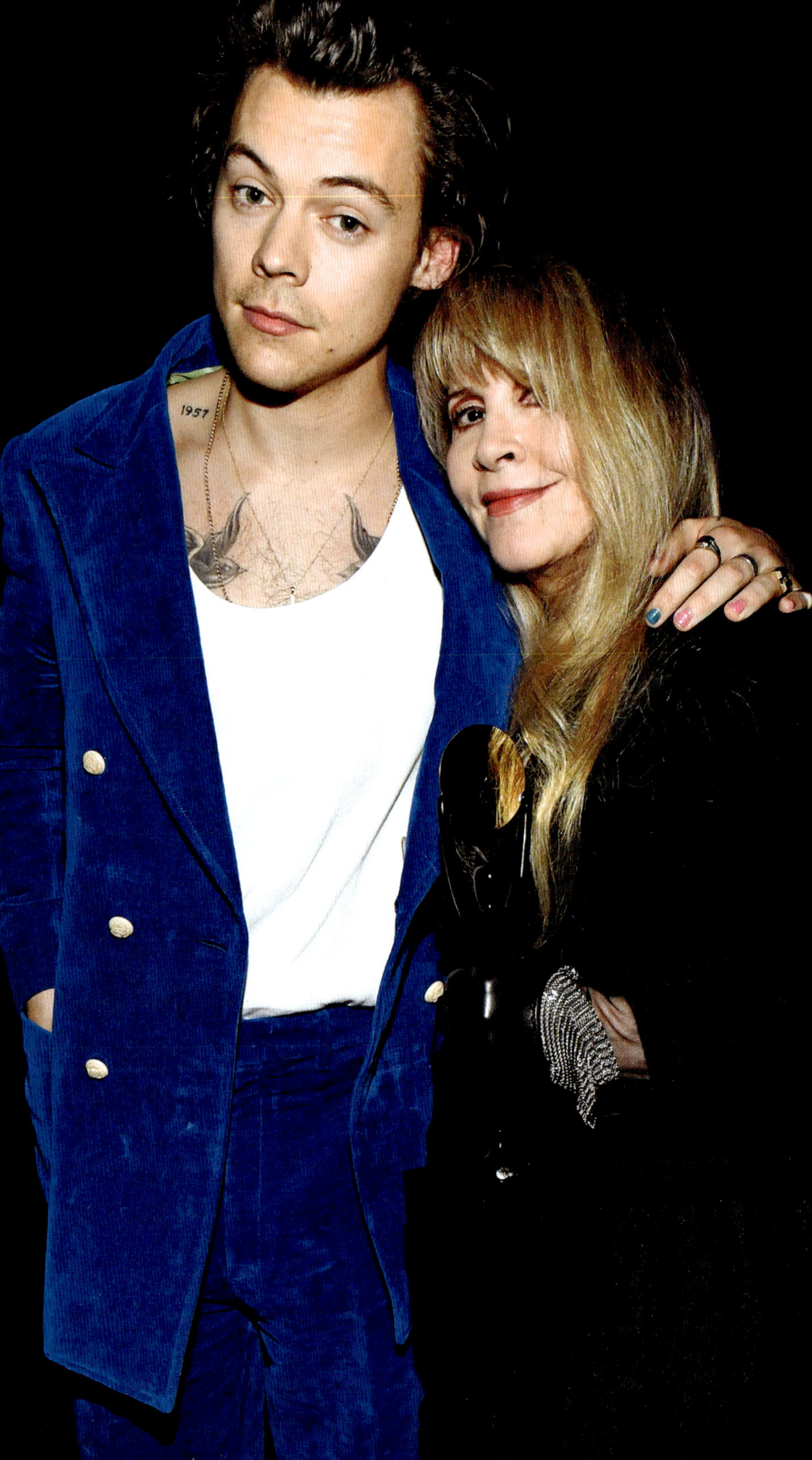
1957

Styles performed "Stop Draggin' My Heart Around" with Stevie at the 2019 Rock & Roll Hall Of Fame induction ceremony.

47. HARRY STYLES

"Sunflower, Vol. 6" 2019

Stevie's deep friendship with a soulful pop superstar.

WHEN NICKS HEADLINED IN LONDON'S HYDE PARK IN JULY 2024, the date of the show heartbreakingly fell on Christine McVie's birthday. Given that McVie had died only a year and a half before, Nicks was feeling particularly emotional during the show. "One thing my mom used to say to me when I was little was when I was hurt, she'd go 'Stevie, when you're hurt you always run to the stage,'" she told the audience. "That's what I've been doing ever since Chris passed away, is running to the stage. The only people that have been able to help me to get over this have been all of you."

On that night, Nicks also leaned on her dear friend Harry Styles for support. The British pop superstar made a surprise appearance during the encore to sing "Stop Draggin' My Heart Around" and "Landslide" with Nicks. The latter performance was especially somber, as the lyrics about life changes and the passage of time clearly resonated in a much deeper way.

Of course, by the time of this Hyde Park appearance, Nicks and Styles had performed "Landslide" together multiple times. When he released his 2017 self-titled debut album, she joined him at the Troubadour in Los Angeles to sing that tune and a harmony-rich take on "Leather and Lace." A few years later, when Styles released 2019's Fine Line, Nicks once again showed up and sang "Landslide" with him at the Forum. Nicks celebrated the milestone by giving him a note in which she compared *Fine Line* to Fleetwood Mac's

"Harry writes and sings his songs about real experiences . . . He taps into real life. He doesn't make up stories. He tells the truth, and that is what I do."

—STEVIE NICKS TO *VARIETY*

Rumours. "We cried," she told *Variety* of the new album. "He sang those songs like he had sung them a thousand times. That's a great songwriter and a great performer."

Unsurprisingly, Styles grew up a Fleetwood Mac fan. "In my family, we listened at home, we listened in the car, we listened wherever we could," Styles said in his hilarious (and from-the-heart) 2019 speech inducting Nicks into the Rock & Roll Hall of Fame as a solo artist. "'Dreams' was the first song I knew all the words to, before I really knew what all the words meant. I thought it was a song about the weather. But I knew it was a beautiful song about the weather." Also unsurprisingly, he noted it was somewhat surreal to become friends with Nicks, telling NPR that "it borders on an out-of-body experience." (Of note: He scored points in their first backstage meeting by bringing her carrot cake with her name on it in frosting.)

The respect and admiration are clearly mutual. "Harry writes and sings his songs about real experiences that seemingly happened yesterday," Nicks told *Variety* in 2020. "He taps into real life. He doesn't make up stories. He tells the truth, and that is what I do." And when *Vogue* asked Nicks to name one of her favorite Styles songs, she chose *Fine Line*'s "Sunflower, Vol. 6," a sunny, Beatles-esque pop-rock gem with pirouetting grooves and a cheerful vibe.

In the same interview, Nicks shared a video treatment she dreamt up for the song that would show a "bee relationship," as she put it. "I called [Harry] and said, 'I have an idea. You're gonna be a bee, and the sunflower would be your girlfriend, and you guys would get married and live in a beehive with your little bee children." Styles was skeptical. Nicks added: "When I finished, the other end of the phone was silent. I said, 'No, really, think about it. It'll be fantastical like a Francis Ford Coppola movie.' He's like, 'Yeah, okay.'"

During his Rock & Roll Hall of Fame induction speech, Styles spoke to her legendary status and their lovely friendship. "Somewhere around 2005, 2006, this woman became God, I think we can all agree on that," he said. "On Halloween, one in seven people dress as Stevie Nicks. She is both an adjective and a verb. To quote my father, 'That was rather Stevie Nicks,' and to quote my mother, 'I Stevie Nicks that shit so hard!'"

On this momentous night, he also dueted with Nicks on "Stop Draggin' My Heart Around," handling the vocal parts originally sung by Tom Petty with grace. "If you're lucky enough to know her, she's always there for you," Styles said of Nicks in his speech. "She knows what you need, advice, a little wisdom, a blouse, a shawl—she's got you covered. Her songs make you ache, feel on top of the world, make you want to dance, and usually all three at the same time."

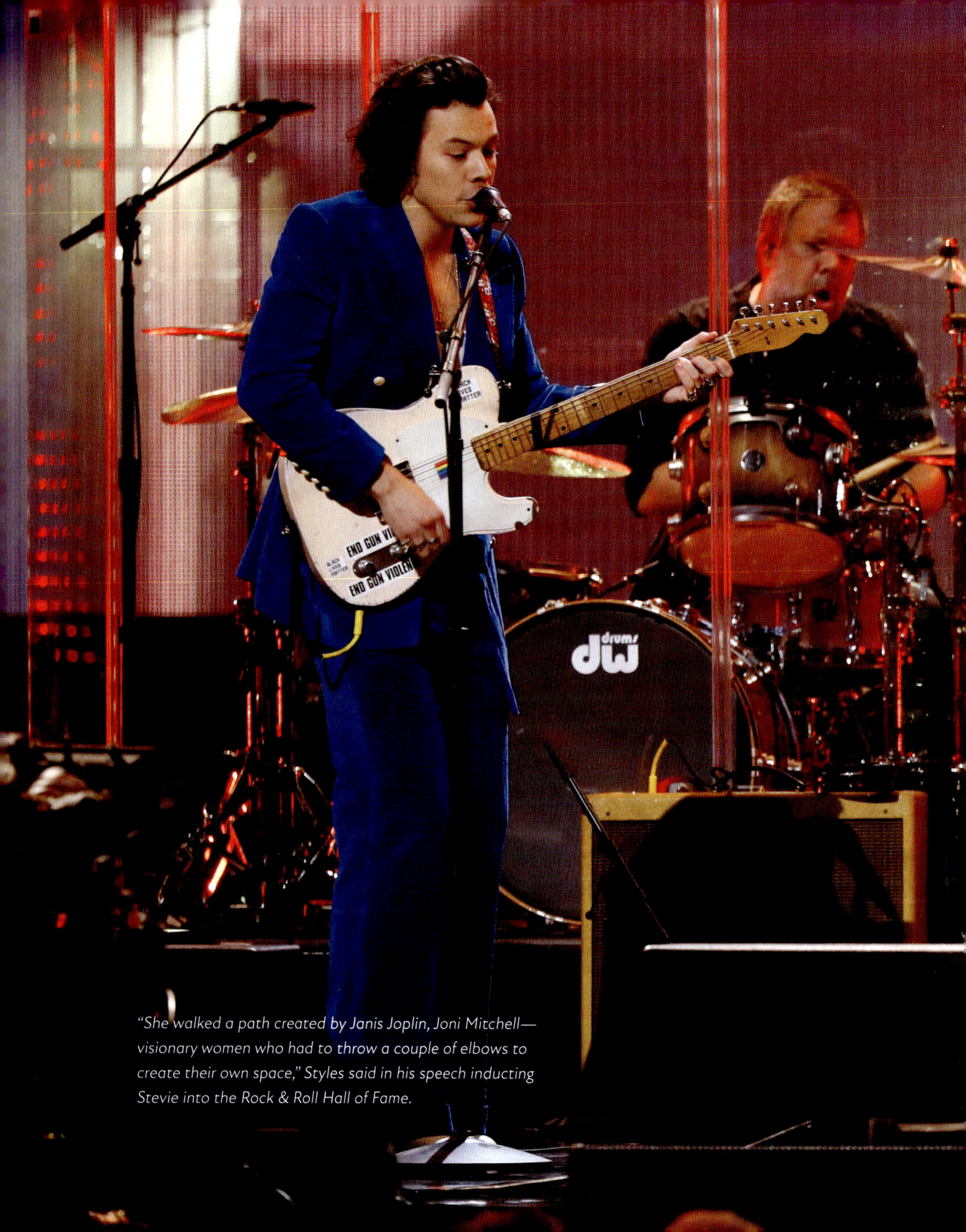

"She walked a path created by Janis Joplin, Joni Mitchell—visionary women who had to throw a couple of elbows to create their own space," Styles said in his speech inducting Stevie into the Rock & Roll Hall of Fame.

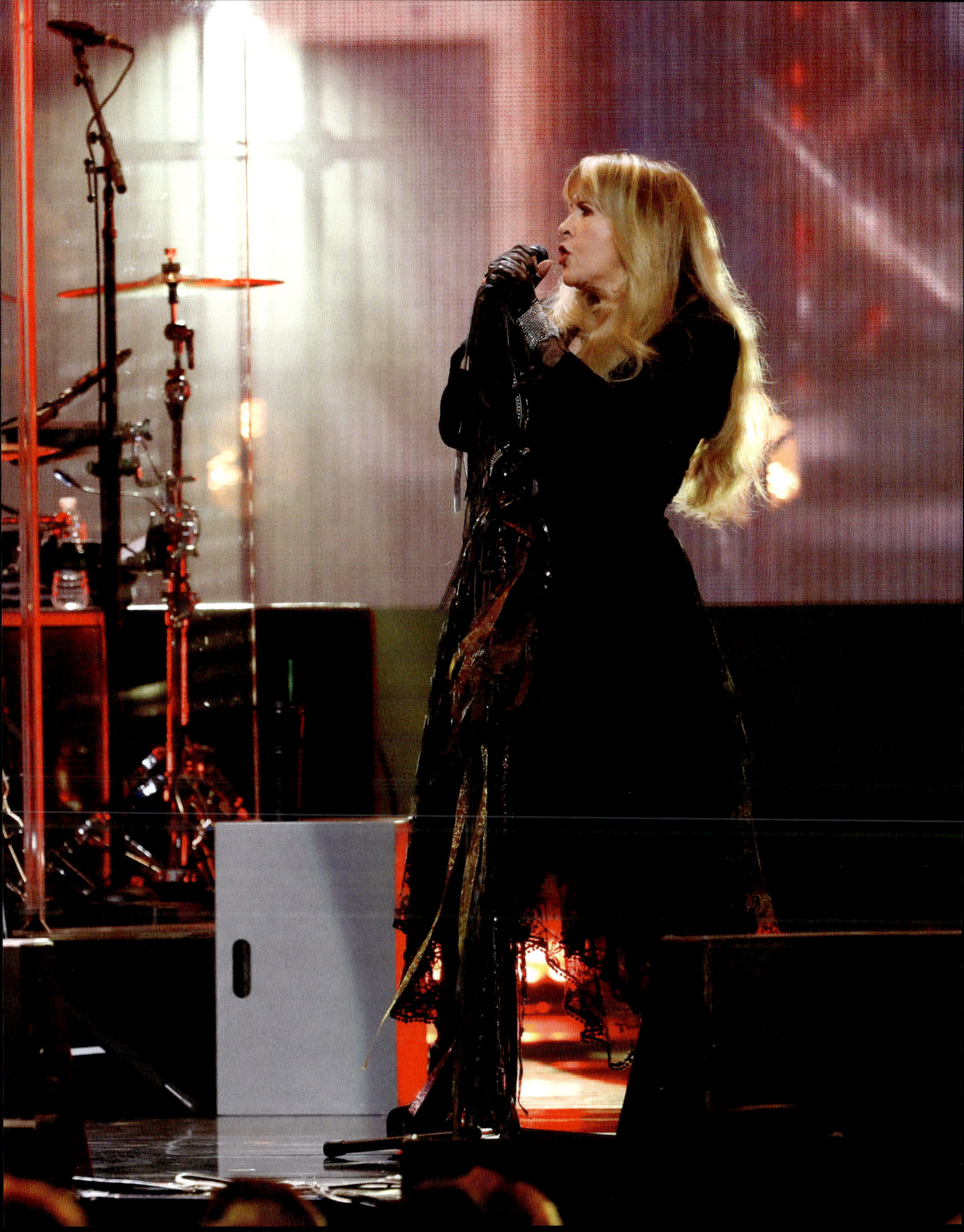

48. DAISY JONES & THE SIX

"Look at Us Now (Honeycomb)" 2023

A fictional Fleetwood Mac gets it right in Stevie's eyes.

**IN 2023, AMAZON PRIME AIRED THE MINISERIES *DAISY JONES &* ***the Six*, based on the Taylor Jenkins Reid novel about a California-based rock band that became famous while navigating drugs, drama, and romance. (Sound familiar?) To create an authentic experience, real-life musicians wrote original songs for the series, led by "Look at Us Now (Honeycomb)," a torchy, *Rumours*-esque duet between Daisy (Riley Keough) and Billy (Sam Claflin) cowritten by Marcus Mumford.

Perhaps unsurprisingly, Nicks loved both "Look at Us Now (Honeycomb)" and *Daisy Jones & the Six*. Nicks took to Twitter/X and observed that Keough (whose Daisy was very Stevie-esque) "soon became my story. It brought back memories that made me feel like a ghost watching my own story. It was very emotional for me."

Nicks was even happier that *Daisy Jones & the Six* nailed the intangible magic that made Fleetwood Mac succeed in spite of turmoil and drama, citing the way the characters always gravitate toward singing even after fighting. "It would blow your mind," she says. "I would be watching and be like, 'Well, there you go.' That's exactly why we did it. That's exactly why Fleetwood Mac stayed together for 50 years. It was all for the music."

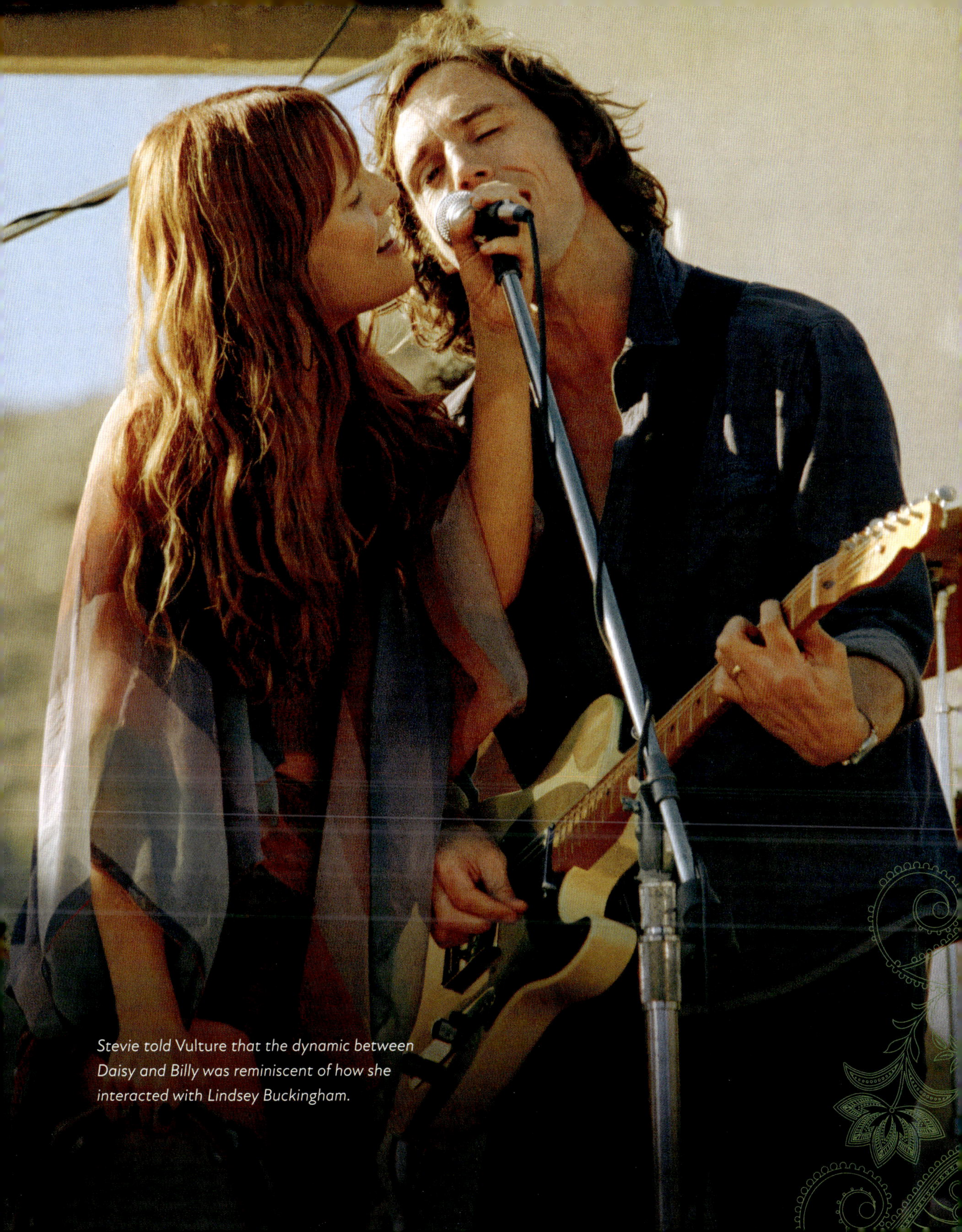

Stevie told Vulture that the dynamic between Daisy and Billy was reminiscent of how she interacted with Lindsey Buckingham.

Stevie in POP CULTURE

Pop culture references are nothing new for Nicks. Actress Lucy Lawless imitated her in a cult favorite 1998 *Saturday Night Live* sketch, "Stevie Nicks' Fajita Roundup." In an absurd premise, Nicks was running a Mexican restaurant; as part of the skit, Lawless sang Nicks tunes rewritten as parodies about food deals (like "Burrito Dreams") or lyrics about a beef tostada meal set to "Gold Dust Woman."

South Park also referenced Nicks several times. One episode used "Landslide" (with permission) as Stan's parents were getting divorced, while another imagined Nicks was kidnapped by terrorists while in Afghanistan for a USO concert. In the kidnapping episode, she was drawn as a goat in a cape—a veiled nod to mean criticism that she sounds like the animal when singing—but she was a good sport about it. "Yes, I was a little goat in a cape," she told the radio station KBCO in 2011. "But who cares? It was hysterical. The fact is, they sent the whole army in to get me [in the episode]."

Much more flattering was the way her music showed up in the 2003 movie *School of Rock* as Jack Black and Joan Cusack talk about how great she is live as "Edge of Seventeen" plays in the background. In addition, in 2011, the popular TV show *Glee* included "Landslide" in one episode and dedicated another to *Rumours*, leading to covers of "Dreams" and "I Don't

Want to Know." Surprisingly, one show Nicks hasn't had a huge presence on is *RuPaul's Drag Race*, although Thorgy Thor did pay homage to her in the third season of *RuPaul's Drag Race All Stars*. However, in 2014, the winner of the second season of *All Stars*, Alaska, created a show called *Stevie Forever* with pianist/Lindsey Buckingham stand-in Handsome Jeremy in which the duo "retell and relive Stevie's history as a rock goddess and all-around badass witch."

In recent years, Fleetwood Mac has become more popular with younger generations; for example, *Rumours* is a perennial top seller on vinyl, outranking most new albums. That's also a reflection of Nicks's charming social media presence. In addition to news about tours and releases, she'll add a personal touch by sharing typed letters or poems in a fancy font (or photos of her Barbie in various fun situations, like celebrating Christmas).

Nicks's influence on music culture is also incalculable. Sonically, many musical acts have been inspired to let their creativity and musicianship run wild. The duo Fleetmac Wood create otherworldly remixes of the band's music, which they pair with immersive concerts. In 2024, Andrew Bird and Madison Cunningham teamed up to do an inventive song-by-song tribute of the *Buckingham Nicks* LP with additional orchestral flourishes and harmonic arrangements.

> "The word 'icon' is difficult for me, because I think of 'icon' as a big Greek statue of a girl in a cape. But I'm good with it, because I've worked hard to be whatever everybody thinks that I am."
>
> —STEVIE NICKS TO *ROLLING STONE*

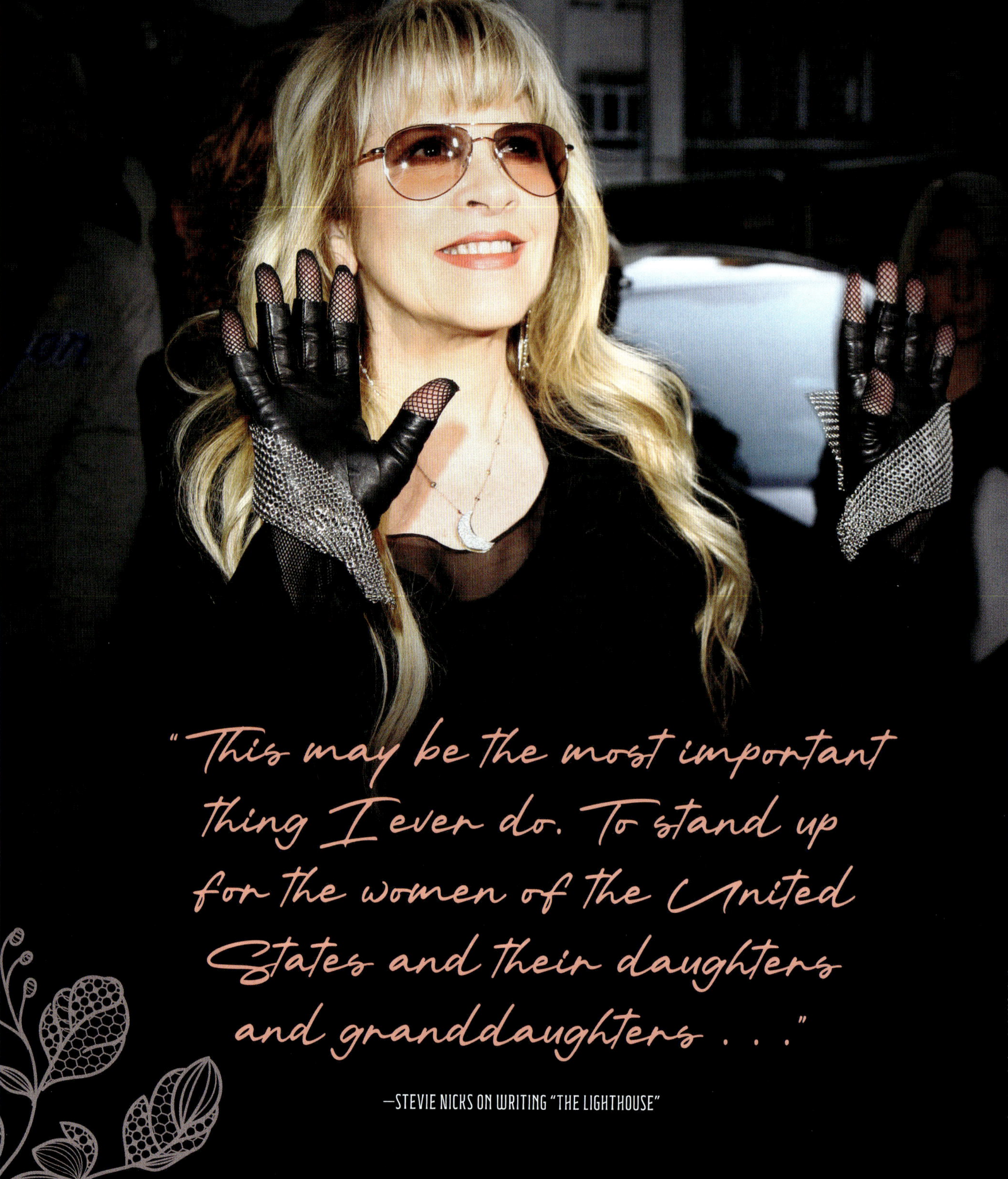

"This may be the most important thing I ever do. To stand up for the women of the United States and their daughters and granddaughters . . ."

—STEVIE NICKS ON WRITING "THE LIGHTHOUSE"

Stevie is a pop culture icon who turns heads wherever she goes.

49. STEVIE NICKS

"The Lighthouse" 2024

An anthem about fighting for your rights.

NICKS BECAME MORE OUTSPOKEN ABOUT POLITICS IN 2024, endorsing Democratic presidential candidate Kamala Harris and encouraging people to vote, because she regretted not doing so until she turned seventy. But one of her boldest political statements yet was a stand-alone single called "The Lighthouse," a stormy rock song about fighting for your rights and clawing back your power from oppressive forces. Nicks initially sings in a delicate, silvery whisper, before unleashing her trademark mighty vocal roar as the music crashes around her like waves on rocks.

Nicks wrote and recorded "The Lighthouse" in less than a day, several months after the Supreme Court overturned *Roe v. Wade*, a 1973 ruling that recognized abortion as a constitutionally protected right in the United States. "Everybody kept saying, 'Well, somebody has to do something. Somebody has to say something,'" Nicks told CBS News. "And I'm like, 'Well, I have a platform. I tell a good story. So maybe I should try to do something.' I was also there. I was, 'Been there, done that.'"

Indeed, the song and the court decision were both deeply personal to Nicks. In 1979, she became pregnant by Don Henley, despite being protected with an IUD. Having a child would have "destroyed" Fleetwood Mac, she told CBS News—the band was at the peak of fame, going into *Tusk*—and she decided to have an abortion. "I would've, like, tried my best to get through, you know, being in the studio every single day expecting a child," she continued. "But mostly, having a child with Don Henley would not have gone over big in Fleetwood Mac, with Lindsey and me; we had been broken up for two or three years. It would've been a nightmare scenario for me to live through."

Stevie and Taylor Swift performed together at the Grammy Awards in 2010.

50. TAYLOR SWIFT

"Clara Bow" 2024

The superstar pop icon expresses gratitude for the trailblazing woman who started it all.

IN EARLY 2010, STEVIE NICKS AND TAYLOR SWIFT COLLABORATED at the Grammy Awards, performing a duet of "Rhiannon" and a stripped-down version of Swift's "You Belong with Me." Although Swift received criticism for her shaky solo vocals, the women sounded dynamic singing in unison, their voices melting together like snow. Later that year, when Swift was chosen for the prestigious *Time* 100 list of influential people, Nicks wrote an essay about what made the then–country star's career so special: talent and ambition. "When I turned 20 years old, I had just made the serious decision to never be a dental assistant. Taylor just turned 20, and she's won four Grammys."

"This girl writes the songs that make the whole world sing, like Neil Diamond or Elton John," Nicks continued. "She sings, she writes, she performs, she plays great guitar. . . . Taylor is writing for the universal woman and for the man who wants to know her. The female rock-'n'-roll-country-pop songwriter is back, and her name is Taylor Swift. And it's women like her who are going to save the music business."

This era kicked off a long-standing mutual admiration and friendship that culminated in Swift's 2024 full-length *The Tortured Poets Department*. In the album's packaging, Nicks contributed a poem that referenced how she and Swift continue to thrive despite fleeting romances and flighty men. In turn, Swift wrote a glowing folk-pop song called "Clara Bow." Although named after the free-spirited actress, the song also mentions Nicks, in the context of holding her up as a paragon of greatness.

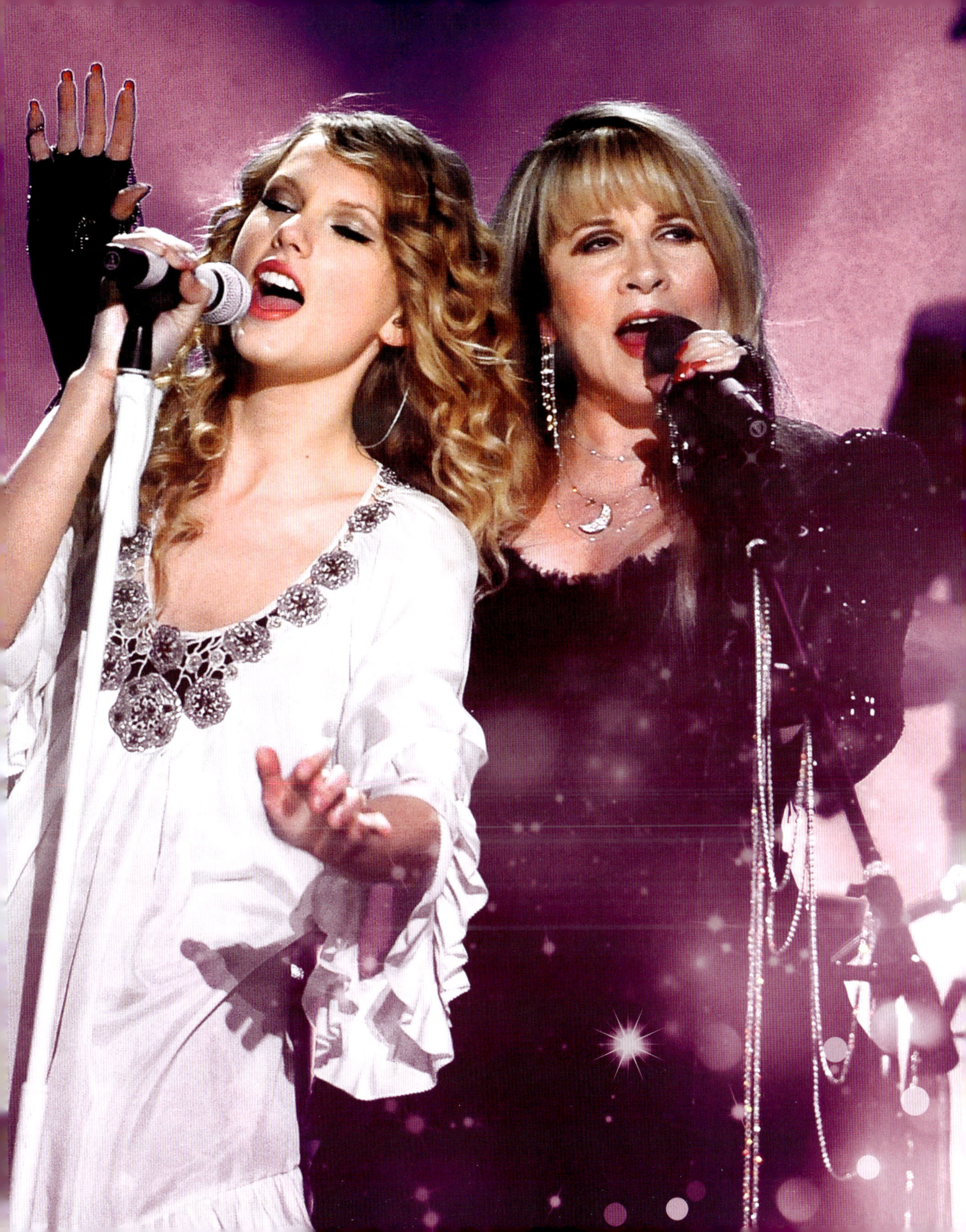

"I picked women who have done great things in the past and have been these archetypes of greatness in the entertainment industry," Swift told Amazon Music. "Clara Bow was the first 'it girl.' Stevie Nicks is an icon and an incredible example for anyone who wants to write songs and make music."

Nicks herself finds inspiration from Swift's music. After Christine McVie died, she took solace in "You're on Your Own, Kid," a song about being brave and finding your own way in life. At a May 2023 show in Atlanta, Nicks thanked Swift for writing it. "When it was the two of us, the two of us were on our own, kids, we always were," she said from the stage, referencing McVie. "And now, I'm having to learn to be on my own, kid, by myself. So you help me to do that."

Poignantly, when Nicks attended the third night of Eras Tour stop in Dublin, Ireland, Swift played a very special acoustic section to honor her friend, mashing up "Clara Bow" and a thematically related song called "The Lucky One" on guitar and then playing "You're on Your Own, Kid" on piano. Swift prefaced this performance with a lovely speech about Nicks, noting she has "really been one of the reasons why I—or any female artist—get to do what we get to do" and praising her trailblazing ways.

"She's paved the way for us, and she's mentored so many artists that you don't even know she's doing it. She's become friends with so many female artists just to be a guiding hand. I can't tell you how rare that is." Calling Nicks "a hero of mine" who excels at keeping secrets, she concluded by noting, "She's really helped me through so much over the years" and then led the sold-out stadium in a well-deserved round of applause for her.

DID YOU KNOW?

In 1983, Nicks referenced classic Hollywood starlets Marilyn Monroe, Marlene Dietrich, and (yes) Greta Garbo in a song called "Garbo," which she later recorded during *The Wild Heart* era. The inspiration for it was the *Buckingham Nicks* LP photo shoot where Nicks, to her chagrin, was asked to pose topless with Lindsey Buckingham. "[In my] dramatic way I thought, 'Maybe the movie stars that came here felt this way. Maybe they felt like they had to do something they really didn't want to do that much, but they did it anyway for art—for music,'" she told the audience at an August 1998 concert. "So I went home and I wrote this song."

"She's paved the way for us, and she's mentored so many artists that you don't even know she's doing it. She's become friends with so many female artists just to be a guiding hand. I can't tell you how rare that is."

—TAYLOR SWIFT ON STEVIE NICKS

Select Album DISCOGRAPHY

BUCKINGHAM NICKS (1973)
BUCKINGHAM NICKS • STUDIO

FLEETWOOD MAC (1975)
FLEETWOOD MAC • STUDIO
Billboard 200: No. 1
Billboard Hot 100 Singles:
"Over My Head" 20;
"Rhiannon" 11;
"Say You Love Me" 11

RUMOURS (1977)
FLEETWOOD MAC • STUDIO
Billboard 200: No. 1
Billboard Hot 100 Singles:
"Go Your Own Way" 10;
"Dreams" 1;
"Don't Stop" 3;
"You Make Loving Fun" 9

TUSK (1979)
FLEETWOOD MAC • STUDIO
Billboard 200: No. 4
Billboard Hot 100 Singles:
"Tusk" 8; "Sara" 7;
"Think About Me" 20;
"Sisters of the Moon" 86

FLEETWOOD MAC LIVE (1980)
FLEETWOOD MAC • LIVE
Billboard 200: No. 14
Billboard Hot 100 Singles:
"Fireflies" 60

BELLA DONNA (1981)
STEVIE NICKS • SOLO
Billboard 200: No. 1
Billboard Hot 100 Singles:
"Stop Draggin' My Heart Around" 3;
"Leather and Lace" 6;
"Edge of Seventeen" 11;
"After the Glitter Fades" 32

MIRAGE (1982)
FLEETWOOD MAC • STUDIO
Billboard 200: No. 1
Billboard Hot 100 Singles:
"Hold Me" 4;
"Gypsy" 12;
"Love in Store" 22

THE WILD HEART (1983)
STEVIE NICKS • SOLO
Billboard 200: No. 5
Billboard Hot 100 Singles:
"Stand Back" 5;
"If Anyone Falls" 14;
"Nightbird" 33

ROCK A LITTLE (1985)
STEVIE NICKS • STUDIO
Billboard 200: No. 12
Billboard Hot 100 Singles:
"Talk to Me" 4;
"I Can't Wait" 16;
"Has Anyone Ever Written Anything for You?" 60

PACK UP THE PLANTATION: LIVE! (1985)
TOM PETTY AND THE HEARTBREAKERS • LIVE, FEAT. STEVIE NICKS
Billboard 200: No. 22
Billboard Hot 100 Singles:
"Needles and Pins" 37

TANGO IN THE NIGHT (1987)
FLEETWOOD MAC • STUDIO
Billboard 200: No. 7
Billboard Hot 100 Singles:
"Big Love" 5;
"Seven Wonders" 19;
"Little Lies" 4;
"Everywhere" 14;
"Family Man" 90

GREATEST HITS (1988)
FLEETWOOD MAC • COMPILATION
Billboard 200: No. 14
Billboard Hot 100 Singles:
"As Long as You Follow" 43

THE OTHER SIDE OF THE MIRROR (1989)
STEVIE NICKS • SOLO
Billboard 200: No. 10
Billboard Hot 100 Singles:
"Rooms on Fire" 16

BEHIND THE MASK (1990)
FLEETWOOD MAC • STUDIO
Billboard 200: No. 18
Billboard Hot 100 Singles:
"Save Me" 33

TIMESPACE: THE BEST OF STEVIE NICKS (1991)
STEVIE NICKS • COMPILATION
Billboard 200: No. 30
Billboard Hot 100 Singles:
"Sometimes (It's a Bitch)"

STREET ANGEL (1994)
STEVIE NICKS • SOLO
Billboard 200: No. 45
Billboard Hot 100 Singles:
"Maybe Love Will Change Your Mind" 57

THE DANCE (1997)
FLEETWOOD MAC • LIVE
Billboard 200: No. 1
Billboard Hot 100 Singles:
"Landslide" (live) 51

ENCHANTED: THE WORKS OF STEVIE NICKS (1998)
STEVIE NICKS • BOXED SET
Billboard 200: No. 85

TROUBLE IN SHANGRI-LA (2001)
STEVIE NICKS • SOLO
Billboard 200: No. 5

THE VERY BEST OF FLEETWOOD MAC (2002)
FLEETWOOD MAC • COMPILATION
Billboard 200: No. 12

SAY YOU WILL (2003)
FLEETWOOD MAC • STUDIO
Billboard 200: No. 3
Billboard Hot 100 Singles:
"Peacekeeper" 80

CRYSTAL VISIONS . . . THE VERY BEST OF STEVIE NICKS (2007)
STEVIE NICKS • COMPILATION
Billboard 200: No. 21

THE SOUNDSTAGE SESSIONS (2009)
STEVIE NICKS • LIVE
Billboard 200: No. 47

IN YOUR DREAMS (2011)
STEVIE NICKS • SOLO
Billboard 200: No. 6

EXTENDED PLAY (2013)
FLEETWOOD MAC • EP
Billboard 200: No. 48

24 KARAT GOLD: SONGS FROM THE VAULT (2014)
STEVIE NICKS • SOLO
Billboard 200: No. 7

50 YEARS—DON'T STOP (2018)
FLEETWOOD MAC • COMPILATION
Billboard 200: No. 65

LIVE IN CONCERT: THE 24 KARAT GOLD TOUR (2020)
STEVIE NICKS • LIVE

BELLA DONNA: LIVE 1981 (2023)
STEVIE NICKS • LIVE ARCHIVE
Billboard 200: No. 127

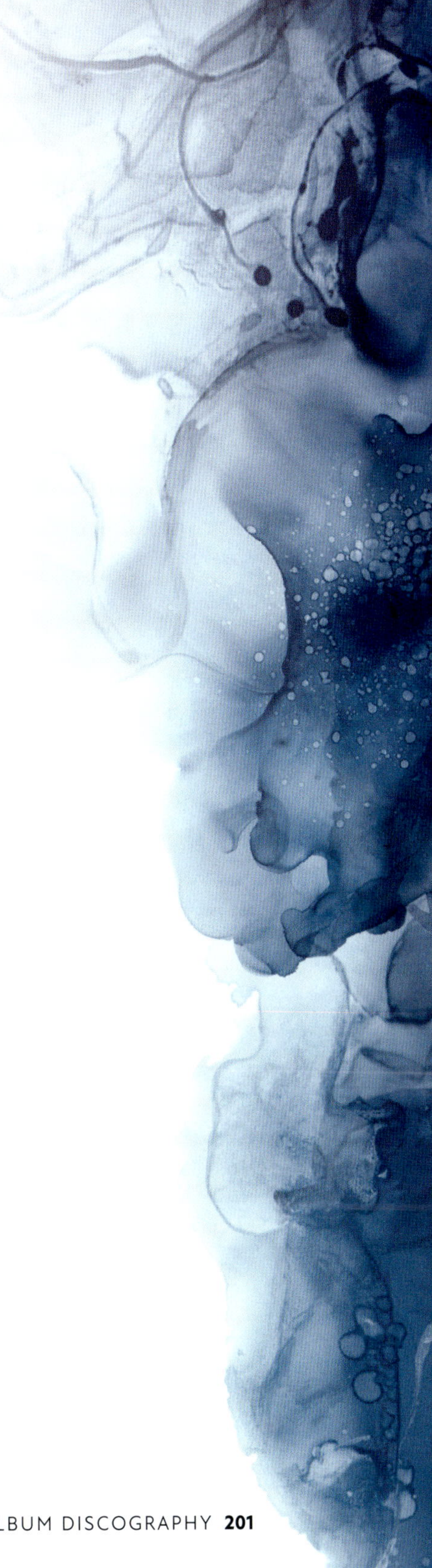

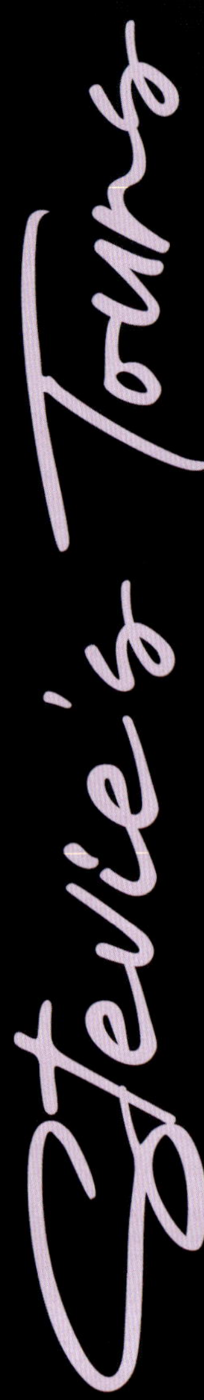

BUCKINGHAM NICKS TOURS

A full accounting of tour dates for Buckingham Nicks does not exist. However, archival reviews, press reports, and live recordings reveal that the duo played shows in New York, Los Angeles, and San Francisco. Among other gigs, they opened for John Prine at the Troubadour in 1973 and in 1974 performed with Hoyt Axton at the Boarding House in San Francisco and with Mountain in Birmingham, Alabama. In fact, Buckingham Nicks closed out their touring in Alabama in January 1975, after they had already joined Fleetwood Mac.

FLEETWOOD MAC TOURS

1975–1976: FLEETWOOD MAC TOUR The first tour with Stevie Nicks and Lindsey Buckingham was a rousing success that found the band moving from theaters into arenas and amphitheaters in the United States.

1977: RUMOURS TOUR A global tour that reached the United Kingdom, New Zealand, Europe, and Japan, with opening acts such as Kenny Loggins and Firefall.

1978: PENGUIN SUMMER COUNTRY SAFARI While recording *Tusk*, the band took a break for a summer US tour. Highlights included a World Series of Rock show in Cleveland before 75,000 people, with openers such as Todd Rundgren and the Cars.

1979–1980: TUSK TOUR A massive yearlong tour that started in October 1979 and wrapped in September 1980 in support of *Tusk*. Christopher Cross opened some shows.

1982: MIRAGE TOUR This tour celebrated the 1982 album *Mirage*, with opening act Men at Work.

1987–1988: SHAKE THE CAGE TOUR Rick Vito and Billy Burnette joined the band, replacing Lindsey Buckingham, as Fleetwood Mac supported *Tango in the Night*. Openers included the Cruzados.

1990: BEHIND THE MASK TOUR The last full tour to feature both Nicks and Christine McVie for a while. Openers included Squeeze.

1994–1995: TOUR Nicks, Buckingham, and Christine McVie were absent from this tour supporting *Time*. Mick Fleetwood and John McVie were joined by Billy Burnette, Dave Mason, and Bekka Bramlett.

1997: THE DANCE The classic *Rumours* lineup reunited for a well-received TV special, album, and tour.

2003–2004: SAY YOU WILL TOUR A Christine McVie–less lineup toured extensively to promote 2003's *Say You Will.*

2009: FLEETWOOD MAC UNLEASHED: HITS TOUR An aptly named tour focusing on the band's many smashes; Christine McVie did not participate.

2013: LIVE A celebration of *Rumours* turning thirty-five, tied to a limited-edition boxed-set release of the album.

2014–2015: ON WITH THE SHOW TOUR Christine McVie rejoined the band, leading to a triumphant victory lap for the classic *Rumours* lineup.

2018–2019: AN EVENING WITH FLEETWOOD MAC With Buckingham no longer in the group, Mike Campbell and Neil Finn joined the band for what became their final tour.

STEVIE NICKS TOURS

1981: WHITE WINGED DOVE TOUR Nicks's first solo tour was a short ten-date run that was recorded for the HBO special *White Wing Dove – Stevie Nicks in Concert.*

1983: THE WILD HEART TOUR After headlining one day at the May 1983 US Festival, Nicks embarked on a five-month cross-country tour.

1986: ROCK A LITTLE TOUR Her first solo world tour, supporting *Rock a Little*, led to the home video *Live at Red Rocks*. In the United States, opening acts included Peter Frampton and Opus.

1989: THE OTHER SIDE OF THE MIRROR TOUR Nicks closed out the 1980s with a world tour promoting *The Other Side of the Mirror*, with the Hooters in the US and Richard Marx elsewhere.

1991: WHOLE LOTTA TROUBLE TOUR Her first solo tour since leaving Fleetwood Mac celebrated the release of the hits collection *Timespace*.

1994: STREET ANGEL TOUR A two-month tour supporting her 1994 album *Street Angel*.

1998: ENCHANTED TOUR Following the success of the reunited Fleetwood Mac, she commemorated the release of her boxed set *Enchanted: The Works of Stevie Nicks* with a tour. Boz Scaggs opened some shows.

"Everyone else changes. I don't change."

—STEVIE NICKS TO *THE GUARDIAN*

1999–2000: PONDERING THE MILLENNIUM A brief tour in Las Vegas and California around the turn of the new millennium.

2001: TROUBLE IN SHANGRI-LA TOUR A tour marked by highs (Sheryl Crow occasionally joined Nicks onstage) and lows (illness and the September 11 terrorist attacks).

2005: STEVIE NICKS: DREAMS Nicks booked four shows at the Colosseum at Caesars Palace in Las Vegas.

2005: TWO VOICES TOUR (WITH DON HENLEY) Nicks reunited with Don Henley for a co-headlining tour where they sang some of their biggest hits solo and together.

2005–2006: GOLD DUST TOUR Vanessa Carlton occasionally opened for Nicks on this solo tour.

2006: HIGHWAY COMPANIONS TOUR (WITH TOM PETTY AND THE HEARTBREAKERS) Nicks joined Tom Petty and the Heartbreakers' summer tour and appeared as guest vocalist on several tracks, including "Stop Draggin' My Heart Around."

2007–2008: CRYSTAL VISIONS TOUR Chris Isaak and Vanessa Carlton opened for Nicks as she toured behind *Crystal Visions . . . The Very Best of Stevie Nicks.*

2010: THIS IS NOT A TOUR A very brief run of shows in August 2010.

2011–2012: HEART & SOUL TOUR (WITH ROD STEWART) Nicks opened for Rod Stewart at various times over a few years.

2011–2012: IN YOUR DREAMS TOUR When not touring with Rod Stewart, she launched solo tours that included Dave Stewart as the opening act in select cities.

2016–2017: 24 KARAT GOLD TOUR A rarities-filled set supporting *24 Karat Gold: Songs from the Vault*, with the Pretenders as openers.

2022–PRESENT: VARIOUS SOLO DATES Nicks continues to tour as a solo artist, booking festivals such as the New Orleans Jazz & Heritage Festival and Bonnaroo, along with headlining shows.

2023–2024: TWO ICONS, ONE NIGHT A co-headlining stadium run with Billy Joel.

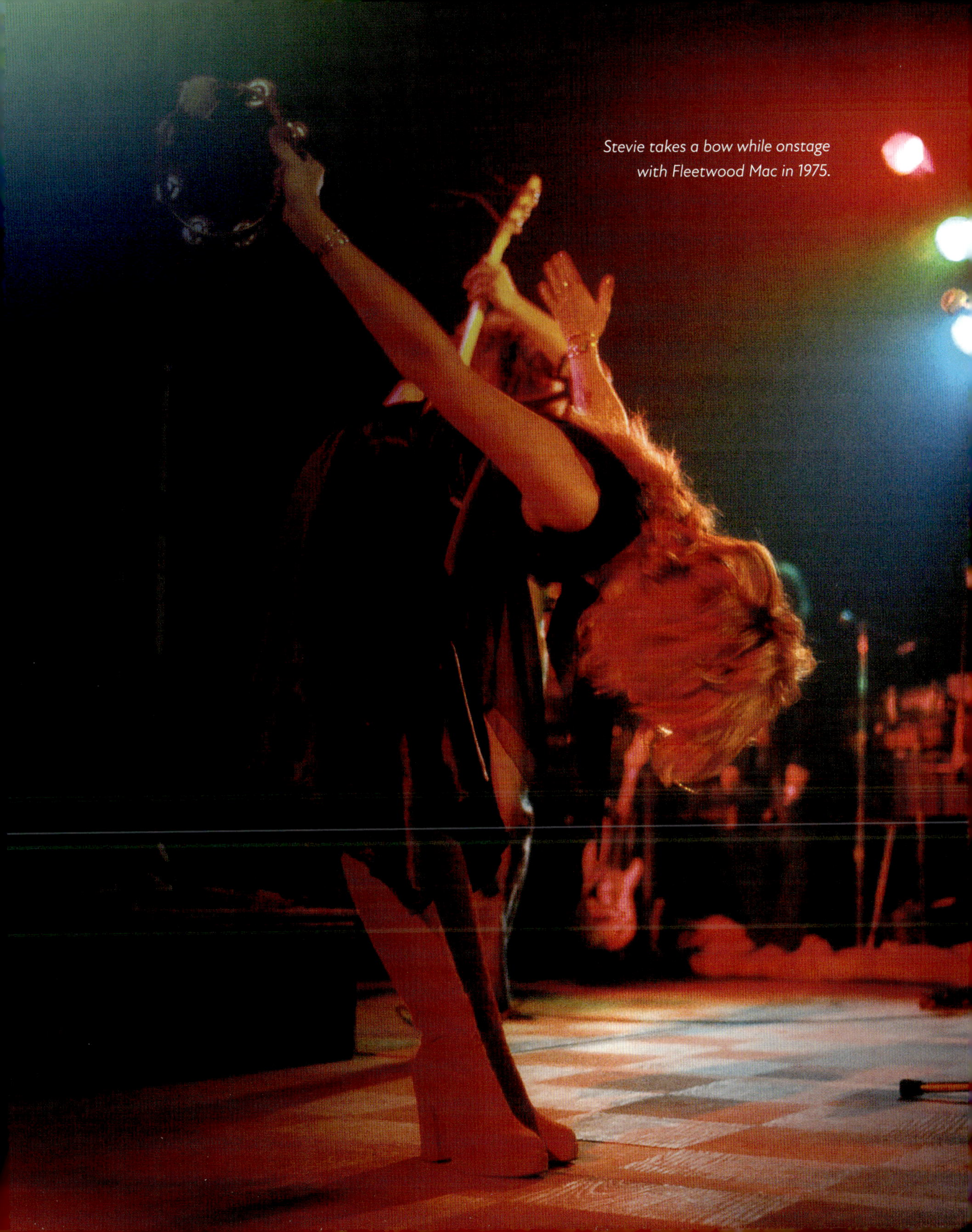

Stevie takes a bow while onstage with Fleetwood Mac in 1975.

Photo Credits

Cover, ii-iii, Fin Costello/Redferns/Getty Images; cover, i, iii, designfourmonths/Shutterstock; cover, ii-iii, 202-203, 204-205, Evgenia Vasileva/Shutterstock; iv-v, 25, 25, 27, 42, 96, 136, 148, 169, Jade ThaiCatwalk/Shutterstock; vii, Fin Costello/Redferns/Getty Images; viii, RocksOffMW; ix, 4, 5, 14, 35, 36, 67, 82, 111, 126, 127, 134, Juli Gin/Shutterstock; x, Larry Hulst/Michael Ochs Archives/Getty Images; x, 1, 3, 10,11, 42, 43, 90, 118, 119, 121, 132-133, 158, 159, 172, 173, 194, 195, endpapers, Back Cover, berez_ka/Shutterstock; 5, Photofest; 6, Michael Ochs Archives/Getty Images; 7, 110, Panzer/Shutterstock; 8, 50, 53, 74, 77, 106, 107, 108, 128, 129, 154, 155, 164, 178, 179, 190, Lace Design Gallery/Shutterstock; 9, Pictoral Press Ltd/Alamy Stock Photo; 9, 34, 53, 110, 165, azure1/Shutterstock; 9, 76, Fedotova Olga/Shutterstock; 11, Photofest; 12-13, Kevin Kane/WireImage/Getty Images; 15, Photofest; 16, Polydor/Photofest; 16, 19, 73, Warongdech Digital/Shutterstock; 17, 18, 72, 142, 143, 150, 201, korkeng/Shutterstock; 20, 21, 54, 55, 124, 125, 162, 163, 184, 185, Caraulan Art/Shutterstock; 21, Michael Ochs Archives/Getty Images; 22-23, Photofest; 24, Pictoral Press Ltd/Alamy Stock Photo; 28, 29, 31, 112, 113, 117, SKY Stock/Shutterstock; 29, Michael Ochs Archives/Getty Images; 31, Michael Ochs Archives/Getty Images; 32, Richard McCaffrey/Michael Ochs Archive/Getty Images; 34, Fin Costello/Redferns/Getty Images; 34, 165, Tatyana Mi/Shutterstock; 38-39, Photoshot/Everett Collection; 40, Jamie McCarthy/Getty Images; 40, 41, 64-65, 102, 103, 152, 153, 174, 175, moobeer/Shutterstock; 43, Michael Ochs Archives/Getty Images; 44, Fin Costello/Redferns/Getty Images; 44, 45, 94, 95, 156, 157, 196, 197, 199, mythja/Shutterstock; 47, Clayton Call/Redferns/Getty Images; 47, Bokeh Blur Background/Shutterstock; 48, Warner Brothers/Photofest; 51, Bob Riha, Jr./Getty Images; 52, 13Natali_L/Shutterstock; 53, Ron Galella/Getty Images; 55, Rick Diamond/Getty Images; 57, Fin Costello/Redferns/Getty Images; 58, Ron Galella/Getty Images; 58, icemanphotos/Shutterstock; 59, PhotoIris2021/Shutterstock; 60-61, Roman Salicki/WWD/Penske Media/Getty Images; 63, Aaron Rapoport/Corbis/Getty Images; 65, Lynn Goldsmith/Corbis/VCG/Getty Images; 66, Richard E. Aaron/Redferns/Getty Images; 68-69, Q3kiaPictures/Shutterstock; 70-71, Kevin Winter/Getty Images; 73, Modern Records; 75, Larry Hulst/Michael Ochs Archives/Getty Images; 78-79, KMazur/WireImage/Getty Images; 80-81, Chris McKay/MediaPunch/Alamy Stock Photo; 83, Richard E. Aaron/Redferns/Getty Images; 84, HB lotus/Shutterstock; 86, LittlePerfectStock/Shutterstock; 88-89, Modern Records/Photofest; 91, Ray Mickshaw/WireImage/Getty Images; 93, CBH/Shutterstock; 94, Pat Johnson/MediaPunch/Alamy Stock Photo; 97, Michael Ochs Archives/Getty Images; 98-99, Tusia/Shutterstock; 101, Fin Costello/Redferns/Getty Images; 102, 104-105, merrymuuu/Shutterstock; Clayton Call/Redferns/Getty Images; 107, PictureLux/The Hollywood Archive/Alamy Stock Photos; 109, Viktoria UA/Shutterstock; 110, Murray Philips/WireImage/Getty Images; 113, Chris Walter/Getty Images; 114-115, Richard E. Aaron/Redferns/Getty Images; 119, Ron Galella/Getty Images; 122-123, Excellent backgrounds/Shutterstock; 124, MediaPunch Inc/Alamy Stock Photo; 127, Blueee/Alamy Stock Photo; 129, Richard E. Aaron/Redferns/Getty Images; 130-131, Warner Brothers/Photofest; 132, Mirrorpix/Everett Collection; 135, Michael Putland/Getty Images; 137, Vinyls/Alamy Stock Photo; 137, Tatyana Mi/Shutterstock; 138, George Rose/Getty Images; 138, 139, icemanphotos/Shutterstock; 141, Ross Pelton/MediaPunch/Alamy Stock Photo; 143, Warner Brothers/Photofest; 144-145, Oganic SL/Shutterstock; 146-147, Kevin Winter/Getty Images; 149, LFI/Photoshot/Everett Collection; 151, Aaron Rapoport/Corbis/Getty Images; 152, Pete Still/Redferns/Getty Images; 157, Fox/Photofest; 159, L. Cohen/WireImage/Getty Images; 160-161, Rudchenko Liliia/Shutterstock; 162, Frank Micelotta/ImageDirect/Getty Images; 165, KMazur/WireImage/Getty Images; 166, Rick Diamond/WireImage/Getty Images; 168, Noam Galai/Getty Images; 170-171, Mike Coppola/Getty Images; 173, Steve Granitz/WireImage/Getty Images; 175, Jim Greenhill; 177, Ingrid Balabanova/Shutterstock; 178, Chris Weeks/WireImage/Getty Images; 180-181, Chris Weeks/WireImage/Getty Images; 183, ZiaMary/Shutterstock; 184, Kevin Mazur/Getty Images; 186, Kati Moth/Shutterstock; 188-189, Kevin Kane/Getty Images; 191, Amazon Prime Video/Photofest; 192-193, Yury Romanov/Shutterstock; 194, Shutterstock; 197, Michael Caulfield/WireImage/Getty Images; 205, Fin Costello/Redferns/Getty Images; endpapers, Rosen-Jones Photography.

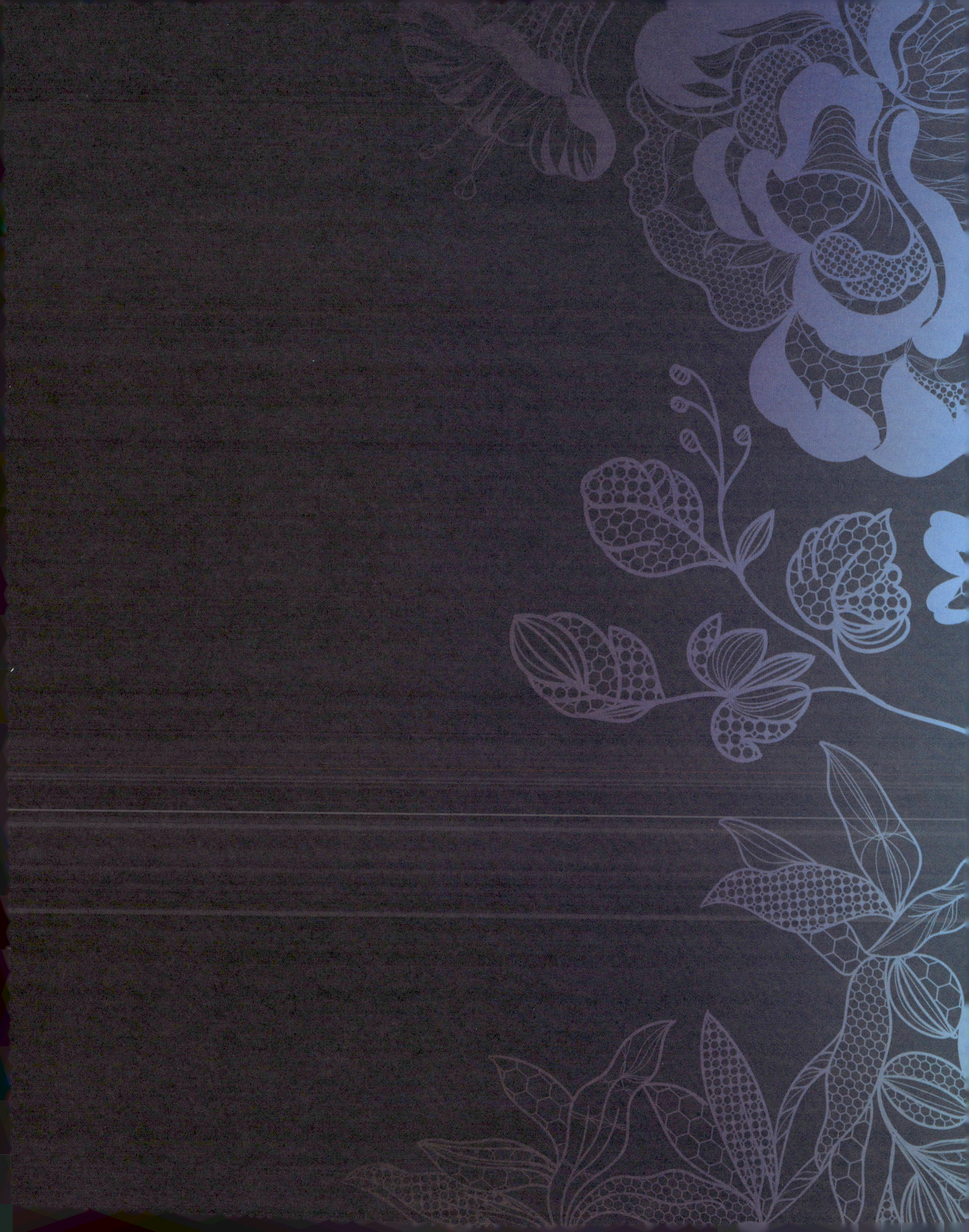

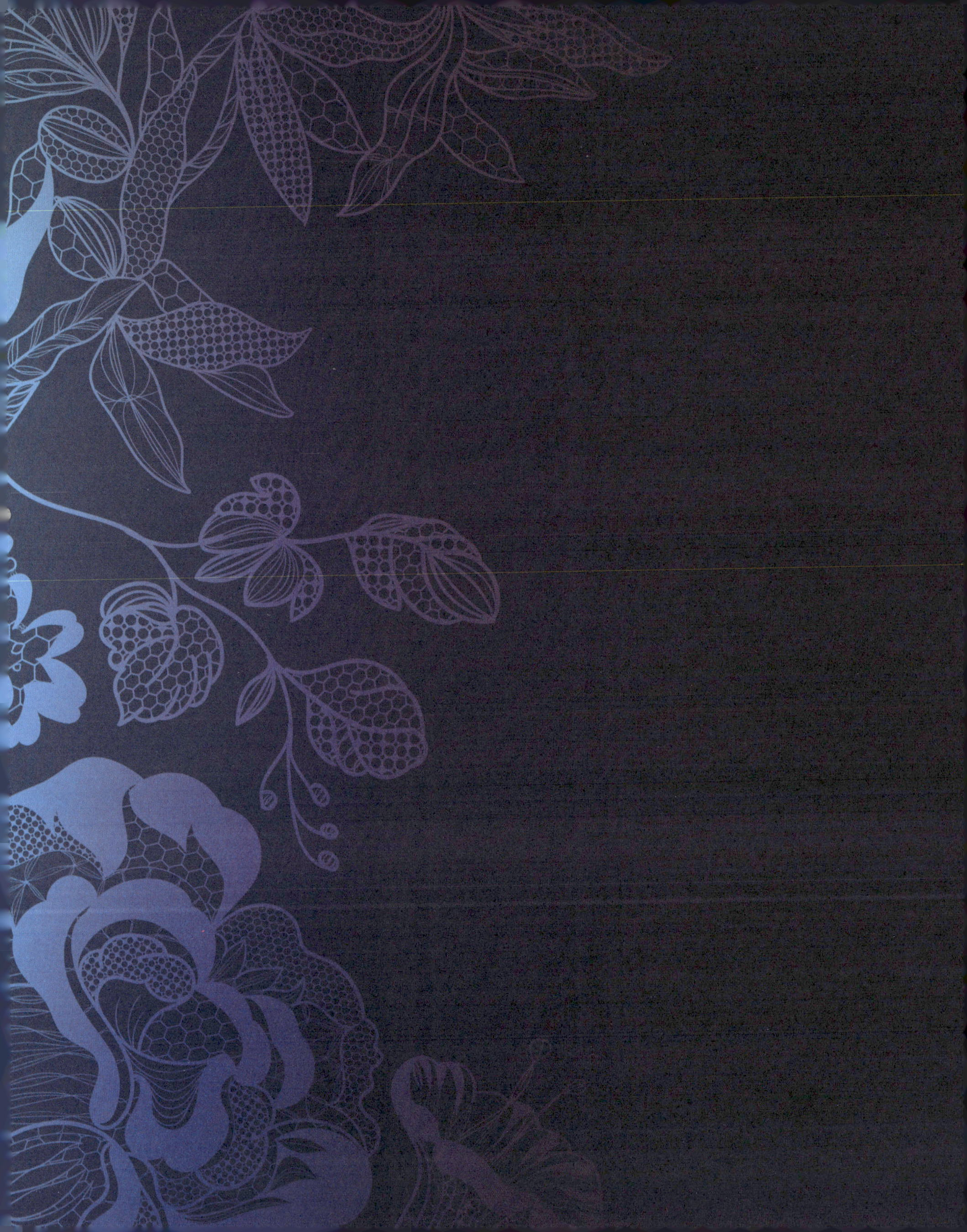